D1570835

ANTIC FABLES

ANTIC FABLES

PATTERNS OF EVASION
IN SHAKESPEARE'S COMEDIES

A. P. Riemer

ST. MARTIN'S PRESS
New York

FOR NINA

© A. P. Riemer 1980

Printed in Australia
First published in the United States of America in 1980

Library of Congress Cataloguing in Publication Data

Riemer, A. P.
Antic fables.

Includes bibliographical references and index.
1. Shakespeare, William, 1564–1616—Comedies.
I. Title.
PR2981.R54   1980   822.3'3   80-13330
ISBN 0-312-04369-4

CONTENTS

ACKNOWLEDGEMENTS

The author expresses his thanks to the following publishers for their permission to quote copyright extracts: William Collins and Sons for *The Complete Works of Shakespeare* edited by Peter Alexander; Routledge & Kegan Paul, Granada Publishing and Beacon Press for the extract from Johan Huizinga's *Homo Ludens*; Oxford University Press for the passages from *Asclepius* in *Hermetica* edited and translated by Walter Scott, vol 1; Routledge & Kegan Paul and The University of Chicago Press for the translation of the passage from Giulio Camillo in F. A. Yates's *The Art of Memory*.

PREFACE

'Antique fables' (according to most modern editions of *A Midsummer Night's Dream*) is Duke Theseus's disparaging description of the curious tale of nocturnal adventures told by the four young Athenians after their strange experiences in the woods outside the city. The authority for this phrase is provided by the First Quarto of 1600. The 1623 Folio, however, following the precept of the Second Quarto, renders the passage in this manner:

> I neuer may beleeue
> These anticke fables, nor these Fairy toyes.

Our sense of the play and the view of Theseus's character that emerges from it make 'antic' a much more likely reading than that encountered in most modern texts; but, scholars tell us, sixteenth-century English did not differentiate between the two words — these fables are both 'antique' — reminiscent of hoary, 'mouldy' tales, and 'antic' — foolish, grotesque and undignified. Without the aid of annotations it is not possible to convey to contemporary readers the rich possibilities inherent in Theseus's remark.

This textual crux is an appropriate emblem for the difficulties posed for modern readers and scholars by Shakespeare's comedies. It is not merely that the passage of four hundred years or so has inevitably obscured nuances of language, social attitudes and psychological suppositions; the changes in culture and the predilections flowing from these changes have made the type of comedy Shakespeare practised to a large extent unavailable as far as the common emphases and preoccupations of criticism and scholarship are concerned. Despite their continuing theatrical popularity, these plays represent cultural attitudes which the modern world does not share in any considerable measure. Our notion of the value and significance of literature, as we have inherited it from the aesthetic philosophy of the last two centuries, is, on the whole, incapable of accommodating the jesting seriousness and solemn levity frequently to be encountered in these plays. The familiar terms of literary discourse (and the attitudes informing them) often impose an improper emphasis on the comedies.

This study attempts to provide a framework wherein the richness and complexity of these plays may be contained without reference to those 'conclusions' that most modern discussions are intent on drawing. It is an essay in the task of dealing with Shakespeare's comedies without considering the 'meanings' that they recommend or urge, and more importantly, perhaps, it represents an endeavour to register the striking variety of intellectual possibilities contained within these plays, yet not combining these possibilities into pseudo-philosophical or ethical systems. It would be foolish to presume that these pages are entirely original in their approach. Any discussion of Shakespeare's comedies must rely on the work of previous critics and scholars, and this study, too, is indebted to the work of earlier (and no doubt more perceptive) criticism. One name, in particular, must be mentioned: the approach to dramatic literature contained in Northrop Frye's various studies, especially in *A Natural Perspective*, embodies a means of examining Shakespeare's comedies that I find most congenial, despite my feeling that there is excessive emphasis on those 'archetypes' which have prompted several facile imitations of Frye's 'method'. The present study stresses, I fancy, the playful, flamboyant 'seriousness' of these plays rather than their 'generic' or 'modal' qualities.

A few words about the procedures adopted in this book may be useful. It is not intended as a comprehensive discussion of the various topics contained in it: that would produce a study of inordinate and unwarranted length. My chief aim has been to provide an approach to these plays that is capable of elucidating what I feel to be their characteristic qualities. In consequence, there is some imbalance in the space devoted to various plays. Several plays, often considered to fall among the comedies, have been largely excluded. The two *Henry IV* plays and *Troilus and Cressida*, though admittedly possessing, at times, 'comic spirit', may not be regarded formally as comedies. *Pericles*, on the other hand, does fulfil the structural requirements of comedy, but its textual difficulty has made it seem inadvisable to engage in lengthy and detailed analysis. The disproportion of space devoted to several of the comedies may also require some explanation. *The Merry Wives of*

Windsor seems to me a totally uncharacteristic comedy and *The Two Gentlemen of Verona* came to seem increasingly dull as I worked on the various drafts of this book. The actual discussion of these plays is, consequently, brief. *The Winter's Tale*, on the other hand, threatened to possess the whole book, but this threat could not be resisted beyond a certain point, since the play came to represent more and more convincingly a distillation of qualities present in a more diffuse manner in other comedies. Each of the seven chapters into which this book is divided possesses a degree of autonomy, with the exception of the fourth and the fifth: the material in these chapters is closely linked and the division was dictated to some extent by my desire to avoid an excessively lengthy section.

All quotations from Shakespeare are taken from *The Complete Works of Shakespeare* (ed. Peter Alexander), London and Glasgow 1951. For the sake of consistency, I have adopted the readings contained in this text, even where privately I would doubt their validity; obvious printing-house mistakes have, however, been silently corrected, as, for instance, in *The Comedy of Errors*, V. i. 73 where the text prints 'unbraidings' instead of 'upbraidings'. The numbering of the lines in the quoted passages is, in almost every instance, identical with that given in the Alexander text, even though the source for these is the Globe edition, on which Alexander's text also relies. This has been done in order accurately to identify the numbering of a prose line.

I am indebted to many friends and colleagues for their assistance, but in particular to Professor G. A. Wilkes for his kindness in offering me much valuable advice while I was writing this study, and to Mrs Ann Parker, for her patience and skill in checking the manuscript and collecting material.

The University of Sydney   A. P. RIEMER

1   *Expounding Bottom's Dream*

Man is but an ass if he go about to expound this dream.

I

Critics have not taken, on the whole, sufficient heed of Bottom's warning: their attempts to expound his strange dream (an apt enough image for Shakespearian comedy) have been, on the whole, futile, for these plays have proved most intractable material for literary criticism. They elude the usual critical preoccupation with commentary and exegesis through their flamboyant, self-regarding refusal to offer serious themes or concerns. Criticism is, of course, a most serious business: it must assume that the works of art coming under its scrutiny have a cultural significance worthy of rigorous examination; it is most comfortable where it is best able to discover striking profundities. The intellectual habits engendered by Romanticism are partly responsible for these ambitions. The elevation of works of art (as well as of the artist) to an almost spiritual plane begins with certain idealistic notions that had their origins in the eighteenth century. Coleridge insisted on the supremacy of the imagination; Arnold took up the thread in his theory of the ennobling function of poetry; and thus the twentieth century came to inherit a particularly solemn attitude towards the importance and value of literature. It is these principles that Shakespeare's comedies challenge so notably. They have resisted most efforts to contain them within the normal categories of literary discussion; their failure to entertain seriously those moral, intellectual and, at times, even overtly philosophical notions that criticism attempts to expose, has placed them in a most peculiar situation where the common preferences of literary discourse are concerned.

In this they are not unique. These spectacularly jesting extravaganzas belong to a type of drama which has appeared occasionally

1

throughout the history of European theatre. Though their particular characteristics are usually very individual, plays within this tradition of comedy—if it may be called that—are distinguished by two features: their flamboyant, often reckless wit, and their remoteness not only from those attitudes that determine most critical preoccupations but also (and more importantly) from many of the concerns of orthodox comic drama. Comedy of the more conventional sort has remained remarkably stable for two and a half thousand years; but throughout this period, a very different comic mode has also made sporadic appearances. Shakespeare's comedies, some of Mozart's later operas, *The Importance of Being Earnest*, *Der Rosenkavalier*, a number of Tom Stoppard's learned fantasias are all remarkable for their apparent lack of concern with social or even moral issues. For this reason, such works have, at times, been decried as escapist and lacking in seriousness; this is so because they appear very often quite deliberately to challenge the concerns of conventional comedies: these concerns, moreover, (for reasons closely connected with their social and, at times political significance) are most congenial to the emphases of literary criticism.

Criticism cannot resist expounding dreams; orthodox comedy, too, is intimately engaged with matters representing general propositions about social issues. The type of comedy to which Shakespeare's work belongs turns its back on these assumptions and comes, therefore, to seem an irreverent challenge to commonly-held attitudes. The usual definition of comedy current in Shakespeare's lifetime demonstrates the strength of the orthodox tradition: the purpose of comedy (according to most Renaissance theorists) is to castigate folly (or vice) and to correct the manners of the age.[1] Later criticism may have come to feel that this prescription is too specific and too limiting to be of general relevance. Yet it identifies a persistent stance adopted by comic writers in most ages, despite great historical and cultural differences, from which the teasing ambivalences of the world that generates Bottom's dream are entirely remote. No matter how much individual plays seem to diverge from the conventional Renaissance definition of comic purpose, throughout the history of orthodox comedy the closely allied concerns of topicality and didactic intention

---

[1] The most familiar statement of this in English Renaissance critical theory is contained in Sidney's *An Apologie for Poetrie*: 'Comedy is an imitation of the common errors of our life, which he representeth in the most ridiculous and scornefull sort that may be; so as it is impossible that any beholder can be content to be such a one'. (From O. B. Hardison, Jr (ed.), *English Literary Criticism: The Renaissance*, New York 1963, p. 121.)

have remained remarkably constant. Most types of comedy, whether Attic *vetus comoedia*, the comedies of Jonson and Molière, or, much nearer home, the essentially *comic* drama of Shaw and Brecht, are intrinsically engaged in the stringent criticism of the follies and foibles of the contemporary world. Even the so-called absurdist plays of the 'fifties and 'sixties of our own century, while giving every sign of elaborating a series of totally unprecedented preoccupations and techniques, belong to this dominant tradition. In *The Caretaker*, Pinter seems to be flirting with fashionable notions about the nature of identity, the impossibility of human communication in the twentieth century and man's need to be, simultaneously, victim and predator. But these are superficial, almost decorative aspects of the play. Its most striking effect, which made it so controversial when it first appeared, is its uncompromisingly frank representation of the familiar and the least comforting aspects of plebeian life in post-war London. The attitudes, aspirations and prejudices of the three characters refer specifically and, at times, insultingly to the audience's familiar experience, the tensions beneath the surface of modern Britain; in this manner, the play confirms its place in the classical tradition of comic drama.

Conventional comedy, thus, habitually brings to the stage the most pressing issues of a civilization, and in this reside both the strength of the tradition and the ephemeral nature of the individual plays within it. In our own century, Shaw and Brecht provide particularly clear examples of this transience. For all Shaw's obsession with Nietzschean notions of the transcendental man and Brecht's Marxism and theories of theatrical effect, both playwrights wrote within the continuing traditions of comedy. Beneath a revolutionary surface, their plays are fundamentally conventional, as indicated by the problems of censorship and persecution experienced by both. The furore over the subject-matter of some of Shaw's plays, particularly *Mrs Warren's Profession*, and the political denigration of Brecht, in his native Germany as well as in exile, exemplify the continuing desire to curb the comic playwright's improper licence—the same desire that also existed in the Athens of Aristophanes and in Walpole's London. Comedy can never resist, it seems, challenging holy cows or ridiculing pomposity: the extreme caution of Ben Jonson (at least in the plays for which he was solely responsible) to stay on the right side of sedition and libel, and the tribulations of Molière and Beaumarchais are eloquent witnesses to the fundamentally radical nature of most comedy.

It is inevitable, in these circumstances, that, despite the continuing strength of the comic tradition, particular plays within it should be subject to decay. Jonson is celebrated in literary history for his position in the mainstream of comic drama; but there is no memorial theatre dedicated to his fame; his comedies are performed far less frequently than Shakespeare's. Something more than relative merit is involved here: Shakespeare continues to be a staple of what might still be regarded as the popular theatre because his comedies have escaped the ravages of time. No matter how much artistic merit or universal truth we may discover in *Volpone* (or in *Tartuffe*) the particular social abuses they depict are no longer a part of the modern world. This is equally true of much more recent comic plays: Shaw has already become a vehicle for 'period' productions, an indication that his preoccupations are no longer entirely pertinent. Brecht's case is similar; though still the darling of theatrical theorists, his aggressively political plays are becoming dated, not because the issues in his plays are no longer pressing, but because the types of abuses and characters he represented emerge so specifically from the society of pre-war Germany.

This is the curious irony implicit in the strength of the orthodox comic tradition: despite its persistence, the plays written according to its broad prescriptions are liable to be forgotten, or at best they have to be preserved by stressing their fantastical ingredients—that is, by attempting to make them resemble the type of comic theatre Shakespeare, for one, practised. In his comedies, the lack, on the whole, of specific reference to contemporary society and manners ensures concentration on other theatrical and poetic possibilities, so that even where particular plays deal with actual situations and people (as is the case, possibly, in *Love's Labour's Lost*[2]), these plays are less explicit in their subject-matter and are therefore better able to survive. But, where the broad pattern of European comedy is concerned, plays of this sort suffer from their own characteristic disability: they are often concerned with a playful artificiality, and they seem to lack intellectually demanding material.

These comedies challenge the canons of literary criticism and cultural attitudes because, when they come to deal with such plays, critics and historians of culture are forced to work within a set of criteria which are only appropriate to the traditional concerns of

[2] See below, n. 13, pp. 16–17.

orthodox comic drama. Criticism, in general, is most at home where literary texts stand for something other than their particular pre-occupations, where exegesis, explanation and explication become indispensable tools. The habits of criticism are, therefore, fundamentally allegorical, in manner if not actually in emphasis, because only thus may the craft of literary discourse justify itself and seek to discover a procedure whereby it may legitimately claim access to skills not available to the laity, and defend itself against those natural accusations of parasitism that follow in the wake of the practice of writing books about books. Art which does not 'say' anything, which has no message or axe to grind, leaves the critical establishment at a loss for words—or else forces it into an attempt to argue that this uncomfortable type of comedy represents nothing other than curious versions of more orthodox and more conventional forms of art.

This problem is acute for critics of English literature because Shakespeare wrote, on the whole, artificial, jesting and stylized comedies. To an extent, this has always been recognized: the nickname 'Romantic Comedy' is a tacit recognition that these plays do not conform to the usual pattern. Yet two hundred years or so of critical effort have attempted to claim that the 'Romantic' comedies are amenable to the same critical, interpretative and evaluative procedures as other comic forms, despite very considerable differences of spirit and manner. Romanticism, as already mentioned, exacerbated the problem, for it insisted upon the special and immediate relationship between the artist and the work of art. Art came to be thought of, and is still so regarded, as confession, as a personal statement of faith or conviction—it is considered to be concerned with things outside itself or its own self-contained integrity. Where works of literature were found to be self-regarding, free of those gestures that point to the world of thought or theory, feeling or experience, the desire to demote them often proved irresistible.

The critical fortunes of Shakespeare's comedies are witness to the general truth of this proposition. Many published accounts defend these plays implicitly or explicitly against the charge of frivolity. Frequently, where praise is bestowed on them—and there are still critics who regard the comedies as fundamentally inferior to the tragic plays—the praise is expressed in terms of a seriousness of purpose or of a commitment to issues that confer on these plays an artistic and intellectual validity similar to the concerns of more conventional literature. In consequence, the critical orthodoxy of our own century has tended to bring Shakespeare's comic plays into line with the dominant tradition of European comedy. As a result, their essential nature has come to be misunderstood, or, at least, an improper emphasis has been placed upon them. This is so because Shakespeare's comedies, as the other comedies of this 'alternate' tradition, are incapable of sustaining the evaluation imposed on them by modern critical efforts. This difficulty is nowhere more apparent than in the curiously teasing problems posed by the endings of several comedies: it is here that many conventional notions and traditional preoccupations of criticism are in danger of breaking down.

II

For a century or so, *Don Giovanni* was usually performed without the *buffo* sextet at the end of Mozart's score.[3] This jesting, stylized and seemingly 'unserious' finale was regarded as mere pandering to the tastes of the original Prague audience, who insisted on leaving the theatre with a jolly tune ringing in their ears. Mozart's final words, it was assumed, are to be found elsewhere—in the dark, threatening tonalities accompanying the Don's damnation. The *Sturm und Drang* power of the music was not only preferred to the original ending, it was considered to embody Mozart's true intentions concerning the significance of the career of the lecherous grandee of Seville. Significantly, the conclusion to *Don Giovanni* is very similar to the final passages of many of Shakespeare's comedies: a deliberately artificial, stylized and theatrical episode comes hard on the heels of more striking and emotionally more compelling material. What an operatic tradition had effected in its alteration of Mozart's work, criticism has attempted to achieve in its interpretation of the endings of Shakespeare's comedies.

The classical model for the misgivings of critics about the concluding moments of Shakespeare's comedies is provided by Dr Johnson:

> It may be observed, that in many of his plays the latter part is evidently neglected. When he found himself near the end of his work, and, in view of his reward, he shortened the labour to snatch the profit. He therefore remits

[3] G. B. Shaw attended a performance of *Don Giovanni* at Covent Garden in May 1891; in a generally acerbic review of this performance printed on 13 May 1891, he made specific reference to the widespread practice of omitting the opera's final pages. See *G. B. S. on Music*, Harmondsworth 1962, p. 71.

his efforts where he should most vigorously exert them, and his catastrophe is improbably produced or imperfectly represented.[4]

These comments pertain to Shakespeare's plays in general, but it is among the comedies that later scholars and commentators have found confirmation of Johnson's view. All too frequently it is assumed that the usual happy ending is, as in the case of the *Don Giovanni* sextet, a sop to the audience's expectations and a nonchalant fulfilment of the conventional-demands of the comic stage. Shakespeare, in other words, is thought not to have had his heart entirely in it. Whatever a comedy has to say—and, according to many critics, the best of them have a great deal to say—is considered to be said irrespective of the frequently cavalier way the curtain is rung down. We are often warned not to make too much of these endings because they are no part of Shakespeare's essential outlook or of the interpretation of the world embodied by his comedies.[5] Others have argued that these finales represent something other than a conventional means of concluding a comic action. It is sometimes said that the very casual way in which the tensions, problems and threats in many of the comedies are resolved may be taken to betray Shakespeare's fundamental dissatisfaction with the comic form—that the artificiality and improbability of many of these endings are intended to indicate that life is not like this, that the realities of existence are otherwise.[6] Few of those holding such views would admit that they are recommending these plays as *tragedies manquées*, but many would agree that their assertions stress the ironic or even the satiric potentialities in comic drama. This represents the major critical and interpretative problem about the endings of Shakespeare's comedies. The question that is most difficult to answer, or the one that leads to the most varying answers, is the following: what signs are incorporated in these endings that enable us to strike the required attitude towards the events and the reversals of fortune they contain?

[4] S. Johnson, 'Preface to Shakespeare' in *Selected Works* (ed. Mona Wilson), London 1957, p. 498.
[5] This attitude is expressed succinctly by L. C. Knights in a comment on *Measure for Measure*: 'It is significant that the last two acts, showing obvious signs of haste, are little more than a drawing out and resolution of the plot'. ('The Ambiguity of *Measure for Measure*', *Scrutiny* X No. 3, January 1942, p. 232.)
[6] I. Donaldson, '*All's Well That Ends Well*; Shakespeare's Play of Endings', *Essays in Criticism*, XXVII, No. 1, January 1977, pp. 34-55, contains a very thorough statement of this view of the comic ending.

Initially, it would seem that both Johnson's misgivings and those of later critics are fully borne out by a significant number of the comedies. Shakespeare seems to have done nothing to avoid the improbability of these endings or the suggestions of haste implicit in the manner in which the narrative strands are often resolved. The details of this are too well known to require full discussion—a few examples must suffice. At the end of *Twelfth Night*, finding Olivia unavailable to him, Orsino hastily offers marriage to Viola, thereby assuring the satisfactory resolution of the play's problems. Bertram in *All's Well That Ends Well*, having spent some two and a half acts attempting to avoid his liaison with Helena, accepts her as his wife only when his affairs have reached an impasse; moreover, Shakespeare seems to have the temerity to ask us to accept this without question. The least probable and the most problematic of these finales is in *The Winter's Tale*—in this late work suggestions of immaturity or of inexperience in handling the requirements of a taxing form cannot arise.

Many misgivings have been occasioned by the spectacular *coup de théâtre* of Hermione's restoration. For much of the play, she is assumed to be dead, a casualty of the narrative. The audience is led to entertain expectations for the marriage of Perdita and Florizel and for Perdita's reunion with the contrite Leontes; the return of Hermione seems beyond the possibilities contained by the play. When, in the last act, the natural and expected climax of the play—the recognition of Perdita's true status, her restoration to Leontes and the removal of the impediments to her marriage to Florizel—arrives, it is reported in the conversation of the three Gentlemen in V. ii. This seems an inexplicable anticlimax: it is profoundly unsatisfactory to be fobbed off with reportage when we expect a suitably emphatic and moving scene of joy and wonder. But the anticlimax is, of course, a lure—the reunion is understated to allow full dramatic scope to the last scene: Paulina's elaborate conjurings with which she claims to bring Hermione's statue to life. This is the improbability of the play's conclusion; its perfunctoriness is to be found in what follows. Hermione's 'explanations' seem to dispel the magical intensity and transcendental beauty of her restoration; as she tells Perdita, she is alive because

> Knowing by Paulina that the oracle
> Gave hope thou wast in being, have preserv'd
> Myself to see the issue.
>
> (V. iii. 126)

A failure of tact or of imagination is not difficult to suppose here. The literal-minded tenor of these lines and the improper questions about the dramatist's motives that they introduce make the episode seem perfunctory and careless—more so, indeed, because Hermione's explanations appear to be so unnecessary. Shakespeare's age was not supremely committed to the rational explanation of supernatural phenomena; nor is there sufficient reason to suppose that Shakespeare might have been diffident about dealing openly with the magical—*The Tempest* demonstrates no such nervousness. The last moments of *The Winter's Tale* appear to be distressingly gratuitous.

But the finale of *The Winter's Tale* (like the endings of other comedies where similar carelessness has been detected) is an instance of another commonly observed feature of these plays, representing the opposite of rushed or nonchalant construction. This is the elaboration of the denouement, a deliberate complicating of the manner in which the intrigue is resolved. Far from seeming careless or nonchalant, many of the plays perplex and elaborate their resolutions in a most striking manner. Intrigue is piled on intrigue; the route whereby the desired outcome is reached is often circuitous and tortured. Fresh characters are, at times, pulled out of the hat at the last moment, materially altering the course of events, sometimes retarding, sometimes advancing the achievement of the conclusion. This is not restricted to the comedies of any one period. One of the earliest, *The Comedy of Errors*, contains an extraordinary delaying of the resolution when the totally unexpected character of the Abbess intervenes in the action in Act V. The sudden arrival of Mercade a few minutes before the end of *Love's Labour's Lost* blocks the anticipated happy ending. *Measure for Measure* is especially remarkable in that it is possible to regard almost all of the last three acts as an elaborate and protracted denouement which twists and turns in a thoroughly complicated and potentially confusing manner. Most noteworthy is *Cymbeline*, in which the resolution is constantly delayed by fresh shifts in the situation and by the intrusion of yet new narrative strands and peripeties until almost the very end.

Criticism has come to recognize both aspects of the Shakespearian comic finale—the seemingly careless rounding-off, against all canons of probability and without any concern for sustaining the dramatic illusion, on the one hand, and on the other, the elaborate, indeed painstaking, prolongation of the intrigue and the holding-back of the resolution. But criticism has often failed to acknowledge that these two views of the subject are in contradiction: we read, often enough, that Shakespeare treated his finales in a most perfunctory manner, and that the exigencies of comic drama (at times alleged to be uncongenial to his real attitudes and notions) forced him into these monstrous elaborations. It is probably through a recognition of such contradictory attitudes that a relatively recent orthodoxy has appeared claiming that the final moments of Shakespeare's comedies represent an ironic, almost bitter commentary on one of the traditional ingredients of comedy: the insistence that all should end happily, that the characters, or at least the sympathetic ones, should be promised a life of perfect felicity.[7]

It is hardly surprising that our disillusioned age, with its penchant for the ironic and the satiric, should feel profoundly distressed that after the treachery, disdain, cruelty and unkindness which some of the characters in these plays inflict on others, happiness comes to be conferred on them with a stroke of the playwright's pen. Viewed objectively, in the light of what we believe to be 'accurate' psychological data, and seen also in terms of our communal morality, the assumptions embodied in these happy endings are little short of outrageous. How are Leontes and Hermione able to pick up the threads of their marriage after sixteen years of presumed death, and in the light of those brutalities he committed against his wife and daughter? How can Helena ever trust Bertram; what sort of married life will the Count and Countess of Rossillion enjoy after the play ends? Will Orsino and Viola establish a lasting relationship, given the erotic and amorous confusions which brought them to the altar? And, most pressing of all, how will the puritanical, indeed almost fanatical Isabella cope with her new status as Duchess of Vienna?

These questions will crowd into our consciousness if we allow them. Recent criticism, brushing aside the claim that nothing beyond the confines of a play is of any relevance, has insisted that they are an intrinsic, though unstated, part of Shakespeare's design. They are such

[7] These attitudes are best illustrated by theatrical practice. In several instances, directors have staged explicitly what they believe to be the implications of Shakespeare's 'sub-text'—emphasizing Jaques's melancholy words at the end of *As You Like It*: 'I am for other than for dancing measures' (V. iv. 187); requiring from Isabella in *Measure for Measure* a horrified response as she receives the Duke's offer of marriage; stressing the bitterness of Feste's song at the end of *Twelfth Night*. Some of Jan Kott's theories (especially the chapter entitled 'Shakespeare's Bitter Arcadia' in *Shakespeare Our Contemporary*) were influential in the emergence of this theatrical tradition during the last two decades.

obvious propositions, it is sometimes argued, that to draw attention to them would be a lapse of artistic integrity—no-one could fail to perceive that at the end of *All's Well That Ends Well* Bertram accepts Helena with bad grace, merely because he has been nonplussed and bullied into acknowledging her as his lawful wife.[8] Shakespeare would not be Shakespeare, such theories assert, if he did not force us into recognizing these truths; it is assumed that the comedies would be no more than escapist fantasies if such realities were not firmly registered. The fabric of life cannot hold out the promises the comedies apparently make—we must, therefore, reach the conclusion that these endings are ironic, bitter-sweet reflections on the invalidity of the comic world. It has been argued that *All's Well That Ends Well* incorporates within its title a disillusioned comment about the impossibility of these affairs ending 'well'.[9]

Yet these views are sophistications. They are attempts to make the comedies palatable despite the inability of modern social, psychological, moral and even political attitudes to condone what these plays seem to be offering. Misty-eyed optimism is as unacceptable to the modern world as are the fantasies of wish-fulfilment. Art and the task of the artist are held to be more demanding, more in keeping with reality as we see it; and our view of reality, as already intimated, cannot tolerate the promise of a brave new world. But modern notions of the function of art are better able to tolerate these suggestions than to come to terms with those fundamental characteristics of Shakespeare's comedies which are so amply illustrated by the comic endings: an art existing for the sake of its own conceit. Uncomfortable though this notion might be, it is the principle represented by Shakespeare's comedies—a principle shared by those other works of art that also display the attitudes of this essentially aristocratic form of comedy. These plays refuse to relate to the world of mundane reality in a direct manner; they are incapable of being treated as explicit comentaries on or critiques of life. They represent an art of patterns and ambivalences, and an art which is essentially devoid of extractable meanings or significances.

---

[8] Such a view of Bertram is to be found in Clifford Leech, 'The Theme of Ambition in *All's Well That Ends Well*', *E. L.H.* XXI, March 1954, pp. 17-29.
[9] Donaldson, in the article cited above (see n. 6), is particularly illuminating in this respect.

III

A survey of Shakespearian comedy demonstrates varying degrees of this artificial, jesting mode. Some plays impress by their apparent engagement with weighty moral issues, others suggest a concern with relatively subtle psychological discriminations, and others again, particularly the last plays, seem deeply influenced by mystical convictions about the possibility of reunion and reconciliation. No art as rich or as varied as Shakespeare's comedies may be contained within distinct categories; the range of his comic interests was obviously generous, each play appears to have been written not from the perspective of a particular programme, but out of a fascination with the potentialities contained by a story, a set of characters, a combination of incidents and situations. A pattern may, nevertheless, be detected within this complex group of plays. Each contains at times isolated incidents, at times extended passages which imply considerable leaning towards the use of comedy as a form of theatre relying on its own internal symmetries or resonances. The allure of artifice for Shakespeare when he turned his attention to the comic stage, while by no means an *idée fixe*, is such that no play fails entirely to give some instances of it, and almost every comedy comes, finally, to rely on artifice for its artistic and theatrical effect. Isolating, therefore, those aspects of Shakespearian comedy which are most contrary to the basically moral emphases of Renaissance literary theory and the critical preferences of later ages is not to impose on these plays a set of dominant preoccupations; it is, rather, to bring into focus an essential element profoundly out of sympathy with the 'official' attitudes of Shakespeare's age. The predominantly didactic preoccupations of Renaissance critical theory paid scant attention to flamboyant artifice; though eloquent on the subject of the moral value of poetry, critics remained relatively silent on the matter of how particular 'poems' embodied delightful teaching, that concern with important issues for which the poet's art was constantly praised. The suspicion is hard to escape that these statements were designed to pacify the growing puritan opposition to literature, especially the theatre, and that they are exclusive to those defences and apologies which were written with these challenges particularly in mind. Elsewhere, through the actual literary preferences of the age, the delight of literature is most often praised.

This is certainly true if the title-pages of many publications are to be trusted. The plays of the period (especially the comedies) were frequently promoted or described as mirth-provoking, jesting, pleasant and conceited. It seems that public priorities during Shakespeare's lifetime were firmly grounded in the modes of popular entertainment. The stature of Renaissance drama is far removed, of course, from what we believe to be the common features of such entertainment—the mindless, the sensational and the vulgar. The literature of the Renaissance, especially its drama, does not always escape mindlessness, vulgarity or sensationalism, but it possesses qualities that are obviously finer and much more thoroughly intellectual, imaginative and spiritual than the mass-entertainment of our own day. Yet literature of imaginative and spiritual greatness need not necessarily possess a didactic intention, and Shakespeare's comedies are supreme examples of a literary art that remains, essentially, 'mirthful'. This type of Renaissance drama and these aspects of the literature of the period must be seen in conjunction with a facet of Renaissance culture which has been the cause of considerable problems, if not, indeed, of distress, to modern theories of literature. Shakespeare's age displays a widespread love of elaboration and embellishment which seem to have been valued quite independently of the context in which they appear. The popularity of what is usually termed the practice of Rhetoric is the clearest indication of this aspect of the culture of the Renaissance.

Ample evidence has survived from the sixteenth and the seventeenth centuries to suggest that the post-romantic notion of an organic form had little relevance in the period. Art which was discontinuous, episodic and even fragmentary, was valued as highly as sustained and consistent art. Where the theatre is concerned, it is clear that audiences took as much aesthetic pleasure from the performance as from the material performed. Such a notion is alien to the contemporary world, although relatively recently (as late, perhaps, as the forties of this century) there still persisted the cult of the virtuoso actor whose delivery of a celebrated and demanding passage was thought to be as integral a part of a dramatic performance as the director's *mise en scène*. All that we know of the circumstances of performance in Shakespeare's time—both from contemporary testimony and from the evidence of the plays themselves—suggests that we must reconsider our commonly held opinions. The fundamental theatrical impulse behind much Renaissance drama is very similar to the impulses of nineteenth-century opera—to provide not only a consistent work of art (though consistency was not enforced rigidly in either case) but also opportunities for the display of the actor's (or singer's) skill and command of technical resources. Shakespeare's comedies, especially, offer many opportunities for virtuoso displays, and—contrary to once-held superstition—there is little evidence to be gleaned from the plays to suggest that he was in the least embarrassed by the need to provide them or that he took great pains to overcome their potential ill-effects.

There is, on the contrary, every reason to believe that Shakespeare's art engaged with those aspects of literature for which modern criticism has no adequate vocabulary—art as performance rather than as statement or demonstration, the employment of technique to produce an essentially impersonal work of art, rather than the subjugation of skills and talent to the communication of a vision. To deny the visionary element in literature is, however, the most difficult task for modern criticism, since our equipment is designed to deal with what an artist has to say, not with the qualities of the work of art itself. Literature occupies, of course, a particularly ambiguous position among the arts; it uses words, the commonplace tools for the communication of ideas; it seems, therefore, unable to avoid dealing with the world of ideas. But the manner of its commitment to it (the relationship, that is, between the work of literature and the ideas it incorporates) is far less constant than modern critical theories would hold.

Critics and historians of culture have for long experienced considerable difficulty in reconciling their insistence that Shakespeare was committed to the ideas and suggestions to be found in his plays and their recognition that the Renaissance barely, if at all, acknowledged such a possibility. As early as the critical writings of Coleridge, we encounter the thesis of a duality in Shakespeare.[10] This duality is usually expressed in terms of a subconscious conviction about 'life' communicated by the artist, even though consciously he is only aware of the technical problems inherent in the telling of a story or the writing of a poem. Later writers greatly elaborated these notions. In Yeats and in Eliot, both in their critical views and in the declared principles behind their poetry, we find the insistence that the lack of a conscious design is an essential prerequisite for the production of great art: only thus may the fundamentally important and revealing ideas, notions

---

[10]Coleridge's views on this topic are to be found most clearly stated in the lecture entitled 'Shakespeare as Dramatist' in T. Hawkes (ed.), *Coleridge on Shakespeare*, Harmondsworth 1969, pp. 83-104.

and feeling be communicated. In the criticism of Leavis and his followers, this attitude received institutional sanction; the word 'cerebral' (standing for the artist's conscious and deliberate use of his tools-of-trade) became a term of abuse.

With Shakespeare's plays, this is much complicated by the considerable difference between his comedies and his other theatrical works. He seems to have had a highly developed awareness of decorum in the various types of drama he wrote. By ancient precept, tragedy is a 'serious' form. It is inevitable, therefore, that it should seem to be concerned with the communication of significant ideas, and to be engaged with the moral, ethical or political implications of its material as well as with its inherent abstract qualities. There is no doubt that this requirement was honoured, in the main, by most of the tragic dramatists of the English Renaissance. In Shakespeare's tragedies we may observe a more or less consistent attempt to suggest the universal significance of the particular events and personalities represented on the stage. Some critical accounts may have exaggerated this aspect of Shakespearian tragedy; several lapses and inconsistencies that have been detected—notably the grandiloquent heroic element in *Othello*, the cause of many misgivings—may be closer to the flamboyant display of the comedies than to the more solemn intention of the tragedies. Nevertheless, it is impossible to examine the tragedies without recognizing that they constantly reach out towards the universal implications of their individual concerns.

Comedy, on the other hand, seems to have been the medium best suited to the indulgence of brilliant playfulness and to the concentration on the abstract possibilities inherent in dramatic material and conventions. Shakespeare developed the latent possibilities for flamboyant extravagance from the traditions of comedy he inherited, even though the comedies of many of his contemporaries and successors pursue a more orthodox path. Because the specific conventions of comedy were always much less well-defined than those of tragic drama, comedy offered the greatest scope for the type of witty display (without too much concern for what it might signify) that we meet in many of Shakespeare's comedies. In these plays we discover a concentration on such facets of the comic tradition almost to the exclusion of all other and much more orthodox features; thus emerges the extraordinarily individual brand of comedy that Shakespeare developed from the secondary elements in the comic tradition of his time.

Love's Labour's Lost represents the clearest and (inevitably for that reason) the most extreme instance in Shakespeare of a comedy concerned with the jesting, playful and essentially 'meaningless' display of comic ingenuity. Its status as a considerable work of art is, nevertheless, not compromised; its critical fortunes afford an insight into its unique nature. The tradition of the play's triviality was well established by the time of Johnson's edition. He found many 'mean, childish and vulgar' passages in it, even though he had to concede that 'there are scattered, through the whole, many sparks of genius; nor is there any play that has more evident marks of the hand of *Shakespeare*'.[11] In the nineteenth century, it was usually written-off as journeyman work (if Shakespeare's at all) representing the young dramatist's pandering to the unfortunate tastes of the period, a tiresome essay in bravura of little intrinsic merit. Clearly discernible beneath this evaluation is the attitude that a *jeu d' esprit* cannot possess the compulsion associated with literature of the highest order. It presumes, as a matter of unstated principle, that *King Lear* is more important than *Love's Labour's Lost* because of its greater gravity and larger significance—a judgement, in short, based on the relative merits of tragedy and comedy.

Such views, applicable to other comedies as well, have been replaced in this century by the discovery in these plays of an alleged engagement with certain serious and pressing issues that appear to excuse or make more acceptable what might otherwise seem inanities. *Love's Labour's Lost* is at times seen as a trenchant critique of Elizabethan culture, an exposé of its hypocrisies, its superficiality, its addiction to verbal formulae and its love of elaboration at the expense of honesty, truth, candour and emotional sincerity.[12] The bitterness of Shakespeare's disillusionment is often said to be discernible beneath the play's jewelled surface. Interestingly, it was claimed on at least two occasions that this play is a *pièce à clef* in which we are required to recognize not merely general representatives of certain social, moral and intellectual abuses, but specific personalities of Shakespeare's time whom the dramatist castigated for such abuses.[13] Both the looseness of

---

[11] S. Johnson, note on *Love's Labour's Lost*, in *Selected Works*, p. 543.

[12] Derek Traversi writes that the play is a 'renunciation of literary affectation', an 'affirmation of natural propriety' and a rebuke to the over-sophistication 'that has been the prevailing fault in the court of Navarre'. D. Traversi, *Shakespeare: The Early Comedies*, London 1960, pp. 37-8.

[13] The two major attempts to identify specific personalities in the play were both published, curiously enough, in the same year. They are: F. A. Yates, *A Study of 'Love's*

its construction and the absence of narrative interest have prompted critics to regard it as a return (no doubt unconscious) to the vehement satirical strain of Aristophanic comedy.

The play's notorious ending has added fuel to this fire. The extraordinary peripety in Act V—the intrusion of death into the world of aristocratic pastorale, the indecorous 'sentencing' of the young nobles by their ladies to do penance by confronting the world of reality, and Berowne's explicit comments about this violation of the decorum of a comic ending—has been cited as evidence that this *coup de théâtre* points to the ironic condemnation of the King of Navarre and his associates. Shakespeare is said to indulge, in other words, in theatrical shock-tactics: having lulled his audience for four and a half acts into the pleasant enjoyment of a comic extravaganza, he shows them, at the last moment, the hard face of reality. The concluding songs have been taken as a highly metaphoric embodiment of the play's basic point of view: the embroidered and alluring world of spring (presided over by the cuckoo, the emblem of treachery) gives way to the 'plain style' of the winter song, to unembellished, honest reality, symbolized by its patron, the owl, the representative of wisdom.

These possibilities are by no means excluded from the play. Much of it is directly concerned with the follies of fashionable learning and with the craze for philosophical cabals and coteries. The recognizable targets of many an Elizabethan satirist are obviously (and deftly) picked off. None of the 'Academy' escapes censure: the King and his friends are clearly unable and quite unwilling to persist in their fanatical resolve to remove themselves from the world. Armado's fantastical diction is as much ridiculed as Holofernes's scholastic nonsense. The ladies demonstrate very neatly that the extravagant declarations of love made by their swains are superficial—change the costume, change the token, and none is able to distinguish his 'true' love. And above all, as so often in Shakespeare, there is the figure of Costard, with his sturdy common-man's good sense that tells him exactly how much more than a remuneration a guerdon is worth, to ensure that we recognize the truth of this world. Shakespeare's attitude seems quite clear, and the purpose of the play appears quite obvious—it is an uncompromising condemnation of folly and self-delusion, an instance of the ancient function of comedy as an

---

Labour's Lost', Cambridge 1936, and M. C. Bradbrook, *The School of Night*, Cambridge 1936. The latter, in identifying the Ralegh-circle as the main satirical target in the play, has been the more influential.

instrument of social criticism. Yet the play refuses to be so contained. What convinces the critic or the student in the study will not work on the stage. *Love's Labour's Lost* is more complex and more ambiguous than received opinion is willing to grant. The relationship between its various facets and the question whether these contribute toward a coherent set of meanings (in the post-romantic sense) are the major problems facing any interpretation or explication of this crucially important comedy.

Certainly the play expresses very fully the allure of this world which, in most modern accounts, it appears to castigate so sternly. Theoretically, the King's opening speech may be taken as a collection of shop-soiled clichés which were as outmoded in the 1590s as they were to become later. But its vitality, exuberance and rhythmic drive demand recognition. It is possible, of course, that Shakespeare experienced the same difficulties Molière encountered when he found himself incapable of writing a bad sonnet for his poetaster to recite in *Le Misanthrope*. Also, the charm of the King of Navarre's green retreat could be taken to represent an attempt by Shakespeare to establish the strength and force of these aspirations, even though they come, ultimately, to be revealed as foolish or even, perhaps, as immoral. He could be thought to have refused, in other words, to score easy points: the play's effect may be thought to depend on the vitality with which unfortunate practices are depicted, so that their condemnation at the end is not facile but fully justified. These are, however, rationalizations; literature, especially drama, rarely operates in this manner without including specific signs of such ambitions. The opening speech of *Love's Labour's Lost* is an instance of poetic display which neglects to concern itself exclusively or even primarily with demonstrating the nature of its inherent values.

> Let fame, that all hunt after in their lives,
> Live regist'red upon our brazen tombs,
> And then grace us in the disgrace of death;
> When, spite of cormorant devouring Time,
> Th' endeavour of this present breath may buy
> That honour which shall bate his scythe's keen edge,
> And make us heirs of all eternity.
>
> (I. i. 1)

In part, of course, this introduction serves to depict the character of the King and the nature of his court—pompous, learned, articulate. The shortcomings of this view of life (with which modern criticism is preoccupied almost to the exclusion of all else) are thereby registered. But the speech has other important effects and functions. In a way, we are not listening here to the King of Navarre, for, within the structure of the play, his character is merely beginning to exist for us. We attend, indeed, to an actor, and (more importantly, perhaps) to Shakespeare himself fashioning this impressive display of rhetorical skill and traditional imagery. And, because we are attending to a skilled poet, the performance cannot but be enthralling. The poetic display is, moreover, notable for its restraint: this is not merely the young writer of genius showing off his ability, the effect is transcended by the artistry which makes the rhetorical elaboration (as in the play on 'grace' and 'disgrace') merge into the poetic and emblematic commonplaces—'brazen tombs', 'devouring Time', 'scythe's keen edge'. The rhythms of these lines and congruence between the verse structure and the grammar of this complex sentence reveal a shaping and organizing literary intelligence that makes the linguistic members of the passage serve the needs of the passage itself. Moreover, the tactful introduction of the epithet 'cormorant' prevents these commonplaces from becoming too commonplace.

The King's speech is a skilled display by Shakespeare the craftsman; we are in the presence of a sportive performance which is not entirely germane to the suggestions involved in the play, though it is by no means wholly irrelevant to them. The allure of this speech is considerable, and it must remain a memorable and attractive experience for the spectators, no matter what shortcomings are revealed in those that maintain such sentiments. The sportiveness creates its own values of exhilaration and even, perhaps, of joy; these lines are exciting because of their poise; an audience cannot but become involved with the world they depict. A most subtle and complex relationship is established, as in so many other instances, between the audience's enjoyment of the theatrical representation and the moral or ethical judgements it might wish to make. In the earlier scenes of the play, at least, this enjoyment of the poet's skilled performance seems to predominate. The King and his nobles dwell in a linguistic universe which is grandiloquent and polished. Nowhere else, perhaps, in Shakespeare's earlier drama do we find the blandishments of sonorous and elegant speech so beautifully illustrated. The four young men, though sharing this world of brave words, are nicely differentiated: none of the others speaks with the same degree of exaltation as the King, each is given his own characteristic accents. Berowne, for instance, is far more sceptical and questioning than his friends; his speeches in the opening scene are more brittle than the others', yet we recognize that he inhabits their world.

> Why, all delights are vain; but that most vain
> Which, with pain purchas'd, doth inherit pain,
> As painfully to pore upon a book
> To seek the light of truth; while truth the while
> Doth falsely blind the eyesight of his look.
> Light, seeking light, doth light of light beguile;
> So, ere you find where light in darkness lies,
> Your light grows dark by losing of your eyes.
>
> (1. i. 72)

A major part of Shakespeare's intention in the early episodes of the play seems, therefore, to have been devoted to the creation of this richness of language that is its own justification.

The elaborately ornamented world of *Love's Labour's Lost* is often regarded as a term within the play's dialectic of ideas. The language created for the King and his nobles is considered to reveal their attitude towards life and to give it substance. This mode of language is thought to enter into a generally dynamic relationship with other attitudes and with other linguistic worlds in the play. By this process, the various worlds are taken to be contrasted, judged, adjudicated and weighed. The purpose of art, according to such views it must be stressed once more, is fundamentally moral; literature is a species of *regulum vitae*. It is, nevertheless, questionable how far *Love's Labour's Lost* engages with such issues. Naturally, a comparison of its four orders of existence is not entirely avoided. The king and his nobles, the wordy representatives of 'learning', are contrasted against the insistence of the Princess and her ladies on plain-speaking honesty. Standing against these worlds (and against the other types of 'learning' represented by the fantastical Spaniard and the schoolmaster) we find the vernacular village-society of Dull, Costard and Jaquenetta, with Sir Nathaniel as a member of this world who has bettered himself through his association with Holofernes. But the play may not be reduced to a diagrammatic or even to a consistent demonstration of the nature of the world depicted in it. The contrasts do not contribute towards coherent moral or ethical statements, despite certain loud protestations by critics to the contrary. To impose such a scheme on it is to pervert or to overlook several by no means negligible aspects of its structure.

One example is striking. At the end of IV. i., we are given an exchange between Rosaline and Boyet (with some assistance from Margaret) consisting of a series of *risqué* puns in the manner much liked apparently, by sixteenth-century audiences. Some sensibilities find it offensive that the representatives of sincerity should engage in this sort of mild obscenity; comfort may, however, be drawn from the observation that the Princess leaves the stage just before the commencement of this passage. More problematical is the function of this passage within the design of the play. A characteristic critical response is to ignore it, to regard it, that is, as a piece of stage-business, quite out of harmony with the significance of these characters, intended to indulge the tastes of the audience or the whims of the actors. Refuge may also be taken in the convenient supposition that this part of the play is a theatrical addition by a hand other than Shakespeare's. But these are strategies to avoid the essential issue: this episode is an integral part of the play, and it must therefore have an effect on the total impression the play makes.

It cannot be said (as it may be in the case of the disquisition on child-actors in *Hamlet*) that the passage is so out-of-key with the rest of the play that it may be safely overlooked. The protracted puns on 'hitting' resemble a number of similar passages in the play. Moth and Armado have several contests of this sort (principally at the beginning of III. i.), Holofernes's fantasia on prickets and sorels in IV. ii. and his burlesque scholastic dispute with Sir Nathaniel in V. i. belong to this category of incidents; they occupy a considerable portion of this relatively brief play. While it is possible to see in these cases instances of a critique of the various abuses of language committed by the pedants, euphuists and courtly wits of the late sixteenth century, these passages are, nevertheless, intrinsically the same in effect as the punning exchange between Rosaline and Boyet: fantastical, elaborate flights of verbal ingenuity in which the 'significances' of literary criticism play a relatively minor part.

These aspects of *Love's Labour's Lost* point towards the possibility that the play consists of a string of bravura set-pieces loosely strung together on a slender narrative frame— a view implicitly held by those that would dismiss it as an immature extravaganza of little artistic merit. But, as a performance of dazzling skill, the changes rung by Shakespeare on the dramatic and poetic modes of the late sixteenth century in *Love's Labour's Lost* are without peer. The play is a compendium of poetic, rhetorical and theatrical devices which furnishes its own fascination; but it incorporates, as well, a rich though evanescent combination of feelings. The play constantly borders on parody, to the extent of its seeming to parody itself; yet this parody involves emotional overtones of surprising complexity.

The surest sign of this is to be found in our engagement with the characters at those moments when they appear most vulnerable. Sir Nathaniel's humiliation during the pageant in Act V, together with Costard's charitable concern for the old parson, provide the most striking instances. There are, nevertheless, others as well: Armado, most consistently the butt of the satire in the play, is presented with some warmth; at the other end of the scale, Berowne's struggling and almost horrified admission that he loves Rosaline incorporates an indulgence towards him which must be recognized. The play is, in consequence, a series of shifting emotional and intellectual responses—their multiplicity and the rich variety of linguistic styles contribute towards the creation of a jewelled, memorable world. We must, of course, laugh at the pretentious folly of the young King and his friends when they decide so pompously to enter the rigours of a retreat from the world; but, simultaneously, the play makes us feel, perhaps with a bitter-sweet regret, the attractiveness of such folly. In this stylized, formal world, we encounter a playful pageant of foolish exuberance, a holiday where our normal judgements are suspended. The rich inventiveness of the playwright's imagination—always controlled by his indulgent recognition of the weakness as well as the achievements of human extravagance—provides its own value. We are unable to say what Shakespeare 'means' by the play because all attempts to make it directly relevant to the *real* world of the late sixteenth century (or of the twentieth, for that matter) are blocked by the smiling insistence that this is no more than a sport. A refusal to allow itself to be taken solemnly, while offering itself with great seriousness, is a characteristic of the rather odd manner of comedy Shakespeare practised.

Love's Labour's Lost, then, is a pleasant, conceited jest. It finds much of its value in its exuberance, variety, display of virtuoso skill, and in its ability to evoke contradictory feelings about the strange, dream-like world of the King's park, flourishing in a perpetual spring yet harbouring the serpent of death. The play is simultaneously flippant, trivial and serious, but its seriousness is not that of the pulpit or of the soap-box; it is, rather, the seriousness to be encountered when an artist arranges his perfectly fashioned pieces into a pleasing shape. The ability of the artist, or of the work of art, to remain unimpressed by artistic achievement, while in no way denying its importance or excellence, is a measure of this curious comic effect. No other play of Shakespeare's demonstrates so clearly or so simply the fundamental qualities of his art of comedy; and, indeed, for all its marvellous freshness, Shakespeare's command of his artistic resources was not mature enough fully to sustain this most difficult of tasks undertaken in *Love's Labour's Lost*. But the play points to the comedies that were to follow; these, while dealing with more recognizably conventional theatrical devices, never abandon entirely the pattern of this early comedy. It would have been unthinkable, of course, for later plays to duplicate the manner of *Love's Labour's Lost*; its lack of narrative interest is, ultimately, a liability; yet in its attempts to weld abstract bravura devices to the exigencies of stage comedy it represents a preoccupation also to be encountered in many of the later plays. For all its oddity, therefore, *Love's Labour's Lost* is the epitome of the characteristic mode of that comic tradition which did not follow the more orthodox comic endeavours of European culture. Its promise was fulfilled some two hundred years later, when a great artist, in full maturity, explored some of the potentialities of comedy which are apparent in Shakespeare's early work.

Cosi fan Tutte is the last of the series of collaborations between Mozart and the greatest of his librettists, Lorenzo da Ponte. Here, too, the comedy retains an ambivalent poise between jest and teasingly 'serious' overtones. And, as in Shakespearian comedy, notably *Love's Labour's Lost*, we are never certain how far we may take it to be a commentary on life. The symmetrical artificiality of its world is such that it is always tempting to regard it as a merely sportive extravaganza; yet the artistic care and musical inventiveness lavished on it frequently beckon the listener to delve beneath the surface for deeper significances. The endeavour is liable, though, to frustration; music is much more capable of parody than poetry, and in *Cosi fan Tutte* we often encounter impish parodies of established musical styles precisely at those moments when the drama seems to take on serious overtones. This is nowhere more apparent than in the opera's best-known passage, Fiordiligi's 'Come scoglio' which, for all its musical brilliance, pathos and apparent sincerity of feeling (a feeling to be frustrated as this tale of amorous treachery unfolds), is a parody of some of the more outrageous clichés of eighteenth-century *opera seria*.

The work mirrors the peculiar patterns of aristocratic comedy in its apparent lack of moral focus. It is a jesting, cynical fable about the inconstancy of love. When two gallants, in order to test their mistresses' fidelity, pretend to go to the wars, but return disguised as 'Albanians' to woo each other's sweetheart, the intrigue is manipulated by a cynical bachelor, Don Alfonso, and the worldly ladies' maid, Despina. Musically and verbally, these two deliver the disillusioned commentary on the folly of love. At the end, after the ladies' inconstancy has been discovered by their apparently enraged suitors, the opera does not conclude with a moral statement. Instead, the marriages arranged for the ladies and their Albanians proceed despite the revelation of the deception—characteristically, both the musical score and the libretto remain unspecific about the pairing in which the lovers enter into perfect bliss in the course of the elaborate finale. The comedy opts out of moral judgements, or at least out of the demonstration of the necessity to achieve a morally commendable state—*Cosi fan tutte*: that's how it is. Comedy of this sort closes with the laughing injunction that we must not confuse its elegant patterns with the world of mundane reality. Yet the world of mundane reality, here as elsewhere, cannot be entirely banished. We are made aware that this is a world apart; in it the conflicts and pressures of our quotidian experience have different consequences from those in the ordinary world. This type of comedy denies, in a way, the 'real' world, but not, as often thought, through supine escapism or wish-fulfilment. Rather, it insists that the world it creates is complete, isolated and self-sufficient. The laws of ordinary experience do not apply here absolutely. The artifice is self-regarding, and thereby it seeks to represent its own justification.

Compared with Mozart's elaborate sport, possessing the fascinating intricacy of a Chinese puzzle, as well as its utter 'uselessness', *Love's Labour's Lost* seems to come down very firmly on the side of moral statements. For, unlike *Cosi fan Tutte*, this comedy ends in separation and in a mood of autumnal regret. The prospect of happiness is delayed for a year and a day, and a year and a day is too long, as Berowne says, for a comedy. The gallants must do penance by engaging in activities of the sort from which characters in a comedy are usually protected. The possibility arises, therefore, that Shakespeare was indeed intent on bursting the bubble of artifice (as many commentators have felt he was doing). Are we being reminded of stern reality and of the necessity to learn the experience of the winter-world? The ending of the play seems to incorporate these suggestions.[14] But the conclusion is so abrupt, the arrival of Mercade with his embassy of death is so pat that there is more than a suspicion of the jesting playfulness of essentially amoral comedy. Instead of preaching, Shakespeare does the unexpected: he ends a comedy in a way in which a comedy should not end. We take note, prepared to take comfort from our awareness of the moral delinquency of this strange world. But all that Shakespeare seems to be doing is to remind us that this is a very peculiar ending for a comedy. Admittedly, the ladies speak about morality when they impose penance on their swains; we are not allowed to forget that these young men have been found wanting. Yet the emphasis falls as much (if not more) on the theatrical oddity of this conclusion. Berowne reminds us of this throughout. We are constantly urged to remember that we are watching a play, not a substitute for reality.

> *Berowne*　Our wooing doth not end like an old play:
> 　　Jack hath not Jill. These ladies' courtesy
> 　　Might well have made our sport a comedy.
> *King*　Come, sir, it wants a twelvemonth an' a day,
> 　　And then 'twill end.
> *Berowne*　　　　　　　　That's too long for a play.
> 　　　　　　　　　　　　　　　(V. ii. 862)

The barrier of artifice protects us from the full moral or ethical potentialities of the situation: the theatre reminds us that it is the violation of its own conventions that seems to make the finale so extraordinary. The end of *Love's Labour's Lost* is one of Shakespeare's games.

Some historians of culture insist that this playfulness is intrinsic to many civilizations, especially to the Renaissance. John Huizinga (not without meeting opposition, it is true) made large claims for the play-spirit during the sixteenth and seventeenth centuries when he wrote:

[14] Philip Edwards, in an admirable discussion of the play argues that it is the priorities of comedy, rather than the immaturity of the young men, that are subjected to the stern lessons of reality. Shakespeare 'behaves unfairly to the creatures of comedy, not because he thought them lacking in the sagacity and maturity he might expect of people in life, but because he wished, in a jest, to protest that a certain form of comedy was not capable of showing the vicissitudes of things'. *Shakespeare and the Confines of Art*, London 1968, p. 48.

the whole mental attitude of the Renaissance was one of play. The striving, at once sophisticated and spontaneous, for beauty and nobility of form is an instance of culture at play. The splendours of the Renaissance are nothing but a gorgeous and solemn masquerade in the accoutrements of an idealized past.[15]

This formulation is probably too sweeping to be accepted at its face value; but it identifies, at least, that stance or spirit which informs Shakespeare's comic drama. The greatest of his comedies, indeed, owe something to the 'accoutrements of an idealized past'. That was to occur, however, some years after *Love's Labour's Lost*: in this earlier play, we may note some of the characteristics Huizinga distinguished in another great poet of the time.

There are two play-idealizations *par excellence*, two "Golden Ages of Play" as we might call them: the pastoral life and the chivalrous life. The Renaissance roused both from their slumber to a new life in literature and public festivity. We would be hard put to it to name a poet who embodies the play-spirit more purely than Ariosto, and in him the whole tone and tenor of the Renaissance are expressed. Where has poetry ever been so unconstrained, so absolutely at play? Delicately, elusively, he hovers between the mock-heroic and the pathetic, in a sphere far removed from reality but peopled with gay and delightfully vivid figures, all of them lapped in the inexhaustible, glorious mirth of his voice which bears witness to the identity of play and poetry.[16]

The playfulness of Shakespearian comedy is akin to the ambivalent, teasing spirit described here; the jesting, merry, conceited comic world defies conventional estimates and evaluations: it establishes artistic possibilities which demand to be taken at their own level. That level has little to do with the specifically social and moral emphases of many literary forms or theories of literature. It consists, most disconcertingly for the critic, but most wonderfully for the reader or the spectator, in the self-regarding mixture of levity and sentiment that distinguishes the Shakespearian comic world. *Love's Labour's Lost* is the most complete and thorough instance of Shakespeare's remoteness from the normal preoccupations and modes of comic theatre; it is an emblem, however, of a spirit shared by most of his other essays in the form.

---

[15] Johan Huizinga, *Homo Ludens* (1949), London 1970, p. 206.
[16] Ibid.

2

Experiment and Excess

I

Love's Labour's Lost is not the only Shakespearian comedy to play elaborate variations on the usual modes of comic theatre. In most of them we may discern a constant fascination with the possibilities of altering and elaborating the familiar ingredients of comedy. It is difficult to escape the feeling that Shakespeare's lifelong interest in writing comedies may have arisen from his recognition of the potentialities offered by this type of theatre for playing witty variations on normal and accepted modes.

Shakespeare's originality has become proverbial. His plays, in comparison with even the most accomplished writing of the period, show a remarkable freshness in their treatment of conventional material. Though not at all a revolutionary or an iconoclast, he was clearly not content to accept established practice at its face value. We are made aware in his works of a questioning spirit examining the customary poetic and dramatic forms of his time, and seeking ways of transforming them into quite unprecedented shapes. This originality (often thought to reflect his particular feelings about life and experience) frequently took the form of experiments with the technical characteristics of a particular dramatic genre—an interest, in short, in those abstract patterns in any literary work which are not intrinsically connected with meanings or themes. This is especially true of his comedies.

The Comedy of Errors (one of the earliest of the surviving plays) already contains a fair measure of experimentation with dramatic form. Basically, it is, of course, a conventional Neo-Plautine farce, an adaptation of *Menaechmi*. Though Shakespeare is acknowledged to have shown great verve and theatrical skill in his handling of this material, the actual contents of the play adhere fairly faithfully, with a couple of notable exceptions, to the manner of the routine Latinate

farces of the period. It includes, however, several significant inno-
vations. The best known of these is the addition of the twin-slaves
motif to the twins of the original play. Shakespeare clearly took some
delight in the opportunities this complication of the source material
offered for theatrical display. It seems, too, that (as so often in the later
plays) we have to reckon with a degree of exhibitionism, a 'showing-
off' dramatic skill, whereby the young dramatist goes one better than
his older and more practised rivals. *The Comedy of Errors* may have been
designed as a spectacular example of how to write a conventional farce,
and where stagecraft and plotting are concerned, the demonstration is
brilliantly successful. But the play goes beyond merely providing an
object-lesson in the writing of farces. The material Shakespeare added
to the original Plautine framework points to a persistent characteristic
of the later comedies: this may be termed a leaning towards excess, a
piling-on of plot-strands, complications and perplexities, the aims of
which are hard to understand, unless they be taken as directed towards
theatrical flamboyance.

The 'excess' in Shakespeare's comedies assumes considerable importance in some of the later works; in *The Comedy of Errors*, these
departures from traditional material are overshadowed by in-
novations of a more unusual character. The most important of these is
the solemn scene at the beginning of the play. As often noted, the long
account of Aegeon's woes and the threat hanging over his life
throughout the play make strange bedfellows with the knockabout
farce of the middle section. It is sometimes overlooked that the motif of
a father searching for his lost children is a conventional ingredient of
Roman comedy[1]—Shakespeare demonstrates, therefore, a degree of
'learning' in his choice of a frame to contain the major interest of the
play. The treatment of this material is, however, extraordinary. The
verse is grave and measured—this is the language of tragedy, although
the language of a type of tragedy which even by the late 1580s was fast
becoming outmoded. The danger of the old man's situation is stressed,
not lightly sketched in, as in some cognate instances. But it is the verse,
with its elevated overtones, that is the most remarkable departure from
the normal means of beginning a comedy. In later plays also, notably
in the sober, death-dominated conversation at the beginning of *All's*

---

[1] This motif is particularly evident in Plautus's *Captivi*: Tyndarus and his master are
purchased as prisoners-of-war by a man who proves later to be Tyndarus's real father;
in *Rudens* a girl, Palaestra, is rescued and protected by Daemones: in this case, too, it is
revealed that she is his long-lost child.

Well That Ends Well, a Shakespearian comedy commences without those unambiguous 'signals' that indicate the presence of a comic world.

When the farcical material of *The Comedy of Errors* begins in the second scene of the first act, the contrast is striking. Shakespeare demonstrates considerable skill in the modulation of tone between the two scenes, while sustaining for a moment the interest in old Aegeon's affairs:

> *Aegeon* Hopeless and helpless doth Aegeon wend,
> But to procrastinate his lifeless end.
>
> *Exeunt.*
> *Enter Antipholus of Syracuse, Dromio of Syracuse, and First Merchant.*
> *Merchant* Therefore, give out you are of Epidamnum,
> Lest that your goods too soon be confiscate.
> This very day a Syracusian merchant
> Is apprehended for arrival here;
> And, not being able to buy out his life,
> According to the statute of the town,
> Dies ere the weary sun set in the west.
> There is your money that I had to keep.
>
> (I. i. 157; I. ii. 1)

Though the old Syracusian vanishes from the play until the last scene, the suspense of the comedy is much enhanced by our learning that both of the long-lost sons are in Ephesus, and that the revelation of their identity is the way to save the old man from death.

While the dramatic and narrative function of the first scene is quite obvious—making much tighter a structure that might otherwise devolve into a string of farcical variations on the theme of mistaken identity—criticism has been notably reluctant to regard the introduction of this alien material merely in that light. To an extent, this is justified, for the sufferings of Aegeon receive more emphasis than they require: Shakespeare dwells on the old man's plight by elaborating his long discourse on the circumstances in which his family came to be separated, and on the Duke's reiteration of his inability to alter the rigours of the law, despite his pity for the old merchant. The possibilities for pathos in this situation are all exploited. It may consequently seem that this pathos-filled 'tragic' material reveals Shakespeare's dissatisfaction, even at this early stage of his career, with the brutalities of farce. His personal preferences (as scholarship sees them reflected by the later plays[2]) are regarded as being too sensitive and too responsive to tolerate the potentiality for human suffering buried in the conventions of rowdy farce.[3] He could not but register a protest, it is thought, or indicate the limitations of the world of farce—though why, in such circumstances, he should have turned his hand to producing one remains unasked.

But there is no reason to accept a hypothesis that Shakespeare wished to temper the more unpleasant elements in this type of comedy. It is safer to assume that this material serves a more direct dramatic and theatrical function. One obvious reason for its inclusion is the need to increase suspense, an essential element of this type of drama. But the structural function of the first scene is more significant; its significance may be gauged if it is related to still another innovation in the play, the sudden appearance of the Abbess towards the end of the plot. Aegeon in his account of his family's misfortunes mentions that his wife accompanied him on the disastrous sea-voyage that led to the loss of his sons. In the second scene, while Antipholus of Syracuse is alone on stage, he is given a short soliloquy (reminiscent of the opening scene in its gravity of style) in the course of which the mother is casually mentioned:

> He that commends me to mine own content
> Commends me to the thing I cannot get.
> I to the world am like a drop of water
> That in the ocean seeks another drop,
> Who, falling there to find his fellow forth,
> Unseen, inquisitive, confounds himself.
> So I, to find a mother and a brother,
> In quest of them, unhappy, lose myself.
>
> (I. ii. 33)

But Aemilia is sacrificed to the needs of the dramatic action. The expectations about the resolution of the play's dilemma are quite clear: all that is required is for the two Antipholuses to be present on

---

[2] E. C. Pettet discussing the 'dark comedies' writes of Shakespeare as 'uncertain of his medium . . . struggling, not always with success, to refashion it so that it might correspond with radical changes in his vision'. *Shakespeare and the Romance Tradition*, London 1949, p. 157.

[3] 'With echoes of mortal and intestine jars, he [Aegeon] strikes a full note of pathos, the pity of age, and suffering, and frustrated hope. And these are plangent cries with which the heedless rollicking brutality of the comedy makes nothing but discord.' H. B. Charlton, *Shakespearian Comedy*, London 1938, p. 71.

stage simultaneously for the bubble of confusions to burst, and for the old man to be saved from the executioner's block. The comic momentum is generated by the series of feints and delays whereby this *cognitio* is constantly averted. The perplexity is resolved in a different way. In V. i. the nearly demented Antipholus of Syracuse, pursued by what seems like the entire citizenry of Ephesus, takes refuge in 'some priory'; as the rabble is about to follow him, its progress is checked by the appearance of a figure of obvious authority. The Abbess addresses them commandingly: 'Be quiet, people/Wherefore throng you hither?'. The effect is familiar, but striking. The course of the action is diverted, just as it is in Greek drama when the god descends, or when Sarastro suddenly appears in *Die Zauberflöte* to frustrate the designs of Monastatos on the hapless Pamina, or, nearer home, when the impressive presence of Prospero presides over the action of *The Tempest*. The importance and effect of this *coup théâtre* are confirmed a few moments later when, learning from Adriana the reasons for the pursuit of the man to whom she is offering sanctuary, the Abbess is given a speech not only of dignity and authority, but one which also incorporates powerful suggestions of the benevolent magical medicine of Renaissance Platonism:

> The venom clamours of a jealous woman
> Poisons more deadly than a mad dog's tooth.
> It seems his sleeps were hind'red by thy railing,
> And thereof comes it that his head is light.
> Thou say'st his meat was sauc'd with thy upbraidings:
> Unquiet meals make ill digestions;
> Thereof the raging fire of fever bred;
> And what's a fever but a fit of madness?
> Thou say'st his sports were hind'red by thy brawls.
> Sweet recreation barr'd, what doth ensue
> But moody and dull melancholy,
> Kinsman to grim and comfortless despair,
> And at her heels a huge infectious troop
> Of pale distemperatures and foes to life?
> In food, in sport, and life-preserving rest,
> To be disturb'd would mad or man or beast.
> The consequence is, then, thy jealous fits
> Hath scar'd thy husband from the use of wits.
>   *   *   *
> Be patient; for I will not let him stir
> Till I have us'd the approved means I have,
> With wholesome syrups, drugs, and holy prayers,

To make of him a formal man again.
It is a branch and parcel of mine oath,
A charitable duty of my order;
Therefore depart, and leave him here with me.
(V. i. 69; 102)

This is a vivid *volte-face* in the development of the action. The audience is not prepared at this stage for a lengthy sermon; the play is clearly winding down, and what is anticipated is the denouement. The Abbess's intervention seems an irrelevant and unwelcome intrusion into the logical development of the action. Yet it does signal the beginning of the resolution. The dramatic illusionist pulls a rabbit out of the hat to the amazement and consternation of all: the Abbess is the long-lost Aemilia, and it is in her power, therefore, to resolve the tangled web of confusions and to save her husband from death. Her spectacular intrusion into the play at such a late stage is a means of both stressing and obscuring the course of the denouement. It is a theatrical trick of great panache. The exalted diction and the teasing references to mysteries beyond the confines of the normal comic action assume a curious position within the play's total effect. When, in the last moments of the play, Aemilia presides over the satisfactory resolution of conflicts, her language catches once more a mystical ritualistic tone: the departure from the audience's expectations, the rabbit-out-of-the-hat, receives vivid emphasis.

The playfully solemn nature of this resolution, and the manner in which the return of Aemilia prefigures an important motif in later comedies may be taken as signs of an engagement with transcendental issues. These must be acknowledged, but the finale also represents the culmination of Shakespeare's witty transformation of the conventions of Latin farce. The audience is presented with a play familiar enough in outline, even if it has no direct knowledge of the Plautine original, but this familiar comic formula is twisted and turned into a most unusual shape. The play opens with a pathetic tale told in a stiff, formal tragic diction, the echoes of which reverberate thoughout the ensuing action. The expected *cognitio* fails to arrive; it is achieved, instead, by way of a seemingly irrelevant detour into the language of medicinal magic. *The Comedy of Errors*, no matter what else it might be, is a witty experiment in the transformation of the usual ingredients of a particular kind of comedy. Within its admittedly narrow limits, the play is a bravura performance, outdoing previous attempts in this genre, dazzling the audience by its variety of characters, effects and styles, and achieving its climax in a curiously roundabout and elaborate manner. The artistic impulse behind it seems to have been largely abstract and technical; an attempt to write a particular type of play in an unexpected manner, and in such a way that its novelty would engender delight. It is an experiment in technique.

II

Other comedies also represent witty transformations of the conventions of comic drama; in later works, though, the experiments with comic forms assume complex and sophisticated patterns. *Love's Labour's Lost* is an attempt to write a comedy without a normal happy ending—a particularly striking jest because the play's divertissement-like nature would make a conventional finale seem particularly apt. Most of the earlier comedies are, indeed, distinguished by this type of experimentation. *The Taming of the Shrew* plays with levels of theatrical illusion through its employment of the play-within-a-play device. *A Midsummer Night's Dream* derives much of its effect from the mingling within the one play of an amazing variety of comic motifs and characters—the fairy play, the comedy of frustrated love, bucolic farce, a parody of high tragedy, and, a form at least cognate with comedies, the marriage-triumph of mythological creatures. It is, nevertheless, in the comedies of the middle period that Shakespeare's experiments with the forms and conventions of comedy bore richest fruit—even if the harvest is not entirely to the liking of modern tastes. The so-called dark comedies or problem plays have for long been objects of critical fascination as well as misgivings. These plays seem to violate so radically conventional comic modes that they have been assumed to represent Shakespeare's disillusionment with the world of comedy.[4]

There is no denying that *Measure for Measure* and *All's Well That Ends Well* both incorporate material that fits the comic mould most uncomfortably. In *Measure for Measure*, Angelo's designs against Claudio and Isabella and the scenes dealing with prison life propel the play towards melodrama, if not exactly towards the 'tragic' intensity

---

[4] For a statement of such an attitude, see Phillip Edwards, *Shakespeare and the Confines of Art*, London 1968, pp. 114–15, 119. 'The comedy-fabric, as Shakespeare has woven it in *All's Well* and *Measure for Measure*, is simply not strong enough to bear the weight of the human problems pressed on to it, nor the weight of their religious solution. He seems not to be able to convince himself, and he does not convince us, that the Christian idea can fully come alive within the tragicomic form.' (p. 119)

discerned by some of its critics.[5] The first three acts have little of the comic in them, either structurally or emotionally. There is little humour, no lightness of touch, and the emphasis on elaborate philosophical dialogue and on the presentation of psychologically complex states is much in excess of the usual habits of Renaissance comedy. It is only in the prolonged and prosaic resolution of the action during the last two and a half acts that the play seems at all comic. Here, intrigue and action replace contemplation and the dramatic clash of absolutely opposed views of the world. The pattern of deceptions and unmaskings, the humiliation of Angelo, the chief antagonist, and the proposed marriage between the Duke and Isabella, the hitherto dedicated novice, emerge from the familiar world of comedy; but their presence in this play has caused much critical regret.

The peculiarity of the last three acts of the play may be the reason why an attempt has been made to discredit the form in which it has survived. The stylistic disjunction between its two parts is obvious and well known. After the action has reached an apparently tragic impasse in the irresolvable clash between Claudio and Isabella—Claudio making an eloquent plea for life, Isabella stressing with equal force her dedication to her chastity—disaster seems the only possible resolution. At this point, however, there is a remarkable change in the action. The hitherto highly-charged verse gives way to prose as the disguised Duke draws Isabella aside and begins the prolonged intrigue to save Claudio and to unmask Angelo by means of the startling revelation of the Deputy's former liaison with the unfortunate Mariana.

Many regard this as a crude device, a failure of Shakespeare's imagination and a compromise of his artistic stature through the adoption of the superficialities of intrigue-comedy.[6] Others, again, find elaborate reasons to claim that the last three acts are not Shakespeare's, basing their views on the tacit assumption that he would have been incapable of allowing his play to devolve into such crudities.[7] Both sets of attitudes have at their base the suspicion that

[5] 'It is true to the spirit of Shakespearean comedy that the note of tragedy should . . . be drawn into its moments of resolution.' D. Traversi, *Shakespeare: The Early Comedies*, London 1960, p. 38. (In the context of *Love's Labour's Lost*.)

[6] 'In *Measure for Measure* . . . a coherent psychology is sacrificed to the exigencies of a striking story pleasing to an unsophisticated audience. And this *because* of the audience; for Shakespeare's better judgment would have taken him another way.' J. I. M. Stewart, *Character and Motive in Shakespeare*, London 1949, p. 15.

[7] See, for instance, J. Dover Wilson (ed.), *Measure for Measure* (New Cambridge Shakespeare), rev. edn, Cambridge 1950, Introduction, p. xl.

Shakespeare should not have written a play like this, that the union
between the elevated concerns of the first two acts and the intrigue that
fills much of the last three is inartistic and inexplicable.[8] Hence, it is
claimed, either a redactor of debased literary tastes has left his mark on
the play, or else Shakespeare sold out to commercial interests,
providing a play that would suit his audiences but not the highest
standards of his art. The affinity between *Measure for Measure* and
Fletcherian tragicomedy has been noted: Shakespeare or his reviser
is regarded as attempting to score an easy success by writing an
example of fashionable entertainment for the popular stage.[9] The
dating of *Measure for Measure* would suggest, nevertheless, that it is
earlier than the earliest of the Beaumont and Fletcher tragicomedies.[10]
Since the reasons for supposing that the surviving text represents a
revision by another hand are flimsy, Shakespeare must be credited
with the authorship of the play as a whole, no matter how unpalatable
that might be to many. To suggest that it is a 'pot-boiler' intended to
make a quick profit out of an emerging theatrical craze could be valid,
but the terms in which such suggestions are often put reveal a value-
judgement about Shakespeare's artistic aims which must not remain
unexamined. Equally, *Measure for Measure* may be regarded as a
remarkable experiment with certain forms of Renaissance comedy.

The play is a compendium of a number of familiar comic motifs.
Most significant is its incorporation of the basic situation in many
comedies, the difficulties experienced by young people in bringing
their love to the happy conclusion of marriage. The main impulse
behind the action of the play, the condemnation of Claudio for
adultery, seems outside the normal patterns of comic drama. But it is
no more than a displacement of the time-honoured dilemma of love-
comedy: how to find a way to overcome the mercenary and legalistic

---

[8] E. M. W. Tillyard saw the inconsistency in the play as arising from differences in the
material from which Shakespeare derived the two portions of the play, and from his
recreation of the character of his heroine. 'With significant action denied to Isabella,
Shakespeare must have seen that to carry the play through in the spirit in which he
began it was impossible; and after III. i. 151 he threw in his hand.' *Shakespeare's Problem
Plays*, London 1950, p. 132.

[9] The attitude was formerly widespread, and accepted as representing known facts. See,
for instance, Robert Bridges, 'The Influence of the Audience on Shakespeare's Drama'
in *Collected Essays*, London 1927, pp. 8–9. This essay was first published in 1907
appended to a volume of Shakespeare's works.

[10] *Measure for Measure* was probably first acted in the summer of 1604. *Philaster*, generally
thought to be the earliest of the 'Beaumont and Fletcher' tragicomedies, is more
difficult to date, but it is unlikely to have been performed before 1609.

opposition of middle-aged or elderly people to the marriage of the hero and the heroine. Claudio and Julietta are in love; they claim that in the eyes of the law they should be regarded as married; and it is stressed that the main impediment to the open admission of their liaison is (as so often in comedy) the question of money. These matters are stated by Claudio when he gives an account of his sorry plight.

> Thus stands it with me: upon a true contract
> I got possession of Julietta's bed.
> You know the lady, she is fast my wife,
> Save that we do the denunciation lack
> Of outward order; this we came not to,
> Only for propagation of a dow'r
> Remaining in the coffer of her friends.
> From whom we thought it meet to hide our love
> Till time had made them for us.
>
> (I. ii. 138)

In many comedies, as in *A Midsummer Night's Dream*, the opposition to the young people's love is expressed in violent terms, involving, at times, even the threat of death. In *Measure for Measure*, this characteristic is also present, but it is displaced from the centre of interest. Angelo is not only more threatening but also much more compelling than those cardboard figures of stern authority in the other comedies whose main function is merely to provide the necessary tension and suspense. Claudio and Julietta by contrast (except for his great *cri-de-coeur* in III. i.) seem to be merely mechanisms to launch the action—the audience cannot engage with them in the way that it is able to engage with Angelo, Isabella or even with the curious figure of the Duke.

The Duke himself represents another common comic type. In his disguise as the Friar, he is the witty or resourceful intriguer working to promote the happiness of the young people and, at times, his own profit as well. The political substratum of the play, the Duke's desire to learn the moral state of his realm and to test Angelo's integrity, is a version of the intrigues indulged in by the 'witty slaves' for their own benefit. Interestingly, we occasionally meet representatives of this character-type in the comedy of the period (as in *Much Ado About Nothing*) who are priests or friars. But in *Measure for Measure* these conventional motifs are to an extent obscured by the Duke's other function—the disguised figure of authority that intervenes at the last moment to save the situation from disaster. Some of the minor characters also reflect conventional comic types. Lucio, for instance, is the cynical realist who often acts as a foil for the hero's romantic ardours. But his rôle in this play is complicated by several un-characteristic features: he resembles to some extent those cynical and depraved characters like Parolles in *All's Well That Ends Well* who must be rejected by the comic world; yet he becomes a sincere advocate of Claudio's cause, even though his championship is no more elevated than his insistence that adultery is too common an offence to be treated so harshly.

The play thus rearranges its fairly conventional comic material in a significantly novel manner. Our interest and our fascination are engaged by those aspects of comedy which are usually kept in the background or are employed merely to commence the action. The language of confrontation between the hostile elements in this dark world, as much as the actual threat under which some of the characters languish, may be seen as an extrapolation of the normal ingredients of love-comedy to their ultimately tolerable extent. The same claim may be made for the deceptions of the last three acts. Substitution is often encountered in comedies as a means of resolving the usual comic dilemma—as in the farcical substitutions for Anne Page in *The Merry Wives of Windsor*. In *Measure for Measure*, the motif is represented by the gruesome search for a head to present to Angelo in place of Claudio's, and by the bed-trick which is to appear once more in *All's Well That Ends Well*. Because these devices are often so displaced or exaggerated in *Measure for Measure*, the play's essentially comic ancestry is largely obscured. It is because of these characteristics that the play has at times been seen as representing an attempt to explore the tragic poten-tialities of comic material. But it must be differentiated from an earlier essay in precisely that mode in order to demonstrate that *Measure for Measure* is a particularly complex set of variations on comic themes, rather than an employment of comic devices for the purposes of tragedy, or else a comedy which, in some unaccountable manner, went sour on its author.

Romeo and Juliet is a remarkable instance of the employment of the language, devices and conventions of comedy in a tragic play. Perhaps because the ingredients of Renaissance love-comedy are employed here for a very unusual purpose, the characteristic features of this type of comedy are more clearly evident than in many of Shakespeare's regular comedies. The characters conform, on the whole, to the familiar type-figures of Renaissance comedy. Romeo's impetuous ardour is contrasted with Juliet's greater caution and the finer depth of feeling she exhibits from time to time. Capulet and his wife are the blustering parents who insist on their daughter's marriage to the somewhat pallid approved suitor, represented in this play by the wooden County Paris. The Nurse is the garrulous, worldly confidante often encountered in comedies, while Mercutio is the hero's cynical friend whose function is to cast doubts on the youth's extravagant claims for the greatness of his passion. Friar Lawrence represents the conventional schemer who attempts to bring the young people together by means of trickery and deception.

The language of the play also emerges from the world of Renaissance comedy. The raucous quarrel between the retainers of the Capulets and the Montagues is filled with the usual tonalities of comic servants. The Nurse's thinly veiled sexual innuendoes, as well as her fund of reminiscences and anecdotes drawn from the world of folklore and popular superstition, belong to the dispensation of comedy. Mercutio's flights of fancy, the domestic bustle of the Capulets as they prepare for Juliet's wedding, and the passages of lyrical intensity in the love scenes all possess comic analogues. Even the lamentation over Juliet's supposedly dead body in IV. v. has something of the comic, perhaps parodistic, exaggeration to be encountered in some 'tragic' episodes in the comedies of the period. For several acts, the play seems to be a version of the 'love will find out a way' species of comedy; except, perhaps, for the deaths of Tybalt and Mercutio, there is little in it that would make a happy ending aesthetically or dramatically unacceptable.

Considerable critical attention has been paid to the classification of this tragedy which seems so contrary to normal sixteenth-century practices. The catastrophic outcome does not depend on any imperfection or moral fault in the major characters. The attempts to make Romeo's youthful impetuosity the cause of the disaster have not been convincing; to call the play a tragedy of fate seems half-hearted.[11] There is no need, however, to seek after arcane moral propositions: *Romeo and Juliet* is simply a fairly conventional Renaissance love-comedy in which all does not end well, but, on the contrary, ends in disaster. This is not to imply that Shakespeare lacked interest in the

---

[11] Both possibilities are discussed by Donald Stauffer in 'The School of Love: *Romeo and Juliet*' in *Shakespeare's World of Images*, New York 1949, pp. 53–59. Stauffer, while recognizing the element of 'rashness' in the lovers, nevertheless argues that *Romeo and Juliet* is concerned with the extra-human moral order represented by Fate.

potentialities contained in the material for pity and pathos. Rather, the pathos in the play emerges precisely because we see the world of conventional comic expectations frustrated. The motifs and devices of comedy are so clearly to be discerned in this play that there is a particular terror in the scene in the Capulets' tomb, when we realize that the end is not to be happiness and reconciliation. Because *Romeo and Juliet* is *not* a comedy, the comic analogues are more simply in evidence than they are in most of Shakespeare's comedies.

Measure for Measure, on the other hand, represents a different type of endeavour. It remains comic in so far as it fulfils the ancient formula that comedy is a fiction which begins in adversity and ends in hapiness. The displacement of these motifs is so thorough that the play may be taken, in part at least, as a technical exercise—an experiment in exploring how far a comedy is able to tolerate emphasis on brutality, greed, lasciviousness, and on the complicated means of arriving at the aniticipated happy ending, without shattering the mould of comic conventions. This must be insisted on: the ingredients of this play, which to many seem so alien to the world of comedy, are nothing other than the stressing of conventional comic material, especially that which produces the necessary tension and suspense. Other comedies also involve threats potentially as grave as the ones encountered here; the difference is that the arrangement of the narrative as well as the general 'tone' in the other comedies frequently provide reassurances that the situation will be saved from catastrophe.

The reassurance in *Measure for Measure* is in fact established very early. By the end of the third scene, we have learnt that the Duke has not left Vienna, and that he intends to exercise a paternally watchful care over his realm. The clearest analogy to this is, of course, Prospero's soothing words to Miranda in *The Tempest*, comforting her fears for the shipwrecked passengers, and thus containing the suspense and threat to the 'court party' within tolerable limits. But the special difficulty of *Measure of Measure* is the Duke's extreme reluctance (if not, indeed, negligence) in exercising his authority to solve the play's conflicts. This is so marked that several critics have suspected Shakespeare of making a definite point of it; moral reservations have been expressed about the Duke's probity, and considerable weight has been given to Lucio's slander concerning 'the Duke of dark corners'.[12] Otherwise, these

---

[12] The tradition seems to have begun with Hazlitt. 'As to the Duke, who makes a very imposing and mysterious stage-character, he is more absorbed in his own plots and

aspects of the play have been employed in arguments about its providential concerns,[13] or in attempts to demonstrate that the Duke's curious passivity was intended as a flattering vindication of James I's reluctance to mingle with his people during the early months of his reign.[14] In any event, such theories grow out of a sense of dissatisfaction: a character who is meant to gain our approval and provide the necessary reassurance of comedy acts in a manner quite contrary to such expectations.

But the Duke is an instrument of the comic design. He is reluctant to act because Shakespeare has fashioned a comedy in which the denouement, usually restricted to a portion of the last act, occupies a considerable portion of the play. Necessarily, a denouement must be articulated in terms of action and events—the conflicts of the comic world are resolved by events, chance meetings, sudden changes of heart, and the revelation of hitherto unsuspected truths. The celebrated (or notorious) *volta* at III. i. 153 of *Measure for Measure*, when the Duke draws Isabella aside, signals the beginning of the denouement: the unmasking of Angelo begins here. Quite appropriately, the dramatic mode changes to prose. The intense moral and poetic confrontation of the previous scenes gives way to the intrigue and bustle of the winding-down of the action. This is conventional comic practice: the beginning of the finale is signalled by a passage of deliberately theatrical artifice through which the course of the action alters for the benefit of the sympathetic characters in an unexpected and, at times, unlikely manner. It is only the relatively large proportion of the play occupied by this finale that makes it seem so contrary to Shakespeare's normal practices: the conventional comic finale in *Measure for Measure* is extended in a remarkable manner.

Yet the prison scenes, the grim search for a substitute head, the curious contrast between busy intrigue and the sickening sense that death cannot be avoided, all achieve a theatrical effect unlike anything else in the drama of the period. The effectiveness of these scenes is beyond question; their dramatic viability should also be acknowledged; the

---

gravity than anxious for the welfare of the State; more tenacious of his own character than attentive to the feelings and apprehensions of others.' *Characters of Shakespeare's Plays*, 4th edn, London 1848, pp. 313–14.

[13] Most notably by G. Wilson Knight, in *The Wheel of Fire*, rev. edn, London 1949, pp. 74, 80, 82–3.

[14] For an extended examination of this possibility, see J. M. Lever (ed.), *Measure for Measure* (The New Arden Shakespeare), London 1965, Introduction, pp. xlviii-l.

tension created by the contrast of the static, emblematic opening scenes and these episodes of swift action is striking. As in *The Winter's Tale*, a stylistic disjunction heralds a radical change in the narrative. This stressing of artifice and artificiality might well be called baroque, for Shakespeare draws attention to the theatrical skill with which seemingly incompatible ingredients in a play are brought into unity. Admittedly, the modulation in the third act of *The Winter's Tale* is accomplished more elegantly than the Duke's rather abrupt way of altering the play's course and mode of organization in *Measure for Measure*. Yet this earlier example of theatrical virtuosity is not the poor thing it is usually taken to be.

Measure for Measure then is an experiment in changing the emphases of comic drama while retaining its decorum. This is not to deny that the play engages with the moral and philosophical implications of its material. The issues isolated by modern criticism—the examination of sexual morality, the probing of the question of authority, and the presentation of the difficult dilemma of the relationship between the law and its dispensers—are important aspects of the work. But their relation to a consistent *Weltanschauung* (tacitly assumed by most critics) is more problematical. Modern criticism has been able to stress these aspects of the play only by neglecting (or all but neglecting) the considerable number of episodes that come after the last of the great, emblematic conflicts in the first scene of Act III.

For all its oddity nevertheless *Measure for Measure* conforms with the essential nature of Shakespearian comedy because it displays these seemingly elevated concerns in a fantastical, almost playful manner. The great issues enter into a curiously ambivalent, hypothetical relationship with the play's other material—some of it grave and thoughtful, some of it theatrical and 'witty'. The play is, essentially, a vehicle for the display of brilliance. The sobriety and sombre tone that pervade much of it (not merely the first two acts) make these terms seem inappropriate; but this 'darkness' is merely another facet of the characteristically *inclusive* nature of Shakespeare's comedies—structures which do not display or illustrate a single consistent set of themes or meanings, but rely, instead, on that copiousness which was so much praised by the Renaissance. *Measure for Measure* is notable for the unusually varied effects and concerns it incorporates within its design; the 'seriousness' of issues displayed in it may, indeed, stretch the decorum of comedy beyond its proper limits. But it is a bold and, on the whole, a successful experiment to exploit the capacity of comedy to include such variety. It sacrifices much of that diverting quality which distinguishes many comedies. But, despite the resulting oddity, this manner of comic experimentation held considerable fascination for Shakespeare at the time that *Measure for Measure* was written.

III

All's Well That Ends Well belongs to the same period. It, too, has seemed confused and very uneven in achievement.[15] It shares the sobriety of *Measure for Measure*, and includes, like that play, passages of considerable coarseness and an amount of apparently inappropriate 'comic' business for a play of such seriousness. Its greatest offence has been its curious treatment of Bertram, the leading male character (most hesitate to call him the hero). Dr Johnson expressed vividly the complaint that many modern commentators would also make:

> I cannot reconcile my heart to *Bertram*; a man noble without generosity, and young without truth; who marries *Helen* as coward, and leaves her as a profligate: when she is dead by his unkindness, sneaks home to a second marriage, is accused by a woman whom he has wronged, defends himself by falshood, and is dismissed to happiness.[16]

Johnson's views cannot be faulted if the play is to be regarded as a coherent moral document. No amount of allowance for the social and ethical priorities of the Renaissance will account for the play's oddity, or for the hiatus between its apparently high moral tone and its curiously a-moral features. For this reason, it has been dismissed as one of Shakespeare's failures, a work lacking direction or artistic coherence. It continues, nevertheless, to fascinate, even if only for its peculiarity, and no matter how unpalatable it is to modern audiences and critics, many sense that its material is organized in a strangely compelling way. The comedy is, indeed, a unity; but it is a unity forged out of its almost complete artificiality.

Whatever moral or spiritual propositions it may deal with, *All's Well*

---

[15] So judged by W. W. Lawrence in *Shakespeare's Problem Comedies*, rev. edn, New York 1960, pp. 32–77.
[16] S. Johnson, Note to *All's Well That Ends Well* in Mona Wilson (ed.), *Selected Works*, London 1957, p. 553.

That Ends Well represents another set of variations on the comic conventions of its period. It is a more 'witty' play than *Measure for Measure* because it is concerned with a thorough and deliberate reversal of the motifs of Renaissance love-comedy. Consistently, it teases its audience through veiled suggestions, false expectations and misleading innuendoes. This play, while apparently filled with ethical problems of the sort that threaten its comic integrity, has a good claim to be regarded as Shakespeare's most abstract comedy, the one most concerned with the witty transformation of familiar devices. In it the usual conventions of love-comedy are turned upside-down. Instead of confronting the hostility of their mercenary elders, the young people in the play, Bertram and Helena, are disunited. Their marriage, instead of meeting the type of financial and social opposition often encountered in comedies, is actively encouraged; even that figure of potentially tyrannous opposition, the King of France, encourages it. In many of the comedies of the period, the youth is usually ardent, reckless and totally dedicated to the cause of love; in this play Helena is given this type of personality except for the episode when she decides to sacrifice her love for Bertram's well-being. Bertram himself expresses the formal opposition to their marriage which is traditionally the preserve of materialistic old-age.

The broad pattern of reversals in the comedy is accompanied by many specific verbal and theatrical touches that constitute a form of game played at the audience's expense. Several times, Shakespeare establishes certain expectations and embodies seemingly important signs in the play, only to frustrate these expectations or convert these signs into different significations. The opening scene illustrates this teasing quality of the play. It is characterized by the reticence of both Bertram and Helena. The traditional landscape of comedy seems to be established in the contrast between the sombre, death-oriented world of the Countess and Lafew and the two (largely silent) young people. The Countess and Lafew converse about sadness, suffering and the past—the King's illness, Bertram's imminent departure, and the memory of the excellent Gerard de Narbon. Though this is not the way a comedy usually begins, we may glimpse here some of the traditional values of the elderly people of the comic world. By implication, Bertram and Helena, although they say little, appear to provide the contrast of youth. With assured stagecraft, these two are isolated and contrasted against a predominantly aged world. Their affinity is stressed: each has lost a father, each is reserved (even, perhaps, secretive) and formal in behaviour. This effect is achieved because they say relatively little—like the sinister Don John in the first scene of *Much Ado About Nothing*. They are enigmatic, and the audience thus suspects that there is something significant about their silence.

Helena's reply to the Countess's reprimand that she seems to grieve excessively for her father reinforces this sensation:

> *Countess*   No more of this, Helena; go to, no more,
> lest it be rather thought you affect a sorrow than
> to have—
> *Helena*   I do affect a sorrow indeed, but I have it too.
>
> (I. i. 45)

Her words are quibbling. The verb 'to affect' had several possible meanings at the time the play was written, besides the common meaning of false suggestion (in which sense it is used by the Countess in this extract). It could also mean to aim or aspire towards a goal, or to like, love or cherish someone or something.[17] The drift of Helena's quibble is plain enough: she indicates that she would prefer the Countess and the others to think that her dejection is caused by her father's death, but she implies that its real cause is to be found elsewhere. This reply carries, in addition, a possibility of faintly indecent overtones. 'Sorrow' may be taken as a periphrasis for childbearing as in the prophecy of Eve's sufferings in Genesis iii. 16.[18] There is no question, of course, of Helena's being pregnant: but it is important to recall that this speech occurs very early in the play, while most possibilities are still open. One, among several, is that she cherishes the sorrow she bears. This is a vague (and ultimately misleading) signal that we may expect a set of complications appropriate to a comedy about the frustrations of young love. Through this lure, the predicament of Bertram and Helena momentarily appears to be like that of Claudio and Julietta in *Measure for Measure*. In her jestingly solemn reply to the Countess she appears briefly to assume the characteristic traits of some of the young women in Renaissance love-comedies. In general, throughout the opening scene of *All's Well That Ends Well*, Helena is presented in a notably ambiguous way. She seems to possess and to demonstrate possession of an almost anti-comic gravity, yet in her reply to the Countess, and

---

[17] *OED*, *affect*, vl, 1 and vl, 4.

[18] The word is used in this sense by the Mother in Middleton's *Women Beware Women*: 'Curse of sorrows' (I. i. 5).

in her subsequent badinage with the foul-mouthed Parolles, she exhibits the freedom and liveliness of those sprightly young women who take on the world to prosper their love. The signals sent out by the opening moments of the play are, therefore, particularly ambivalent and misleading.

The first of Helena's two weighty soliloquies in the opening scene is an instance of this double perspective. Most commentators take the speech as an expression of her unrequited love for Bertram. Yet nothing in it suggests explicitly that she is *not* lamenting the frustration of mutual love. Indeed, several teasing suggestions intimate the contrary:

> my imagination
> Carries no favour in't but Bertram's.
> I am undone; there is no living, none,
> If Bertram be away. 'Twere all one
> That I should love a bright particular star
> And think to wed it, he is so above me.
> In his bright radiance and collateral light
> Must I be comforted, not in his sphere.
> Th' ambition in my love thus plagues itself:
> The hind that would be mated by the lion
> Must die for love. 'Twas pretty, though a plague,
> To see him every hour; to sit and draw
> His arched brows, his hawking eye, his curls,
> In our heart's table—heart too capable
> Of every line and trick of his sweet favour.
> But now he's gone, and my idolatrous fancy
> Must sanctify his relics.
>
> (I. i. 76)

Some of the details of this speech are odd. Favours were tokens of fidelity exchanged by lovers; we must attend to the text very carefully (more carefully, perhaps, than a theatrical audience is able) to understand that she carries an image of his *features*, not his gifts of love. To be undone commonly means to have been ruined through seduction.[19] Helena's claim to be undone causes a momentary surprise (coming, as it does, relatively soon after the quibble on sorrow). The astronomical conceit in 'collateral light' is apt, but the adjective carries a genealogical sense which helps to confuse the issues for a moment. Later in the speech, she seems to suggest that her relationship with

---

[19] *OED, undo,* v8d.

Bertram was intimate enough to permit her to sketch his visage—until we realize that she is speaking figuratively about the strong impression of him engraved on her heart. At the end of the speech, we return to the ambiguities of 'favours'. These obfuscations are quite deliberate, they aid the general supposition that we are witnessing a common comic situation—the sorrows of young lovers, possessing strong sexual desire for each other, who experience, in this instance, not merely parental opposition, but the prospect of separation as well.

These are traditional motifs of love-comedy, represented most clearly in Shakespeare by *The Two Gentlemen of Verona*, an almost entirely routine and predictable play. We are given a strong reminder of it in the third scene of *All's Well That Ends Well* after the Steward has come to the Countess with news of Helena's intention to travel to Paris to attempt the King's cure and to win Bertram as her husband. The Countess's reply recalls the traditional responses of parental authority:

> You have discharg'd this honestly; keep it to yourself.
> Many likelihoods inform'd me of this before, which hung
> so tott'ring in the balance that I could neither believe nor
> misdoubt. Pray you leave me. Stall this in your bosom; and
> I thank you for your honest care. I will speak with you
> further anon.
>
> (I. iii. 113)

These words echo the Duke of Milan's speech to Proteus in *The Two Gentlemen of Verona* when the young man informs him of the plan by Valentine and Silvia to elope. The tone of outrage, the dark hints that the liaison had already been suspected, the insistence that only circumspection prevented action, and the veiled promises of reward are to be encountered in both.

> Proteus, I thank thee for thine honest care,
> Which to requite, command me while I live.
> This love of theirs myself have often seen,
> Haply when they have judg'd me fast asleep,
> And oftentimes have purpos'd to forbid
> Sir Valentine her company and my court;
> But, fearing lest my jealous aim might err
> And so, unworthily, disgrace the man,
> A rashness that I ever yet have shunn'd,
> I gave him gentle looks, thereby to find
> That which thyself hast now disclos'd to me.
>
> (III. i. 22)

Yet even here, before the peculiar inversion of comic motifs becomes apparent in *All's Well That Ends Well*, a perceptive member of Shakespeare's audience might have been struck by a curious reversal: these apparently outraged tones of conventional authority are not usually adopted by women in the comedies of the time; they are the prerogative of angry fathers. A traditional ingredient of love-comedy is here given a faintly bizarre flavour.

Subsequently, the transformation of orthodox devices multiplies rapidly. In a painful interview between Helena and the Countess, the conventional confrontation between the young lover and his mistress's angry father becomes a conflict between two women. It is during this impassioned scene that we have the first substantial hint of the play's ancestry in the story of Giletta of Narbona. At the beginning of the confrontation, the Countess displays the anger and outrage implicit in her words to the Steward. She torments Helena by insisting that the girl should call her 'mother'. Her barbed comments finally elicit a veiled confession of love, whereupon she attacks her victim with a show of violence:

> Yes, Helen, you might be my daughter-in-law.
> God shield you mean it not! "daughter" and "mother"
> So strive upon your pulse. What! pale again?
> My fear hath catch'd your fondness. Now I see
> The myst'ry of your loneliness, and find
> Your salt tears' head. Now to all sense 'tis gross
> You love my son; invention is asham'd,
> Against the proclamation of thy passion,
> To say thou dost not. Therefore tell me true;
> But tell me then, 'tis so; for, look, thy cheeks
> Confess it, th'one to th' other; and thine eyes
> See it so grossly shown in thy behaviours
> That in their kind they speak it; only sin
> And hellish obstinacy tie thy tongue,
> That truth should be suspected. Speak, is't so?
> If it be so, you have wound a goodly clew;
> If it be not, forswear't; howe'er, I charge thee,
> As heaven shall work in me for thine avail,
> To tell me truly.
>
> (I. iii. 158)

The last of Helena's inhibitions is overcome by this *tour de force* of mock indignation. She confesses her love and her intention to travel to Paris. Thereupon, Shakespeare produces a spectacular *coup de théâtre*: the Countess blesses Helena's project with words of soothing comfort:

> Why, Helen, thou shalt have my leave and love,
> Means and attendants, and my loving greetings
> To those of mine in court. I'll stay at home,
> And pray God's blessing into thy attempt.
> Be gone to-morrow; and be sure of this,
> What I can help thee to thou shalt not miss.
>
> (I. iii. 242)

'Be gone to-morrow' are words with which young men are usually banished from the sight of their grieving mistresses; in this play, a young woman is peremptorily dismissed into happiness. By the end of its first act, *All's Well That Ends Well* has reversed neatly the world of Renaissance love-comedy.

In the second act, it is quickly established that Bertram, and not the King, will fulfil the traditional function of objecting strenuously to the marriage of the young Count and the poor physician's orphan. He voices the usual objections to a marriage based on inequality of rank and property. The King reminds him of Helena's great service to the crown; Bertram adds, not entirely without reason:

> But follows it, my lord, to bring me down
> Must answer for your raising? I know her well:
> She had her breeding at my father's charge.
> A poor physician's daughter my wife! Disdain
> Rather corrupt me ever!
>
> (II. iii. 109)

The King, in turn, assumes the role of an apologist for love, even where it offends against social status. Ironically though (and with that playfulness which is never far absent from this comedy), in order to get his way, this champion of 'true love' must play the autocrat. At first, he urges the supremacy of love over social priorities in significantly rhymed, aphoristic verse:

> From lowest place when virtuous things proceed,
> The place is dignified by th' doer's deed;
> Where great additions swell's, and virtue none,
> It is a dropsied honour. Good alone
> Is good without a name. Vileness is so:
> The property by what it is should go,
> Not by the title. She is young, wise, fair;
> In these to nature she's immediate heir . . .
>
> (II. iii. 125)

But the diction changes to direct, forceful blank-verse when Bertram insists that he cannot marry Helena because he does not love her. The King begins to speak in the accents of the irate fathers in the comedies of the time:

> Obey our will, which travails in thy good;
> Believe not thy disdain, but presently
> Do thine own fortunes that obedient right
> Which both thy duty owes and our power claims;
> Or I will throw thee from my care for ever
> Into the staggers and the careless lapse
> Of youth and ignorance; both my revenge and hate
> Loosing upon thee in the name of justice,
> Without all terms of pity.
>
> (II. iii. 155)

The traditional antagonists of love-comedy have changed sides. Bertram appeals to the social mores of parental authority; the King uses the peremptory rhetoric of angry fathers and tyrannical dukes to plead the cause of young love. The Duke of Milan's absolutely conventional speech in *The Two Gentlemen of Verona*, when he banishes the unfortunate Valentine, demonstrates the extent to which the King of France's speech relies on our recognition of its departure from conventional modes.

> Why, Phaethon—for thou art Merops' son—
> Wilt thou aspire to guide the heavenly car,
> And with thy daring folly burn the world?
> Wilt thou reach stars because they shine on thee?
> Go, base intruder, over-weening slave,
> Bestow thy fawning smiles on equal mates;
> And think my patience, more than thy desert,
> Is privilege for thy departure hence.
> Thank me for this more than for all the favours
> Which, all too much, I have bestow'd on thee.
> But if thou linger in my territories
> Longer than swiftest expedition
> Will give thee time to leave our royal court,
> By heaven! my wrath shall far exceed the love
> I ever bore my daughter or thyself.
> Be gone; I will not hear thy vain excuse,
> But, as thou lov'st thy life, make speed from hence.
>
> (III. i. 153)

Bertram's refusal of Helena is the outstanding instance in *All's Well That Ends Well* of the reversal and inversion of traditional comic structures. The later scenes of the play are concerned with the unravelling of the situation, and the interest comes, consequently, to be focused on narrative, not on the largely verbal wit of previous scenes. Bertram's callousness, that most uncharacteristic quality in the hero of a comedy, now receives some emphasis: his function hitherto has been largely paradoxical. His protestations of his inability to love Helena are reasonable enough—he persists in saying that he does not love her and that, therefore, he should not be forced to marry her. He says no more, in other words, than the lovers of comedy are constantly saying: that love cannot be commanded or ordained by social considerations. Why he seems so unsympathetic in the first two acts has little to do with his character. He is unpleasant because he stands in the way of the play's basic drive, the desire to see Helena's endeavours succeed. He sets himself up against an eloquent authority which, in this play, represents the goal towards which the narrative aspires. And yet these considerations form merely one perspective in a comedy of multiple perspectives and shifting focuses. Although critical tradition since Johnson's time has singled out Bertram as the play's special difficulty, he is merely a symptom of the nature of the whole. The other major characters, too, are established in the rhetorical and theatrical terms of certain familiar prototypes; yet their actions and personalities are often the opposite in function and effect.

The play is, therefore, a network of contradictory suggestions, strange turnings, odd reversals of expectations and attitudes. It is, in other words, a series of variations on the conventions of a popular from of Renaissance comedy. It is Shakespeare's most surprising and most thorough experiment with comic form. The play's flamboyance and sophistication are further indicated by the unlikely overtones that gather around its chaste and serious heroine's name. Helena's counterpart in the source-story is called Giletta: this is the only instance in the play where Shakespeare did not use a name provided by his source. The reasons for the change are not readily apparent: Helena as a name may be slightly more euphonious than Giletta, and it allows abbreviation into the more homely Helen, with obvious metrical advantages. Yet, whatever the reason for the change, Shakespeare obviously plays with the fact that his heroine has the same name as the legendary adulteress, the cause of immense suffering and woe, Helen of Troy. This is clearly implied in the snatch of song sung by the Clown in I. iii.

"Was this fair face the cause" quoth she
  "Why the Grecians sacked Troy?
Fond done, done fond,
  Was this King Priam's joy?"
With that she sighed as she stood,
With that she sighed as she stood,
  And gave this sentence then:
"Among nine bad if one be good,
Among nine bad if one be good,
There's yet one good in ten."

(I. iii. 66)

The point of this ditty (borrowed, it seems, from an unknown but apparently popular ballad) is obscure; it reinforces, however, the irrelevant comparison between Helena and her legendary namesake. The Countess remarks that the Clown has 'perverted' the song; it seems, therefore, that its words are deliberately altered in this context. Thematically there is little reason for the introduction of this episode since, as already stressed, there is little affinity between this Helena and Paris's paramour. Yet the joking associations hinted at recur in another impertinent flourish a little later in the same scene. Twice in the course of the painful interview with Helena, the Countess names the French capital-city as she is attempting to elicit a confession from the unfortunate girl.

Had you not lately an intent—speak truly—
To go to Paris?
          *   *   *
                  This was your motive
For Paris, was it? Speak.

(I. iii. 209; 222)

These words embody a strange ambiguity. they could refer equally to the city and to the Trojan prince. As far as the action of the play is concerned, of course, only the city is signified; but there seems to be a peculiar delight in accumulating these random and irrelevant associations between the name of the chaste heroine and the fabled whore. Moreover, with a particular type of wit entirely lacking moral associations, these odd possibilities are also reflected by Helena's having to indulge in the shoddy bed-trick to regain her conjugal rights—she must come to Bertram in the dark and in silence, disguised as a woman of easy virtue.

The possibility that these puzzling elements in the play represent an abstract and essentially 'meaningless' wit is reinforced by another curious feature of its nomenclature. None of the surviving versions of the source-story gives a name to the young woman Bertram attempts to seduce in Florence. In the Palace of Pleasure she is described merely as 'a gentlewoman, very poore and of small substance, nevertheless of right honest life & good report'.[20] Shakespeare chose to call her Diana, the name of the goddess of chastity, of the moon and of childbirth, and the protectress of the plebeian classes.[21] The name is, in many ways, quite appropriate: she is chaste and honourable, she heeds Helena's warnings about Bertram, and she safeguards her virtue. She is, moreover, the patroness of Helena's pregnancy because the bed-trick depends on her co-operation. She is, also, certainly *déclassée*, if not exactly plebeian. Yet certain improper suggestions accumulate around her. At the end of the play, when she interrupts Bertram's marriage to Lafew's daughter with her riddling message concerning her possession of Bertram's ring, there is a curious digression as she is vilified by the King and Lafew. She is called 'an easy glove' and 'a common customer', and comes to be identified momentarily with the moral laxity Bertram presumed her to possess. This passage represents the characteristic delay in the resolution that is often a part of comic design; but its function may also be taken as another instance of the curious jesting with names, words and conventional motifs.

The comedy contains, therefore, an amount of odd playing with the names of its leading women characters. These names suggest absolute contrast; yet they are similar in many ways. Both are chaste and virtuous; both are poor and of lowly status. They are resourceful and courageous. This affinity is further stressed by the play's off-beat conclusion: in the King's closing words (addressed to Diana)

> If thou beest yet a fresh uncropped flower,
> Choose thou thy husband, and I'll pay thy dower;
> For I can guess that by thy honest aid
> Thou kept'st a wife herself, thyself a maid.
>
> (V. iii. 320)

there is an implicit suggestion that we are about to witness the beginning of another play called *All's Well That Ends Well*. Their

[20] G. Bullough, *Narrative and Dramatic Sources of Shakespeare*, II, London 1958, p. 393.
[21] P. Harvey, *The Oxford Companion to Classical Literature*, corr. edn, Oxford 1940, p. 143.

function, however, is sharply contrasted: one seeks Bertram, the other strives to avoid him; Helena is pious, grave and solemn, Diana exhibits much more of the usual comic vitality. Through these similarities and contrasts, the two characters are interwoven in the play's complex fabric of jesting suggestions.

The view of the play emerging from these considerations is somewhat different from its usual reputation. Instead of a gloomy, agonized examination of vice and chastity, love and egotism, we have a curiously abstract and formal structure which rings sophisticated changes on the conventions of Renaissance love-comedies. Bertram, who should be the ardent lover, willing to risk all for his mistress, insisting upon the primacy of love above all considerations of wealth and rank, adopts, instead, the attitudes of hostile old-age. The elderly people in the play (its figures of authority) encourage and aid the penniless girl (turned adventuress) in her pursuit of the unwilling male. She, herself, is surrounded by unlikely implications of indecency; her 'rival', who appears to be named as inappropriately as she is, proves to live up to the moral requirements embodied in her name. The apparent moral disapproval of the 'hero' during the first two acts proves, on examination, to be based not on morality but on theatrical expectations. This is a play, in short, which constantly turns its material and conventions inside-out. It is a highly *literary* work despite its being based so much on theatrical traditions and modes. Its real impulse and many of its best effects depend not so much on extractable meanings, views of life or schemes of morality—the usual topics of literary exegesis—but on fundamentally 'meaningless' patterns, suggestions and implications. It is, to stress once more, a witty experiment with the possibilities of a common type of comedy.

Shakespeare's experiments with comic form took an exceptionally radical form in the early years of the seventeenth century. It is perhaps significant that no more comedies seem to have been written after *Measure for Measure* and *All's Well That Ends Well* until the so-called Romances of the second decade of the century. Those plays represent the culmination of Shakespeare's constant fascination with the possibilities of comic drama: they, too, are experiments with comedy, no less extraordinary than the 'dark comedies', though richer and more subdued, more harmonious in their transformation of comic traditions and conventions. Two other plays of the earlier period must be glanced at briefly in any account of Shakespeare's comic experiments. The two *Henry IV* plays from the end of the sixteenth century represent a remarkable attempt to incorporate certain stylistic and conventional elements of comedy in a political chronicle play. In the tavern scenes, in the Gadshill episode and in the provincial episodes of the second part the plays move close to comedy, but they lack the structural aspects of comic drama. The merging of the political and the comic within a comic framework occurs more surely in *Cymbeline*. *Troilus and Cressida* lies outside the province of Shakespearian comedy: it is a unique essay in historical satire which transforms the customary elements of Renaissance comedy—the ardent lovers, the clown figure, the amoral promoter of love, the worldly cynic—almost beyond recognition.

Measure for Measure and *All's Well That Ends Well*, true comedies for all their peculiarity, remain comic because in them the conventions and traditions of comedy, though stood on their heads, are still recognizable. They are flamboyant theatrical extravaganzas concerned with largely abstract and formal preoccupations. It is difficult to see either of them in any other light if we take into account the manner in which each plays elaborate variations on comic decorum. They are essentially witty plays, even though they lack the superficial wit and fantasy usually associated with Shakespeare's comedies. They are not instances of a disillusionment with comedies or of an exploration of the tragic implications of the escapist world of comedy, but extensions of the nature of comedy to its ultimate point.

IV

Playing elaborate games with the modes and conventions of literary forms is a type of flamboyance that leads, inevitably, to excess. Works of art which seem concerned with the ingenuity of their creator, rather than the communication of a coherent view of life, have often been suspected of being self-regarding and exhibitionist. Certain modern novels are notorious instances of this: Thomas Mann's later works (notably *The Holy Sinner* and *The Confessions of Felix Krull*) and most of Nabokov's many works of fiction seem so involved with merely technical details of construction and so little concerned with communicating their authors' 'vision' that they have been, at times, dismissed as mere follies, or, in the case of Mann, as retreats into triviality after the rigours of *The Magic Mountain* and *Doctor Faustus*.

Such literature piles effect on effect; it charms and delights by odd turns of narrative and character, by the curiously roundabout means of arriving at obvious conclusions, or else by the abrupt and unashamed introduction of unexpected developments or changes of fortune. These works often seem, as well, to adopt deliberately artificial modes of narration and construction—the medieval saints' legend in *The Holy Sinner*, picaresque fiction in *Felix Krull*, the salacious tale of sexual perversion of *Lolita*, or the science-fiction fantasy of *Ada, or Ardor*. All these are akin to that insouciance and levity so often associated with comedy and the comic spirit. In 'escapist' entertainment, all absurdities seem valid.

Shakespeare's comedies offer many instances of this type of literary art. In these plays, he goes consistently beyond the normal sportiveness and exuberance customarily encountered in comedy, by redoubling conventional effects and producing even more outrageous, complicated or, at times, even barefacedly improbable theatrical situations. The common features of the comedy of his time are pushed to the limit of viability, seemingly for the delight of so doing. *The Comedy of Errors*, as already noted, doubles the identical-twins motif of the original source. Adding the two Dromios to the two Antipholuses enhances the opportunities for breathless farce, making it possible to increase the misunderstandings and confusions occasioned by the presence in Ephesus of two sets of indistinguishable twins. But the endeavour also increases the danger that the audience, too, will become confused, and it offers, therefore, an opportunity for the playwright to display his skill.

Farce habitually dwells on the brink of chaos. Its characters live in a world which seems to have lost all semblance of logic and probability. In the farces of Georges Feyedeau, this is symbolized by his *haut-bourgeois* set of characters' being frequently thrown into the perplexing confusions of a bordello; in *The Comedy of Errors*, the well-known reputation of Ephesus as a place of sorcery and witchcraft fulfils the same purpose. A large part of the theatrical excitement and pleasure an audience experiences in a farce comes from the manner in which these confusing strands are held together. The playwright teases his audience; he threatens constantly to make the plot so complicated that the audience, too, is in danger of becoming confused. Yet in great farces we are able to keep our heads above water, no matter how precariously. On the whole, Shakespeare succeeds in achieving this in *The Comedy of Errors*. Its action becomes increasingly perplexing, confusion is heaped on confusion, the characters feel more and more that they are living in a world that is fast becoming totally insane. But the audience remains serenely in control of the dizzying complications. The brilliant management of these excesses seems to have been a large part of the dramatist's intention and of the play's *raison d'être*.

Later comedies display similar characteristics. The twin-motif is employed in *Twelfth Night* in an admittedly more subdued manner. *As You Like It* provides an interesting variant in Jaques de Boys's sudden arrival in the last scene to announce Duke Frederick's abrupt change of heart. The youngest of the de Boys brothers is mentioned briefly early in the play, but seems subsequently to have been forgotten. Making him the messenger of glad tidings appears to be one of the essentially excessive flourishes or displays which often characterize the final moments of Shakespeare's comedies. No dramatic or emotional necessity is served by this; it is an instance of the excess to be encountered in other comic episodes—a going beyond the expected, the required or even, perhaps, the tolerable. It is a deliberate infringement of probability—not the probability of the world outside the theatre, but the conventional probabilities of the stage.

As You Like It is not content merely to include the gratuitous arrival of the youngest of the de Boys brothers, at its end there is also the essentially indecorous appearance of Hymen. Until his arrival to preside over the marriage-feast, the play has excluded the supernatural. The world of Arden is fantastical and improbable, but it contains nothing that is impossible. The introduction of Hymen breaks this decorum; the conventions of the masque are conflated with the conventions of comedy. The incursion into a different scheme of reality in the last moments of the play is excessive and startling; it draws further attention to the flamboyant artifice. *As You Like It* would have remained a satisfying and coherent work of art without these instances of excess; but Shakespeare throws them in, as it were, just for good measure. A similar feat may be observed in the last scene of *The Merchant of Venice*. Portia brings news from Venice that some of Antonio's wealth has been recovered; again, this serves no dramatic necessity. The audience entertains no fears for Antonio's welfare—he has been saved from Shylock's knife, and at that point he has ceased to be of any interest. The recovery of his wealth is not included, therefore, from any post-Ibsenish necessity to account for the state of all the characters at the end of a play. Rather, it is once more, a gratuitous gesture of excess.

The tendency towards excess in Shakespeare's comedies is to be seen in other features as well. Significant, though not in need of extended discussion, is the way in which the language of these plays constantly inclines towards the fantastical. This was, and still remains, a common feature of comedy. But in Shakespeare, the verbal fantasias are, somehow, more notable than elsewhere. No doubt, this was a result of his extraordinary linguistic facility and connoisseur's love of collecting odd or interesting expressions. That he saw no need, apparently, to curb this excess of language is nevertheless an indicator of the essential mode of many of his comedies.

The excessiveness of the comedies appears also to possess thematic and philosophical implications. Excess is to be found not merely in events, sudden peripeties or in odd strokes of good fortune. It resides also in the generally benign attitude expressed towards some of the characters who, in the opinion of many, are 'let off too lightly' given the transgressions they commit. In many plays, we encounter characters who are worthy of great censure yet appear to be treated with extreme indulgence. The mirror-image of this, perhaps, is the savagery meted out to others whose transgressions appear to be no more worthy of condemnation than the transgressions of those who seem to receive such benevolence from their creator. The so-called problem plays or dark comedies are outstanding in this respect. Angelo, in *Measure for Measure*, is guilty of hypocrisy, dishonesty, misapplication of the law and of the abuse of his office to such an extent that his being forgiven at the end is often thought to be offensive. Lucio, on the other hand, whose greatest offence is that he enjoys the amenities of Vienna and that he has a sharp tongue, is treated almost brutally, being in danger for a moment of losing his life. It is not entirely appropriate to appeal to political attitudes about *lèse majesté* in Shakespeare's world. If the play were intended as an apologia for James's even-handed judiciousness,[22] as some claim, then Angelo's abuse of a deputy's function should not be treated more lightly than Lucio's slanders of the Duke. Though Lucio is saved, at the last moment, from whipping and hanging, he is still made to marry a punk—Angelo, on the other hand, is received into the commonwealth of comedy.

Bertram, in *All's Well That Ends Well*, is a similar case. As Dr Johnson noted, he does not really repent; he honours his marital obligations only when absolutely cornered: yet the play tolerates him

[22] See J. M. Lever (ed.), *Measure for Measure* (The New Arden Shakespeare), London 1965, Introduction, pp. xlviiiff.

quite cheerfully as a fit husband for the excellent Helena. *Much Ado About Nothing*, a play in some respects similar to the 'dark comedies', presents the same type of moral ambiguity in its treatment of Claudio. Like Bertram, he has little to redeem him. The shallowness of his personality is demonstrated, it would appear, by the way in which his declaration of absolute and unending love for Hero turns into violent contempt after he has been taken in by Don John's transparent calumny of her chastity. The nature of his offence is stressed by the near-hysteria of his rejection of Hero in the marriage-scene of Act IV. He seems as caddish and as little deserving of sympathy as Bertram. Yet he is restored to Hero's love at the end after the most perfunctory of penances. The moral implications of the denouement, here as elsewhere, are apparently avoided. The comedy draws a veil of benevolence over problems and actions which should be the cause of considerable agitation.

A degree of moral laxity is frequently to be encountered even in those comedies where the central characters do not demonstrate such callousness. The apparent blandness of this comic world places few demands on its sympathetic characters. Orsino languishes for Olivia throughout much of *Twelfth Night*, yet does little to advance his suit, except for sending Viola/Cesario on embassies to the lady. Orlando in *As You Like It* is, apparently, too thick-skulled to recognize the in-nuendoes made by Rosalind in her disguise. In *The Two Gentlemen of Verona*, Valentine may be considered to be carrying the code of chivalry much too far in offering to hand Silvia over to the newly-contrite Proteus. It is difficult to escape the impression that these young men are guilty of passivity and even, at times, of stupidity. Incidents such as these may be taken as instances of the mockery that often characteriz-es the world of comedy. Otherwise, they may be seen as testimony to the intrinsic triviality of comedy. There is no doubt that in many of these instances we are required to register gentle, indulgent mockery. Comedy, whenever it deals with youthful love, usually adopts an attitude of mature indulgence: young lovers are attractive often because their ardour and idealism border on the foolish. More important than the mockery, however, is a tendency in these plays towards a benevolence which seems remarkably free from the requirements of poetic justice. There is an absence of the connection between intrinsic worth or an active striving after felicity and the achievement of happiness and good fortune.

The concept of poetic justice is deeply embedded in most forms of narrative. There is a fundamental desire to see a morally ordered world where justice is dispensed according to worth. It may be observed that this desire for justice in literature is simpler than that experience in daily life. Both tragedies and comedies of social criticism frequently exhibit a concern with poetic justice. Characters in fiction do not always reap as they sow, but if they fail to do so, their failure is often recognized as a miscarriage of justice. In tragedies, this sense of justice often seems inexorable and even extreme. Oedipus and King Lear are exemplars of the manner in which natural justice (or revenge) exacts retribution much in excess of the original offence. Oedipus is an unwitting malefactor, yet he must pay the penalty for his transgression. Lear's sufferings are much greater than his crime; Cordelia must die, much to the distress of Dr Johnson who could not understand how her death could be made consistent with the audience's natural desire for justice. But the rigour of tragic justice demands that even the innocent suffer for the transgressions of the guilty. The moral scheme behind the dispensation in many tragedies is similar to the inflexible but grimly just biblical requirement that the sins of the fathers be visited on their sons. The Genesis myth sets the pattern for the basic characteristics of poetic justice in most forms of tragedy: Adam's transgression is regularly and inexorably visited on his offspring until, in some fabulously remote era, the curse is lifted by divine mercy.

This concern with patterns of justice entered into the major comic tradition of the European cultures. The comic dispensation is less vengeful and less absolute, but the impulse to separate sheep from goats is fundamental. In certain bitter forms of comedy, it is true, the virtuous often miscarry, but in these cases the dramatist usually registers a strong protest about the desperate state of a society that permits such things to occur. This is where comedy assumes its most satiric stance, as in some of Brecht's work, notably *The Rise and Fall of the City Mahagonny*. Sometimes, as in *Tartuffe*, the impression is given that the play will end with a miscarriage of justice, that the forces of hypocrisy and greed will prevail. The *deus-ex-machina* fiat from the King at the last moment seems to restore the play to the demands of natural justice, while, through its abruptness and overt theatricality, managing to suggest that in everyday experience such neat resolutions are not to be expected.

Shakespeare's comedies (and the type of comedy that they represent) do not in every case subscribe to such a scheme. In general, of course, because of the usually amiable nature of his comedies, the attractive and sympathetic characters end by becoming the recipients of happiness and good fortune. Jack, mostly, has Jill, and nought finally goes ill, no matter how circuitously such felicity is achieved. But consistently, there is little if any stress on desert: a character's good (or ill) fortune seems remote from his moral status. For the approved one, the benevolence and the geniality of the comic world seem limitless; the impulse towards showering blessings on the nice (even if they happen not to be particularly good) is irresistible, and several none-too-nice characters also manage to achieve this desirable state.

Curiously, the young men in the comedies are distinguished in this respect. In a number of the plays, the women are active, determined and courageous; they frequently withstand risks and dangers in their pursuit of love and happiness. Where the women exhibit these characteristics—in *The Two Gentlemen of Verona*, *As You Like It*, *Twelfth Night* and *Cymbeline*, but most of all in *All's Well That Ends Well*—the menfolk are usually passive, unadventurous and, in the case of Bertram, callous. Posthumus, like the much-maligned Bertram, easily doubts Imogen's virtue and forgets her quickly. Yet these men are received into the realm of happiness. Nothing more than being young, attractive and above all loved is required; the comic dispensation makes no other demands. Is this the mindlessness of comedy? Does it represent a fundamentally unpleasant attitude which suggests that all that these youths have to do is to expect happiness to come to them? Or does it, on the contrary, indicate a celebration of the courage and endurance of these young women who take on the world in pursuit of their ideals? All these views are arguable; all may be demonstrable; but the plays offer little evidence one way or another. In their excessive benevolence, Shakespeare's comedies tease us with possibilities of interpretation or significance, without directing attention unambiguously to any, and even without registering the necessity that we should seek them. Yet the comedies appear to hover on the edge of the significant, the meaningful and even the philosophical. The patterns of benign indulgence are so general that they seem to point towards a statement about the possibilities of happiness.

It is for this reason that on several occasions various providential schemes have been detected in the comedies. An attempt has been made to argue that some of the middle-period comedies deal with the specifically Christian virtue of forgiveness.[23] Elsewhere, it has been

---

[23] R. G. Hunter, *Shakespeare and the Comedy of Forgiveness*, New York 1965, contains a particularly clear statement of the view that the 'dark comedies' deal with schemes of Christian redemption. See especially pp. 106ff.

suspected that the lack of poetic justice and the reluctance to judge or to condemn certain types of characters represent an idealism and the expression of a generally optimistic view of life. This optimism would confer great benefits on a class of characters even though, from the stance of common morality, they often seem unworthy of their good fortune. The probability of this seems to be reinforced by the savagery with which other characters, not always deserving great condemnation, are treated.

The amiable, fortunate young men in these plays are often contrasted with certain characters, well past the first flush of youth, whom Frye has identified as the 'refuser of the festivities'.[24] These characters are subjected to scorn, mockery and humiliation by the more likeable and more fortunate personages. At times, this character-type merges with the conventional antagonist of the comic action, in which cases his humiliation and expulsion seem morally defensible. Shylock is an obvious example. Some characters, notably Falstaff in *The Merry Wives of Windsor* (though not in the *Henry IV* plays), are more ambiguous; their torment and humiliation seem not entirely proportionate to their moral or ethical shortcomings. But the most interesting group of characters is that where scorn and contempt are heaped on representatives of this figure in a manner much in excess of their actual 'transgressions'. Jaques and Malvolio are both treated contemptuously; each is profoundly out of harmony with the society in which he lives and to which he seems to cling. They come to represent, in a not entirely rational way, all that the comic world of love and youth is incapable of tolerating. Parolles in *All's Well That Ends Well* belongs to this class, as does Thersites in *Troilus and Cressida*, that strangely hybrid play possessing some of the characteristics of comedy. In all instances, but with varying degrees of intensity, these characters are antagonistic to the idealized world of love and courtship. With Jaques it is fashionable, disenchanted melancholy; with Malvolio it is the mercenary attempt to better his social standing; and with Parolles and Thersites it is the reductive sexual cynicism which sees nothing but lechery in romantic ardour.

The treatment of these characters is usually harsh. Malvolio is humiliated publicly in the last scene of *Twelfth Night*; Jaques must endure the taunts of Touchstone and the hostility of others, just as Armado in *Love's Labour's Lost* is constantly the target of insults thrown out by the King and his nobles. Parolles is humiliated in *All's Well That*

[24] Northrop Frye, *The Anatomy of Criticism*, New Jersey 1957, p. 176.

Ends Well when he has been exposed for a cheat and a liar, even though at the end the old lord Lafew takes pity on him and offers him shelter. The entire population of Windsor, it seems, is enrolled to torment Falstaff. Propero's stern regimen of Caliban in *The Tempest* is a strangely variant echo of these practices. There is no readily apparent reason why some of these characters should be subjected to such harshness, when others, like Angelo, who infringe the dictates of morality and of the law, are treated with relative indulgence. In other instances, we suspect that the cards have been heavily stacked against some of these people. Some comedies appear to need an expression of or a channeling for cruelty, savagery and even hate; in *The Merchant of Venice* these are concentrated in Shylock with the powerful overtones of the fear of usury, Jews and tyrannical fathers. The happy, misty-eyed benevolence at the end of a number of comedies appears to depend on powerful impulses of exclusion.

These expulsions and exclusions are so little based on moral or ethical priorities that some critics have suspected that they echo various folk-rituals of the English countryside. It is one way of accounting for the excessive humiliation and torment of those characters that fall outside of the comic dispensation.[25] But the reasons for the inclusion of this motif in the comedies must be considered alongside the excessive felicity showered on the sympathetic characters or those who are received into the comic celebration. The chief distinguishing feature of the characters excluded from happiness is that they are incapable of loving or are incapable of attracting love. Their capacity is often only for self-promotion and for the indulgence of mercenary or materialistic desires. By comparison, even those, like Claudio and Posthumus, who are guilty of a lack of trust and readily believe the slanders against their mistresses' virtue, are saved because they are loved and because they adhere to an ideal of love, no matter how much their foolishness compromises their belief. Even where they do not show the capacity for love, as in the case of Angelo, the ability to attract patient and faithful love guarantees them felicity. The comedies seem to offer a circular and, from the moral point of view, unsatisfactory conclusion that those who are not loved are not loved because they fail to attract love. The disdain of comedy is, therefore, concentrated in them.

[25] C. L. Barber, *Shakespeare's Festive Comedy* (1959), New Jersey 1972, pp. 7–8 contains a clear statement of this motif.

The comedies, then, are dedicated to the cult of love. There is little need to detail the powerful rôle played by the concept of love in Renaissance literature; it is a common feature of comedy, even in plays like *Volpone*, which, for all their concern with the exposure of villainy and hypocrisy, usually include some concern with the innocence of love. But it has often been alleged that the importance of love in Shakespeare's comedies is far greater than the exigencies of comic drama demand. An attempt has been made to argue that these plays demonstrate and illustrate the power of love to forge a better world for those that are fortunate enough to fall under its spell. Those that oppose or deny it, or those that attempt to abuse it are excluded from this happy commonwealth with force and vigour. For others, it seems sufficient to be loved; this transcends the ethical requirements of the mundane world—love conquers all, in the most specific sense of the old saying. Where love operates, it is capable of solving the difficulties and antagonisms experienced by the sympathetic characters; its blessings flow freely. Questions of desert recede; the floodgates of benevolence are opened.

The excess in Shakespeare's comedies therefore—the separation, that is, of the characters not through moral discriminations but by some other means—may be part of a larger scheme of values, a concern with the mystical powers of love. Clearly, the powerful current of thought originating in Plato's *Symposium* and running through Ficino's *Commentary* and the many popular treatises of 'Platonic Love' like Castiglione's *The Courtier*, seems to have reached Shakespeare, as it did Spenser and many poets of the English Renaissance. The comedies from one standpoint may be regarded as offering fables of the providence of love.[26] We find in some of them, indeed, complex and thorough structures which suggest this possibility very strongly, even to the extent of incorporating certain recondite aspects of this philosophy or mystique that are not immediately concerned with love itself. This is where a potential set of *meanings* for a number of the comedies may be discovered. The plays appear to embody with some care a declaration of faith and even a recommendation of certain 'philosophical' principles, excess thus becoming a sign of their fundamental stance. These possibilities are explored in Chapter 5.

---

[26] Such an attitude to the comedies informs two studies by John Vyvyan: *Shakespeare and the Rose of Love*, London 1960 and *Shakespeare and Platonic Beauty*, London 1961.

3 *Ideal Landscapes*

I

Most of Shakespeare's comedies are set in a deliberately artificial and stylized world in which the familiar moral and physical landscape of the Renaissance is distorted and rearranged. At times in the past this characteristic of the comedies was thought to have emerged from Shakespeare's ignorance of well-known historical and geographical facts, at other times it was taken to represent his fundamental refusal to engage with 'real' or serious issues. The term 'Romantic Comedy', coined in order to distinguish between Shakespearian comedy and the dominant traditions of European comic drama, places its theoretical justification in these rearrangements of the commonplace.

The comedies offer ample evidence to suggest that the 'real' world finds little representation in them. But a comparison with the history-plays and the tragedies should make it quite clear that this is not the result of ignorance but of conscious and deliberate choice. The tragedies and the history-plays, apart from several celebrated lapses (the talk of firing a cannon in *King John* some hundreds of years before the introduction of gunpowder into Europe, the doublet worn by Julius Caesar) observe with reasonable accuracy the better-known features of history and geography. In the Roman tragedies, especially, Shakespeare shows some familiarity with the ancient world's habits, manners and political forms. Obviously, his knowledge of antiquity lacked Jonson's thorough acquaintance, but, like his much more pedantic contemporary, he too attempted to observe the basic decorum of historical and tragic drama. The Roman plays demonstrate a sure sense of history and geography; they depict a coherent society, very different from that of sixteenth or seventeenth-century England, even if some characteristics of Shakespeare's own world colour his portraits of its inhabitants. By comparison, the comedies abound in confusions. Geography is often ignored: Milan and

64

Verona are sea-ports; Bohemia enjoys a Mediterranean climate while Sicily suffers from severe winters; lions roam the Forest of Arden. History and chronology are treated in an equally nonchalant manner. The Rome of *Cymbeline* is peopled by patricians of the Imperial period as well as by Italian bravoes of the Renaissance. The Athens of Theseus is invaded by the fairy-folk of northern mythology and by the artisans of sixteenth-century England.

It may be possible to explain these confusions and inaccuracies by reference to Shakespeare's alleged carelessness: since most of the comedies depend on a variety of sources, it may be argued that they lack historical or geographic coherence because he did not bother to iron out individual differences, whereas in the tragedies and history-plays such coherence was more or less dictated by the uniformity of the sources. But this, if it offers any explanation at all, is partial, at best. The distortions and the rearrangement of everyday reality in most of the comedies represent artistic necessity—the discovery of an ideal landscape in which playfully ambivalent concerns find a proper and comfortable environment. The comic world is one of freedom and artistic licence; its confusions and inaccuracies serve to remind us that we must not stray beyond the boundary of theatrical artifice. In most of the comedies, we meet people, communities and landscapes bearing little resemblance to provable facts; but this hypothetical world is, nevertheless, the repository of that individual artistic truth for which Shakespeare's comedies are notable. The grave philosophical playfulness of *the Winter's Tale* and the teasing emotional shadings of *Twelfth Night* could not exist outside of the particular habitations which contain them; only in such a world are the comedies able to achieve their delicate balance between the profound and the trivial. Shakespeare's use of this cloud-cuckoo-land is, therefore, essentially conceited and fanciful. A survey of his comedies demonstrates the deep-seated appeal this world held for him; it becomes, in consequence, an important element in his comic theatre.

But the pursuit of the ideal world is neither an indispensable nor a doctrinaire aspect of the comedies. There is no commitment to an intellectual programme in these ideal landscapes as there is, for instance, in Maeterlinck or in *Parsifal*. Shakespeare obviously found the exploration of such a world congenial and enthralling; some of his richest comic moments emerge from it. Yet, as with most other characteristics of these remarkable plays, their basic effects do not depend directly on this landscape. Shakespeare's ideal world, while important and significant, is (like his fascination with philosophical patterns in some of the later comedies) essentially decorative. The centre of a play is almost always elsewhere; the particular type of playfulness his comedies embody very often finds a comfortable domicile in cloud-cuckoo-land (the hypothetical world of impossibilities which is given miraculous birth in a theatrical representation)—but, equally, these ideal landscapes do not represent intellectual convictions on which his comic art is based.

The type of indecorum indicated by the confusions of geography and chronology—the presentation of fantastical worlds—is relatively absent from the earlier comedies. *The Comedy of Errors*, while in no way depicting the antique world, preserves in a minimal sense the traditional setting of Roman New Comedy. *The Two Gentlemen of Verona* (apart, perhaps, from Speed and from Launce and his dog) adheres fairly faithfully to the Mediterranean genesis of its story and of its characters. It has been pointed out that even the much-publicized water-journey from Verona to Milan might have been possible in the sixteenth century.[1] Both plays avoid the radical mingling of different societies, historical periods and orders of existence to be encountered in many of the later comedies. *The Taming of the Shrew* provides the earliest glimpse of the characteristic landscape of later comedies. The signs of this are difficult to recognize because the play maintains fairly consistently the particular decorum of its kind. The Induction is, of course, more English than Italian in flavour, but the play that follows reminds us of the principal features of certain forms of Renaissance Italian comedy. The Italian landscape is mirrored with some accuracy: Padua is precisely the city where a Pisan burgher would have sent his son to study during the sixteenth century; Verona is close enough to Padua for the various journeys of Petruchio and his entourage to be credible. The surnames, it may also be pointed out, are appropriate to the well-heeled inhabitants of the cities of Northern Italy. More important, however, is the manner in which the play reflects the chief stylistic and narrative material of Italianate comedy. The characters conform to recognizable types: Baptista is a witty variant of the *Senex*, the crotchety father strenuously objecting to his daughter's marriage—he appears to have no objection to Bianca's getting married, but by insisting that Katharina must be married first he places seemingly insurmountable difficulties in the way of his

---

[1] Mario Praz, 'Shakespeare and Italy', *Sydney Studies in English*, 3, 1977–8, p. 8.

younger daughter's happiness. There are several dull suitors (one, at least, quite elderly) claiming the privilege of marrying the *ingénue* on account of their wealth and social position. One of these, Hortensio, masquerades as the traditional Pedant. The motif of master and servant exchanging places appears in this comedy, further illuminating its relationship with the conventions of Italian comic theatre.

The coherence of the main portion of the play and its faithful adherence to its prototype may be a consequence of some of its source-material as Shakespeare acquired it. But the issue at stake is that in *The Taming of the Shrew* (for whatever reason) he avoided the mingling of the various societies and historical periods suggested elsewhere by his sources. Moreover, though the material is derivative, its treatment reveals a certain sophistication: Shakespeare seems to have been aware of the context from which this material is drawn: the coherently-maintained Italian flavour of the play does not seem merely a happy accident, a largely unconscious adoption of the ingredients of the source-play for one of the plots. The impression is difficult to escape that Shakespeare's interest was, in part at least, engaged by the possibilities of producing his own version of 'learned' comedy. Act III Scene I reveals a familiarity with and an eager employment of devices with 'erudite' or intellectual overtones. 'The gamut of Hortensio'—

> "Gamut" I am, the ground of all accord—
> "A re" to plead Hortensio's passion—
> "B mi" Bianca, take him for thy lord—
> "C fa ut" that loves with all affection—
> "D sol re" one clef, two notes have I—
> "E la mi" show pity or I die.
>
> (III. i. 71)

—whatever its ancestry, shows how far Shakespeare captured the intellectual ambitions of the tradition from which he drew the material of some part of this play. Despite all this, in one respect *The Taming of the Shrew* is an earnest of things to come. The containment of the play itself within the Induction is the first instance of that toying with levels of illusion which dominates some of the later comedies. If, as seems likely, in one version at least, Sly were present on stage throughout,[2] the intrinsic character of the play would be more clearly recognizable;

---

[2] See J. Dover Wilson (ed.), *The Taming of the Shrew* (New Cambridge Shakespeare), rev. edn, Cambridge 1953, Introduction, p. xvii.

but even with the disappearance of Sly after the first act, its basic flavour remains. The device of the play-within-a-play may possibly be taken as an instance of the playwright's concern with moral or ethical problems arising out of human gullibility and the therapeutic potentialities of art. But its primary effect—as in the case of cognate devices employed in some of the later comedies—is fundamentally aesthetic. It enhances the play's theatricality; the audience is one step farther removed from the pretence that it is witnessing a reproduction of reality. The use of this theatrical trick in *The Taming of the Shrew* is relatively simple and direct; it goes little beyond reminding us that we are watching nothing other than a play; in later comedies, the insistence on the essential artifice of theatre assumes subtle and occasionally profound significances. But it is a sign, no matter how faint, of the characteristic mode of the more mature comedies.

A Midsummer Night's Dream was written, in all probability, only a little later than *The Taming of the Shrew*, yet it demonstrates a flamboyance entirely lacking in the earlier works. It has a daring sophistication, mixing together very different narrative strands derived from widely dispersed cultural sources. The four character-groups are held together not only by narrative causality, but also through the continued concern with the variety of love. The play may, indeed, be seen as a fantasia on love: the domestic strife in the court of the King of the Fairies; the heroic love of Theseus for his newly-vanquished Amazonian queen; the love-difficulties of the four young Athenians; the Apuleian experiences of Bottom the Weaver (with the farcical undercurrent of the sad tale of Pyramus and Thisby) illuminate different facets of the perplexity of love. This unity is achieved, however, in terms of diversity. While we register the conceit inherent in these parallels, we remain conscious of the separation of these worlds. This operates not only on the narrative level (for the human characters meet as a group only briefly at the end) but also in the language. The play is notable for its discovery of individual accents for each group of characters—accents, moreover, which are immediately recognizable. Through their individual modes of speech, the characters carry about with them tokens of their basic isolation from the other orders of existence depicted in the play.

The language of Theseus and Hippolyta is heroic; their diction is elevated and hierarchical. These patternings, often taken to be signs of Shakespeare's immaturity, are instances of his masterful depiction of the world these characters inhabit:

Four days will quickly steep themselves in night;
Four nights will quickly dream away the time;
And then the moon, like to a silver bow
New-bent in heaven, shall behold the night
Of our solemnities.

(I. i. 7)

The other 'royal' pair, Oberon and Titania, as befits their nature, are given wilder, more romantic diction. Their world is in contact with nature and the elements: in some instances, as in Titania's description of the havoc caused by her quarrel with Oberon, the characters almost merge into the natural world with striking effect.

Therefore the winds, piping to us in vain,
As in revenge, have suck'd up from the sea
Contagious fogs; which, falling in the land,
Hath every pelting river made so proud
That they have overborne their continents.
The ox hath therefore stretch'd his yoke in vain,
The ploughman lost his sweat, and the green corn
Hath rotted ere his youth attain'd a beard . . .

(II. i. 88)

By contrast, the young lovers are given the language of sentiment and of society: they are courteous or insulting as circumstances demand, and their speech (as their personalities) is filled with the details of everyday middle-class life. Helena's jibe about Hermia —

O, when she is angry, she is keen and shrewd;
She was a vixen when she went to school;
And, though she be but little, she is fierce.

(III. ii. 323)

—captures exactly the horizons of their world. Lastly, the mechanicals are given the richly inaccurate and pompous speech of self-important artisans.

The multi-layered language and the elaborate mingling of different sets of characters and of different levels of theatrical illusion confer a unique atmosphere on the play. Its range is far wider than the range of effects encountered in the earlier comedies—it is the first comedy to explore levels seemingly much deeper than the pleasant superficialities of normal comedy. Most notable are the frequent suggestions of threat and brutality implied by the action. The songs of the attendant fairies avoid the pretty and the sentimental; they establish a familiarity with the natural world which recognizes its inherent threats:

> You spotted snakes with double tongue,
> Thorny hedgehogs, be not seen;
> Newts and blind-worms, do no wrong,
> Come not near our fairy Queen.
>
> (II. ii. 9)

Puck's reputation as a village prankster is presented in sinister terms:

> Are not you he
> That frights the maidens of the villagery,
> Skim milk, and sometimes labour in the quern,
> And bootless make the breathless housewife churn,
> And sometime make the drink to bear no barm,
> Mislead night-wanderers, laughing at their harm?
>
> (II. i. 34)

The revenge play by Oberon on Titania is announced with obviously cruel overtones:

> The next thing that she waking looks upon,
> Be it on lion, bear, or wolf, or bull,
> On meddling monkey, or on busy ape,
> She shall pursue it with the soul of love.
>
> (II. i. 179)

Amidst these threatening and sinister tonalities, however, we also find language of rare lyrical beauty, the pinnacle of Elizabethan decorative verse:

> Thou rememb'rest
> Since once I sat upon a promontory,
> And heard a mermaid on a dolphin's back
> Uttering such dulcet and harmonious breath
> That the rude sea grew civil at her song,
> And certain stars shot madly from their spheres
> To hear the sea-maid's music.
>
> (II. i. 148)

The play is rich in the language of love, artificial and patterned, no doubt, but possessing verve and conviction:

I swear to thee by Cupid's strongest bow,
By his best arrow, with the golden head,
By the simplicity of Venus' doves,
By that which knitteth souls and prospers loves,
And by that fire which burn'd the Carthage Queen,
When the false Troyan under sail was seen,
By all the vows that ever men have broke,
In number more than ever women spoke,
In that same place thou hast appointed me,
To-morrow truly will I meet with thee.

(I. i. 169)

The ceremonial language of Theseus and Hippolyta includes an extraordinary and haunting fantasia on the baying of hounds:

I was with Hercules and Cadmus once
When in a wood of Crete they bay'd the bear
With hounds of Sparta; never did I hear
Such gallant chiding, for, besides the groves,
The skies, the fountains, every region near,
Seem'd all one mutual cry. I never heard
So musical a discord, such sweet thunder.

(IV. i. 109)

And, of course, this is the play that contains the following:

O Sisters Three
Come, come to me,
With hands as pale as milk;

Lay them in gore,
Since you have shore
With shears his thread of silk.

(V. i. 327)

A Midsummer Night's Dream is, therefore, an extravaganza, a dazzling display of poetic and theatrical skill. The manner in which its outrageously incompatible narrative strands and poetic styles are woven together illuminates Shakespeare's virtuosity. This is the type of play that could so easily have split apart; yet it manages to remain unified: for all its variety, it is the product of a shaping creative intelligence. Some of its language and many of its incidents might well be derivative, but the hand of the master craftsman is evident at every turn. But is it any more than a virtuoso display? Most critics have felt that it must be more than that; only those wishing to use this play as evidence of the general mindlessness of Shakespeare's comedies have been content to regard in terms of a *tour de force* of theatrical skill.[3] Others have attempted to discover in it an engagement with 'serious' issues. There is no denying that the play constantly suggests possibilities beyond the confines of its superficial character: a number of themes may be traced through it, like an elaborate pattern. The chief of these is the concern with the variety of love, its follies, absurdities and dangers, noted above. Most of the characters, at one time or another, find themselves in the grip of a type of love which, to them, seems wild, threatening and even insane. For Titania and the young Athenians it is the irrationality of love; for Theseus and Hippolyta the nuptials they anticipate with such fervour seem to retain an echo of the violence and excitement of their first meeting:

> Hippolyta, I woo'd thee with my sword,
> And won thy love doing thee injuries;
> But I will wed thee in another key,
> With pomp, with triumph, and with revelling.
>
> (I. i. 16)

Love is frenzy; love is conflict. It is also akin to madness, if not madness itself. The Athenian lovers experience a night of hallucinations; Bottom receives an enchantment which he recalls merely as a bizarre dream; the frenzy of love humiliates Titania. The madness of love also entails a type of transfiguration—reminding us of the Apuleian origins of a part of the plot. The play abounds, indeed, in transformations: not only of Bottom into the ass, but the transformations of others as well, especially when the young Athenians experience the senseless alterations of love.

The play appears to explore, in consequence, some dark areas of human experience. It explores these, moreover, in a curious world of half-lights: a world consisting of madness and enchantment, and waking to all-but-incredible realities. Hippolyta's celebrated lines capture the sensation in the play that life is conducted in the quicksands of experience barely standing witin the bounds of the rational:

---

[3] See, for instance, W. Hazlitt, *Characters of Shakespeare's Plays*, 4th edn, London 1848, pp. 133–4.

But all the story of the night told over,
And all their minds transfigur'd so together,
More witnesseth than fancy's images,
And grows to something of great constancy,
But howsoever strange and admirable.

(V. i. 23)

Passages like this have prompted some to see in the play an alarmed recognition that, in certain states, a bush is most easily supposed a bear.

So richly complex is the mixture of worlds in *A Midsummer Night's Dream* that it is understandable that scholarship should have sought after elevated or arcane meanings. Yet it is difficult not to remain sceptical about some of the claims made concerning this comedy: the profundities discovered in it (as in the case of *The Tempest*) fit uncomfortably into a play which is so close to the spirit and the manner of popular entertainment. This comedy, like *The Tempest*, never strays far from the confines of fairy stories. It is very simple in its 'intellectual' material; its virtuosity and flamboyance are directed towards theatrical effect, and towards the inclusion of a variety of emotionally striking possibilities, not towards philosophical profundities. What, to many critics, seems a *paysage moralisé* of infinite suggestibility, may be no more than the evocation of cloud-cuckoo-land on the stage. Yet to see the play in terms of these alternatives is fundamentally incorrect. It encompasses both possibilities; like some of the later comedies, it creates a unique environment, an individual physical and poetic landscape which is richly and deliberately ambivalent. Its many-sided world is an ideal one, for Shakespeare gives flesh to the fanciful and imaginative hypothesis that a world may be created on the stage peopled with an array of creatures, human, superhuman and supernatural, who could not exist (or co-exist) in quotidian life. In this essentially free and untrammelled environment, the dramatist finds opportunity to explore many possibilities. He may contrast the strange, sinister, half-lit world of fairyland with the clamorous ceremony of mythological beings, with the pathos of the tribulations of young love, and with the hilarious comedy of Bottom and his *confrères*—and in the background, there remains that other order of existence, the patently subhuman world of Pyramus and his Thisby. At times, the various extremes spanned by the play are brought together in an episode, and incident, or even in a few lines of verse:

Titania's rapt love-words to the transformed Bottom are simultaneously deeply moving and farcical, transcendental and silly:

> Come, sit thee down upon this flow'ry bed,
> While I thy amiable cheeks do coy,
> And stick musk-roses in thy sleek smooth head,
> And kiss thy fair large ears, my gentle joy.
>
> (IV. i. 1)

The shifting perspectives, the confusions between daytime reality and the hallucinations of the night fit perfectly into this state which could never have existed, which confounds probabilities and possibilities, and yet possesses its own imaginative coherence. The ideal world allows for art to play with those depths that this comedy seems so richly to explore, without commitment to anything but its own integrity. In the environment of the theatre, the distinctions between profundity and levity vanish—the richness of the artistic experience emerges from the simultaneous presence of both.

A Midsummer Night's Dream is a challenging and, in its own way, a thorough exploration of the possibilities of the type of comedy Shakespeare made characteristically his own. Its challenge and its value reside in its demand that we register the complexity and the subtlety of the issues it raises while it maintains, all along, the insistence that the connections between this world and the world of mundane reality are merely hypothetical and illusory. A play remains a play: it creates something that has never been, that cannot exist, except in the context of this particular illusion. Even the generally unsympathetic Theseus grudgingly admits that the poet is able to achieve something akin to this:

> as imagination bodies forth
> The forms of things unknown, the poet's pen
> Turns them to shapes, and gives to airy nothing
> A local habitation and a name.
>
> (V. i. 14)

The ideal world is capable of suggesting all manner of possibilities; but these suggestions always remain provisional, merely one aspect of the ambivalent experience generated by comedy.

II

A Midsummer Night's Dream looks forward to Shakespeare's latter comedies—the so-called romantic comedies as well as the last plays. The world of the later works is less flamboyant and less extraordinary than the world of this extravaganza. Shakespeare's greater tact and the greater subtlety of his art may delude us into feeling that the later plays hold the mirror up to life and reflect our experiences—that is to say, that their concerns may approximate to those attitudes and prejudices which are usually called a view of life. But these suggestions are misleading. Cloud-cuckoo-land is the real setting of most of the later comedies; the schemes and ideas incorporated in them are as playful and as provisional as those of *A Midsummer Night's Dream*. Significantly, extensive use of the pastoral is made in two of them. A particular type of narrative progression is to be found in *As You Like It* and *The Winter's Tale*: each play begins in a treacherous, dangerous world centred or located in a court; and each moves into the pastoral world, where the antitheses of the dangers and threats of the court are embodied. The Renaissance often employed the pastoral (it is said) for purposes of political satire; it is possible, therefore, that each of these plays includes certain themes or preoccupations closer to the orthodox comic modes of their time—the criticism of society and its abuses.

But the status of the pastoral in Renaissance culture is not so simple. There is little doubt that it was used, from time to time, as a vehicle of stringent satire[4]—thus offering its practitioners relative immunity from persecution; but at other times, especially as the seventeenth century progressed, its use was frankly escapist: James Shirley's dramatization of *The Arcadia*, for instance, lacks Sidney's political and moral concerns. Indeed, the pastoral was capable of a variety of uses: its chief and relatively stable characteristic, however, is that it allows remarkable freedom of action and existence for its inhabitants. In it the laws of everyday probability are relaxed, social behaviour is often liberated from the decorum and protocol of the 'real' world. The pastoral is, therefore, an ideal world, determined only by the probabilities imposed on it by the creative artist; in this landscape, writers and poets were able to discover not merely an opportunity for

[4] See the discussion in the Introduction, F. Kermode (ed.), *English Pastoral Poetry*, London 1952, especially p. 15.

dangerous political satire—as in the celebrated passage in *Lycidas* dealing with the corruption of the clergy—but also for the indulgence of the fantasy we find in the forest scenes of *As You Like It.*

One of the problems in *As You Like It* is to what extent we are meant to discover moral and social values in the Forest of Arden. Stern critics have detected a measure of moral delinquency in some parts of the play: it has been suggested that Shakespeare was so enamoured with the freedom of the natural world that he came to recommend it as a panacea for the ills of society he depicted so memorably in the earlier scenes.[5] But it is doubtful whether we may see this (or any other) play simply in such terms—these attitudes presume an artistic purpose for which the plays themselves offer little evidence. The green world of Arden is beguiling and fascinating; but it is to be doubted whether we are meant to discover in it a *regulum vitae* or a statement about social and moral responsibility.

Criticism has largely overlooked one important aspect of the pastoral in the play: the powerful suggestions it contains that we should, to some extent, yearn to escape from it. This is achieved in two ways. In the first place, no particularly cogent reason is given why Rosalind's masquerade should continue as long as it does, or why she does not declare herself to Orlando sooner. It may be taken as a 'testing' of the youth, or as a particularly keen insight into the psychological complexion of a personality requiring oblique and indirect relationships. But these represent surmise. The episodes, as they stand in the play, are a prolonged version of the comic mock-torment, akin to the gulling of Bassanio and Gratiano in the last scene of *The Merchant of Venice.* The prolongation of any aspect of a play's structure usually generates a sense of impatience in the audience: we desire to see its conclusion and culmination. The frustration and the tension in *As You Like It* arise, moreover, not merely because we wish to come to the conclusion of this particular theatrical device, but also because, while it is in operation, it stands so much in the way of the desired outcome: the happy union of Rosalind and Orlando. This desire to see the fortunes of the young people happily resolved is part of the second reason why the pastoral world, for all its allure, breeds

[5] Philip Edwards, in his discussion of *As You Like It* (*Shakespeare and the Confines of Art,* London 1968, pp. 56–63) attempts to overcome his feeling of dissatisfaction at the ease with which complex problems are solved in the green retreat of Arden, by placing emphasis on Jaques's refusal to participate in the dance, and on his decision to seek the 'abandon'd cave'.

impatience in the spectator. We observe in the first act of the play a number of instances of patent injustice—Oliver's denial of Orlando's patrimony, Duke Frederick's usurpation and his tyrannical banishment of Rosalind. As Dr Johnson remarked, an audience naturally finds justice pleasing; we desire, therefore, the righting of these wrongs, and, no matter how enjoyable the holiday sports of Arden might be, our expectations are not satisfied until these injustices are reversed. That, inevitably, requires the return of the sympathetic characters to the social world.

The Forest of Arden is, thus, a holiday world filled with suspense, an environment that is fantastical, gay, appealing and yet, for all that, unsatisfactory because of its limitations. Some of the characters do, indeed, discover there a degree of freedom not available in the ordinary world; but the audience's reaction to this freedom is ambivalent—we are made as conscious of the necessity of leaving the green world as of its allure. Consequently, the sojourn in Arden becomes a game—fantastic, at times exhilarating—but, like all games, basically unsatisfactory. It is as a result of theatrical expectations, not because of its moral implications, that the pastoral world breeds impatience. This essentially paradoxical response to the holiday world is, at times, captured by the characters themselves, usually with memorable effect, as at those moments when Rosalind's gaiety turns to a smiling sadness:

> The poor world is almost six thousand years old, and in all this time there was not any man died in his own person, videlicet, in a love-cause. Troilus had his brains dash'd out with a Grecian club; yet he did what he could to die before, and he is one of the patterns of love. Leander, he would have liv'd many a fair year, though Hero had turn'd nun, if it had not been for a hot midsummer-night; for, good youth, he went but forth to wash him in the Hellespont, and, being taken with the cramp, was drown'd; and the foolish chroniclers of that age found it was—Hero of Sestos. But these are all lies: men have died from time to time, and worms have eaten them, but not for love.
>
> (IV. i. 83)

Later drama often vulgarized such effects—laughter-through-tears has become a totally debased currency. But in *As You Like It* it has freshness and gaiety: in the simultaneous presence of playfulness and sentiment an essential quality of the play is revealed.

These are some of the possibilities of the pastoral world. In it the dramatist may explore varieties of emotion and of human relationships with a freedom unavailable in the world of common experience. The courtship of Rosalind and Orlando is a curious mixture of charm, pathos and hilarity; Ganymede's education of the young swain is, by turns, fantastic and touching. The situation in which a girl disguised as a boy pretends (for 'pedagogic' purposes) to be a girl—especially when the character is impersonated by a boy-actor—is an instance of theatrical flamboyance, as well as a tactful suggestion of ambivalent sexuality. The pastoral landscape holds surprising and delightful potentialities. It is also a meeting-place for a variety of emotional and ethical attitudes. It contains not only the lovers, but also that philosophical melancholiac, the Duke Senior, an elder statesman cast into the Ovidian world of the golden age (only to discover that he has moral qualms about it), and the professional melancholiac, Jaques, who finds the *topoi* of elegant disillusionment in his green exile. As the scenes set in this world unfold, so probability is left farther behind. When Rosalind and her friends arrive in Arden, she still retains some of the characteristics of the outside world. 'Well, this is the forest of Arden' is a matter-of-fact, practical statement, only a little more practical than her subsequent decision to set up in farming. But the nature of this world gradually imposes itself on her: she enters into the dream-existence of ambivalences; half-plucky, half-vulnerable, she plays out her curious masquerade of courtship.

The events of the play (as already hinted) also come increasingly to be determined not so much by moral propositions or by the observation of a particular decorum of what is real, as by the exploitation of the freedom available to the artist when he depicts the ideal world of fantasy. The events of the last act, unexpected and unprepared, thrown off with that legerdemain Dr Johnson found so distressing, are perfectly credible in such an imaginative environment. The measure of their viability is the ease with which Hymen's appearance to preside over the marriage of the 'country copulatives' proves acceptable, natural and proper. In its last moments, the play leaves behind even the minimal decorum of 'reality' it had maintained until then. Even though it had depicted a fantastic landscape where lions roam the forests of northern Europe, where exiled dukes spend philosophically resigned lives in the wilderness, where the most extraordinary changes of heart occur, there is, until the play's last moments, a general insistence that this world is circumscribed by the natural and biological probabilities of life. But all this changes at the end. Hymen descends, mythology invades fantasy as the god among mankind blesses the happy occasion with a sidelong glance at numerology:

> Peace, ho! I bar confusion;
> 'Tis I must make conclusion
>   Of these most strange events.
> Here's eight that must take hands
> To join in Hymen's bands,
>   If truth holds true contents.
> (V. iv. 119)

a little later, the preposterous dramatic event occurs: a new character, about whom we have been told only a little (and much earlier in the play at that) arrives on the scene with astonishing news, barely minutes before the end. Such improprieties may only occur in this version of the pastoral.

There is a naïve-sophisticated optimism in these turns and arabesques. Shakespeare creates, with certain limitations, a world of innocent make-believe where our fondest dreams may be indulged. But a special distinction of *As You Like It* (as of some other comedies) is that this pleasing indulgence is contained within an awareness of its own absurdity. Some characters are present here, as elsewhere, to remind us that this is cloud-cuckoo-land, and that these events are impossibilities. Touchstone and Jaques are sometimes seen as embodiments of Shakespeare's trenchant criticism of the green world, his disillusioned condemnation of these fancies. Their function is, however, somewhat different. The joyful sports are placed at an ironic distance by the acerbic comments of these two characters; yet this distancing and the changed perspective are as sportive as the revels against which they are contrasted. Jaques's well-known monologue on the seven ages of man expresses melancholic disillusionment. But its thematic function in the play is peculiar: it is neither a corrective to the pervasive jollity, nor an instance of despairing sadness which must be conquered. It is a perfomance, a bravura display, both within the fiction of the play and from the point of view of the theatrical audience. Just as Touchstone is the professional *farceur*, so Jaques has some of the characteristics of the professional *déraciné*. His expression of profound melancholy follows the Duke Senior's remarks concerning the privations of old Adam:

Thou seest we are not all alone unhappy:
This wide and universal theatre
Presents more woeful pageants than the scene
Wherein we play in.

(II. vii. 136)

Jaques then embroiders this statement in a fanciful speech filled with well-known rhetorical flourishes and a series of elegantly witty conceits. The fundamentally operatic nature of the speech would not have been lost on Shakespeare's audience, and it would, no doubt, have been savoured for its qualities as a performance.

By such means, Shakespeare incorporates in his pastoral world views quite contrary to the play's basic attitudes. Yet there is no requirement that one set of views should be measured against the other. The most important characteristic of the ideal landscape created in comedies like *As You Like It* is that it is encyclopaedic: the pastoral offers an opportunity for the inclusion of a variety of effects and, at times, of contradictory possibilities. The inclusiveness might best be described through the use of a musical analogy: *As You Like It* resembles a set of variations on a ground-theme. Its theme is akin to the ancient debating topic that a life of solitude is preferable to the busy world of society. This commonplace topic is embellished in a number of artful and elegant ways; the emphasis (as in the musical genre of variations) comes to fall on the amplitude, inventiveness and even extravagance of the performance, not on the result of the debate or on the judicial decision. The nature of the impossible world implicit in the pastoral conceit makes this possible; heterogeneous material is capable of being contained within a unified work of art: the artist may enjoy a freedom not available in those fictions which retain a closer relationship with daily experience.

Touchstone's comments illustrate this dimension in *As You Like It*. Not since Costard's discovery in *Love's Labour's Lost* of the exact monetary values of guerdon and remuneration had Shakespeare given so many *mots justes* to one of his clown-figures. His quibbles and gibes are, nevertheless, good-humoured, if not exactly good-natured—his rôle represents, once more, a bravura performance. He never forgets that he is a court-jester, even if an absconding one: his comments are barbed, but a large part of their intention is still to amuse. His various contests with Jaques bring together the professional clown and the gifted amateur; each, in his own way, demonstrates the extent of his skill. Jaques's description of his first encounter with Touchstone

indicates the mutual recognition of two paractitioners of the same
craft:

> "Good morrow, fool" quoth I; "No, sir," quoth he
> "Call me not fool till heaven hath sent me fortune."
> And then he drew a dial from his poke,
> And, looking on it with lack-lustre eye,
> Says very wisely "It is ten o'clock;
> Thus we may see" quoth he "how the world wags;
> 'Tis but an hour ago since it was nine;
> And after one hour more 'twill be eleven;
> And so, from hour to hour, we ripe and ripe,
> And then, from hour to hour, we rot and rot;
> And thereby hangs a tale" When I did hear
> The motley fool thus moral on the time,
> My lungs began to crow like chanticleer
> That fools should be so deep contemplative;
> And I did laugh sans intermission
> An hour by his dial. O noble fool!
> A worthy fool! Motley's the only wear.
>
> (II. vii. 18)

The shudder that passes across the surface of the play in 'And then,
from hour to hour, we rot and rot' is transformed and converted by the
multiplicity of perspectives—it reaches us through the filter of Jaques's
fantastical, flamboyant report.[6] Decay and death are registered at this
moment in *As You Like It* (as they are elsewhere in the play) but their
status is jesting and hypothetical. Because of their placement in this
ideal world, the play is able to entertain these reminders of death and
of the sadder, darker side of existence in a manner for which 'comic' is
the only appropriate term. This is not a mocking, satiric or despairing
comment on the vanity of human wishes; it is, rather, a recognition
that maturation does, indeed, lead to decay and death; but in the
comic world, even these may be transformed into 'something of great
constancy'. When Shakespeare's drama moves into the impossible and
ideal landscape represented, in this instance, by the thorough employment of the pastoral mode, it becomes possible for these thematic
strands to be liberated from their moral and emotional significances in
'ordinary' experience. The astonishing quality of this manner of comic
drama is its ability to transform sadness into a species of hilarity.

[6] Helge Kokeritz (*Shakespeare's Pronunciation*, New Haven 1953, pp. 58–59) drew
attention to the obscene innuendoes generated by the homonymic puns on
'hour/whore' and 'tale/tail'.

Touchstone is the most engaging of Shakespeare's fools: his folly is flamboyant and essentially good-humoured not because he refrains from speaking home-truths, but because his truth-speaking produces that joy which is, perhaps, the most mysterious element in the experience of comedy. He is no less outspoken than Lear's fool; but the tragic fool produces, at best, a hollow death-rattle of a laugh. The tragic world, which is not cloud-cuckoo-land but a true *paysage moralisé*, cannot tolerate the flamboyant pyrotechnics of a Touchstone. Lear's fool constantly cuts close to the bone; his cutting pains both his victim, Lear, and us, the onlookers. The type of jesting encountered in the comedies has intimate connections with the comic landscape examined in this chapter; this fanciful world requires, it seems, the presence of one of these figures of irreverence, and it is in the plays making the most extensive use of the pastoral (*As You Like It* and *The Winter's Tale*) that the clown-figure achieves his greatest stature. But even where the ideal landscape has not the same degree of freedom we encounter in the pastoral world, the clown still retains an exuberant flamboyance which blunts the spikes of his barbed comments. Feste's dark melancholy in *Twelfth Night* seems, at first, to come closer to the patterns of tragic fooling; yet he remains true to his comic heritage—his *aperçus* rarely wound, mostly they produce sadness. Comedy tolerates sadness: indeed, at times it thrives on it; tragedy is too stern to contain it.

To appreciate the essential nature of the fool in the extravagant world of comedy, it is worthwhile to glance briefly at Thersites, the grim clown-figure in *Troilus and Cressida*, that unclassifiable play, and at Apemantus of *Timon of Athens*, a notably ironic tragedy, for both characters straddle the two modes of fooling. Each is fantastical, each is capable of speaking those home-truths which generate hilarity, yet each displays a bitterness largely absent from comedy. When Thersites refuses to fight with Margarelon, Priam's bastard son, his apologia demonstrates how far he inhabits both worlds:

> I am a bastard too; I love bastards. I am a bastard begot, bastard instructed, bastard in mind, bastard in valour, in everything illegitimate. One bear will not bite another, and wherefore should one bastard? Take heed, the quarrel's most ominous to us: if the son of a whore fight for a whore, he tempts judgment. Farewell, bastard.
>
> (V. vii. 16)

Significantly, both *Troilus and Cressida* and *Timon of Athens* display some features of the ideal world of comedy. The latter is certainly a tragic discourse, but it is markedly different from the more familiar of Shakespeare's tragic plays: its Athens is a cipher, a mental concept in which the features of the familiar world are thoroughly rearranged. Also, the society depicted in the play is not an intensification of normal human societies, as the world of the middle-period tragedies tends to be, but a transformation of mundane experience in a way that is both hypothetical and extravagant. The similarities between these plays and Shakespeare's comedies must not be pressed too far; but the satiric nature of both glances, at least, in the direction of those plays. In each, in consequence, the clown-figure threatens to exceed the normal choric function of tragic fools, and to enter into the fantastical extravagance of words which is the province of comedy.

The Winter's Tale (in some respects the quintessential Shakespearian comedy) also depicts a clown-figure, the astonishing Autolycus, in the artificial world of the pastoral. The function of the pastoral in this play is intimately connected with its gravely jesting display of Platonic optimism; Autolycus himself, an essential element in this 'philosophical' conceit, significantly arrives in the comedy shortly after the transition from the harsh brutalities of Leontes's court to the open-air world of Bohemia. He becomes, in consequence, an emblem, though an unruly and amoral one, of the freedom of the pastoral even more thoroughly than Touchstone is in *As You Like It*. The ideal landscape in *The Winter's Tale* assumes philosophical implications of a characteristically playful sort. The events of the pastoral scenes do not merely furnish a contrast to the cruelty of the court-world, they represent also the fulfilment of patterns and promises implicit in that world, but incapable of being recognized.

The full implications of the fourth act of *The Winter's Tale* cannot therefore be examined until the play's thorough engagement with a group of mystical notions we may identify as representing Renaissance Platonism is explored. But even without taking these matters into consideration, the pastoral world of this comedy may be seen to fulfil some of the functions of the rural sports of *As You Like It*. The threats posed to this world by the presence of the disguised Polixenes, a note consistently heard throughout the sheep-shearing festival, increases the sense of impatience also to be encountered in the Forest of Arden. This, too, is a suspenseful festival: the grace and beauty embodied by

Perdita and Florizel and the joyous anarchy of Autolycus are contained by two important elements that may not be overlooked. The episode provides a powerful contrast to the Sicilian scenes which have been left in suspension. Precisely because the contrast is so great, we are led to anticipate a weaving of the play's fabric back to Leontes and to the consequences of his offence. In addition, the internal dangers of this world (a disguised king delivering sinister warnings dressed in the guise of a disquisition on the propagation of plants) add to the suspense, to the audience's awareness that the decorative beauty of these scenes is fragile and (in this case too) ultimately unsatisfactory.

Artifice, therefore, recognizes its own limitations. The ideal landscape of *The Winter's Tale* is the venue for some of the play's most powerful and most pleasing effects. The emotional relaxation after the tensions of Sicilian madness and intrigue is not only significant but also quite necessary. Nevertheless, precisely because these episodes are, on the surface at least, so relaxed in their artifice, because youthful love and roguish ebullience are given free expression for the first time, we sense that some vital issues are left in suspension. In another type of play, this may serve to achieve nothing other than the stressing of the limitations (perhaps even the treacheries) of the pastoral ideal. In this case, however, the ideal world is depicted in a notably ambivalent fashion: while its artifice suggests, perhaps, that the pressures and cruelties of Leontes's world cannot be resolved in such an essentially easy-going environment, the resolution is, nevertheless, brought about by means of this excursion into the pastoral. Superficially, the issues displayed in the fourth act with such marked flamboyance and artifice are not causally linked to Paulina's ceremonial mock-magic; or, at best, they provide a purely narrative way of fulfilling those patterns of natural providence hinted at in Apollo's oracle which Paulina seizes on through her sixteen-year torment and testing of Leontes. But the function of the idealized landscape of the pastoral is far greater than the mere provision of the conditions for the restoration of Perdita and the reconciliation of the two kings, thus making possible Hermione's return. The pastoral scenes, even without their 'Platonic' implications (which give substance to these potentialities), provide an aesthetic preparation for the joy and wonder at the end of the play.

The marked change of style in the last scene of Act III, when the old Shepherd's relaxed prose replaces Antigonus's agonized verse, introduces an equally marked change of direction in the narrative. It is here that the play moves for the first time into a recognizably comic environment. The fantastical enters into its fabric not only in terms of events (in the reassurance that the abandoned child will be saved from privations and death) but also in atmosphere and diction. Until this moment, no matter how extreme the passions and jealousies depicted, *The Winter's Tale* resides within the probabilities of the social world. Now, the possibilities begin almost visibly to expand. The well-known (and often scorned) landmarks of Shakespearian comedy, happy chance and coincidence, appear and multiply. The Bohemian country-side is a world of radical improbabilities: shepherd-lasses are courted by princelings; the language of rural life reverberates with the accents of antique ecstasies:

> These your unusual weeds to each part of you
> Do give a life—no shepherdess, but Flora
> Peering in April's front. This your sheep-shearing
> Is as a meeting of the petty gods,
> And you the Queen on't.
>
> (IV. iv. 1)

The ideal landscape functions as a powerful and eloquent indication that a play, concerned so far with cruelty and treachery, is to become a celebration of the joy-giving aspects of life. The pastoral establishes these possibilities through its freedom and its liberation, in a way, from the purely human world; its radical mixture of modes, carefully established through the simultaneous presence of shepherds, rogues, disguised princelings and a king's daughter whose very *royalty* shines through her rural weeds and habits, signals an expansion of the play's emotional and poetic concerns. The artifice of the pastoral is a preparation, therefore, for the return to Sicilia as well as an indication of possibilities which have to be acknowledged before the Sicilian world may be restored to grace.

Renaissance Platonism gives substance and form to the complex possibilities embodied in *The Winter's Tale*, and in this way its use of the pastoral conceit transcends the pastoral in *As You Like It*. Nevertheless, in both plays, the mode is a particular instance and employment of those ideal worlds which are so intrinsic to most of Shakespeare's comedies. *As You Like It* anticipates, in many ways, the shape and movement of the later comedy. It, too, moves from the treacherous and constricting social world to a world of actual and theatrical (or poetic) freedom where the characters may discover possibilities of higher value than those encountered in courts and assemblies. And the pastoral of *As You Like It* implies, even if the play does not actually represent, the return to the social world where, we are made to feel, the freedom and contentment discovered in the natural realm may ensure greater justice and happiness. But in each instance, as well, the ideal landscape of the pastoral is used to indicate not merely these thematic possibilities, but also the essential playfulness of comedy which effectively denies such possibilities the status of recommendations or of arguments. Touchstone acts as a most engaging embodiment of that ironic spirit which prevents the dreams of Arden from totally dominating the play. Autolycus in *The Winter's Tale* fulfils a similar function in a much more thorough and fundamental way. He is a figure of anarchic or, at least, amoral energy whose presence in a world tending so much towards idealization is disturbing. The audience finds itself becoming attached to this disturbance in a curious and possibly improper manner. Our complicity with the 'snapper-up of unconsidered trifles' is more sinister than the joyful irreverence we discover in Touchstone's refusal to be impressed by Arden's more sentimental and romantic potentialities. This greater complexity and the greater artistic daring of Shakespeare's use of an ideal world in *The Winter's Tale* (embodied by the clown-figure that cuts across the comfortable consolations of artifice and sentiment) both point towards the unique achievement of *The Winter's Tale*: the playful ambivalence of the comic world about its seemingly elevated issues becomes, in this play, an intrinsic part of its themes and concerns. For this reason, the impact of the idealized world in this play may not be properly recognized until its solemnly 'philosophical' playfulness is further explored in Chapters 4 and 5.

III

The ideal landscape is never entirely absent from Shakespeare's comedies. Two plays, each written towards the end of the sixteenth century, while superficially much closer to the usual habits of orthodox comedy, nevertheless exemplify the allure this world held for Shakespeare. *The Merchant of Venice*, more obviously than the other play, *Much Ado About Nothing*, seems firmly placed in the customary environment of the dominant tradition of comedy. Venice, here, stands for that essentially urban, acquisitive world so often explored by comic dramatists. The news from the Rialto is about wealth, its acquisition, its loss and its replacement. The courting of Portia is accomplished in terms of caskets and metals of varying value; the orthodox comic concern with the difficulties of young lovers (Lorenzo and Jessica in this play) is, for Shakespeare, more than usually financial in emphasis, and the couple ensure that their elopement is comfortably cushioned with a goodly portion of Shylock's ducats. The central motif of the play, Shylock's bond, may, indeed, be seen as a most potent image for the conventional concerns of comic drama; it resembles those exaggerations of man's commercial instincts (like Subtle's discovery of true alchemy in mankind's readiness to be fleeced precisely through its lust for wealth, or Tartuffe's recognition that piety may be a means of fiscal enrichment) which naturally belong to the busy urban world. The play, in its first four acts, seems to subjugate the familiar ideal world of Shakespeare's comedies to the harsh realities of greed and commerce. Venice, for all its exoticism, may appear to be a mere cipher for humanity's corruption in general and for those particular vices of contemporary London that it also represents in *Volpone*.

But *The Merchant of Venice* is not concerned with the ethical and moral implications of its narrative material to the extent that such an account suggests. This is not to deny the importance of commercial values in its structure; rather, these values must be recognized as a part of the play's generally 'romantic' world. Such is the significance of the escape to Belmont in the last act: the abandonment of the discord of the city for the sweet harmonies of a moonlit garden has certain philosophical implications which are discussed in Chapter 5. The movement from city to aristocratic estate may be taken as a sign of Shakepeare's dissatisfaction with the busy world of the first four acts, his desire to endow the play with those 'poetic' qualities that are so often noted in his comedies. Yet the city itself, the Venice of Shylock and Antonio, is essentially exotic—it, too, is located in cloud-cuckoo-land, not for purposes of satiric exaggeration, but for more fantastical ends.

This is an Italian world. Here, as in many Elizabethan prejudices about the Mediterranean, passions and social forms are less circum-scribed than they are in common experience. Here fathers may make extraordinary provision for their daughters' marriages, hopeful youths are able to finance their amorous adventures in terms of commercial sureties, and wealthy merchants seem prepared to enter into bloody and inhuman bonds with Jewish usurers. No matter how diverse the various sources from which these narrative strands are drawn, and no matter how often English usurers were accused of crimes like Shylock's, Shakespeare places them all within a fantastical Italian world. It is its extreme nature, not its universal applicability, that engages dramatic interest. Consequently, Shylock threatens to dominate the play. It was once fashionable to argue that his passionate rapacity and his strange dignity were instances of Shakespeare's engagement with potentialities contained by his material that clashed with his overt comic purposes. The tendency towards melodrama on the one hand, and the sudden recognition of a capacity for suffering in the tormented malefactor, on the other, were both seen as Shakespeare's transcendence of his shoddy, prejudiced material. But Shylock is not a deflection from the play's course: the extremes of his character are the extremes of this world. The Venice of *The Merchant of Venice* is a fantastic dream-city where the unbridled rapaciousness of the usurer is balanced by his human dignity and contrasted against the melancholy of the titular hero. This play is not as flamboyantly indecorous as most of Shakespeare's comedies, yet its coherent social world, especially in the first four acts, is another ideal landscape.

Much Ado About Nothing furnishes a more telling example of the persistent importance of the ideal landscape in Shakespearian comedy. Superficially, this play, too, seems somewhat remote from his more customary comic practices. The world of the play is once more a coherently depicted society; it is the *haute-bourgeoisie* of Messina, a provincial outpost of the Spanish-dominated Kingdom of the Two Sicilies. The inhabitants of the city possess, in the main, Italian names; the great political and military luminary, whose arrival in the city is the occasion of such excitement, is aptly named Don Pedro, in recognition of the Spanish hegemony over Sicily during the sixteenth century. His darkly sinister bastard-brother, the rebellious Don John, may recall the notorious Don John of Austria, the scourge of the Netherlands. The play's historical decorum is far more thorough than the references to Henry of Navarre in *Love's Labour's Lost*; its environment and its inhabitants are portrayed with a coherence that is markedly different from the nonchalant mingling of wildly different societies and historical periods in other comedies. Apart from the aggressively English members of the constabulary, the play reproduces with care some of the major facets of Sicilian society as understood by Englishmen during Shakespeare's lifetime.

But this is precisely why *Much Ado About Nothing* (even more thoroughly than *The Merchant of Venice*) dwells in a Shakespearian cloud-cuckoo-land. It does not possess the obvious exoticism of the other play—until, that is, its passions break loose. It retains, for most of its length, the decorum of middle-class life: the combination of sentiment with fiscal priorities is as appropriate to sixteenth-century London as to this Messina—in this one instance, Shakespeare appears to be addressing himself to the concerns of orthodox comedy. Despite the consistently sustained illusion of a 'normal' world, however, *Much Ado About Nothing* is fundamentally (though tactfully) located in an ideal landscape. Its exotic setting and the curiously volatile and extreme nature of the Mediterranean races—a powerful myth in Shakespeare's England—effectively distance the play's concerns from that recognition of affinity with the familiar world which is customarily encountered in more conventional comic drama. The conceit in this play resides largely in the discovery that this apparently 'normal' world—lacking the usual fantasy of Shakespearian comedy—is as strange and as self-contained as the improbable settings of other plays.

It is in its arrangement of its material that *Much Ado About Nothing* is so different from other comedies. It does not declare its exoticism immediately, as does, for instance, *Measure for Measure*, where the severity of the city's sexual restrictions inevitably place this 'Vienna' in a wholly imaginary context. In *Much Ado About Nothing* Shakespeare depicts a world so apparently ordinary that it is only through accumulation that we come to recognize how extraordinary it is. The opening scene is a striking evocation of a provincial society; the snobberies, the boredom, the incestuous gossip of this provincial backwater are beautifully captured. Leonato, described as the governor of the city, is a mixture of civic self-importance and of a proper deference towards the great ones of the world when they come within his orbit. He receives with approbation the news that only a few of the minor gentry 'and none of any name' were lost in the recent action; he is obviously pleased to be able to tell the messenger that the Florentine Count Claudio, whom the Prince has distinguished with fresh honours, 'Hath an uncle here in Messina'. An actor impersonating this character would not err if he reacted with some show of disappointment when the messenger tells Leonato that he has already delivered the news to Claudio's uncle.

In this self-important, gossip-ridden society, we are introduced to two entirely contrasted young women, both of whom, nevertheless, are characteristic products of such a society: Hero, the *ingénue*, the virtuous young lady lacking all personality or individuality, and her cousin,

Beatrice, a woman of nervous sensibility, intelligence and wit, forced into that clowning and flouting of conventions often displayed by such people in a narrow world like this Messina. She is deliberately provocative and consciously shocking in her comment on the messenger's assurances that Benedick (Singnior Montanto) has returned from the wars.

> He set up his bills here in Messina, and challeng'd Cupid at
> the flight; and my uncle's fool, reading the challenge,
> subscrib'd for Cupid, and challeng'd him at the bird-bolt.
> I pray you, how many hath he kill'd and eaten in these
> wars? But how many hath he kill'd? For, indeed, I
> promised to eat all of his killing.
>
> (I. i. 32)

Leonato's attitude to this flamboyance is emblematic of the world presented in the play: 'You will never run mad, niece'—his words betray both a grudging admiration for and a disapproval of unconventional, un-maidenly behaviour.

When Don Pedro and his suite arrive, the great cosmopolitan world invades Messina; the Spanish grandee, the Florentine nobleman and plain Signior Benedick are greeted with formal courtesy. The greeting is returned with fine *noblesse oblige*:

> *Don Pedro*   Good Signior Leonato, are you come to meet
> your trouble? The fashion of the world is to avoid cost,
> and you encounter it.
> *Leonato*   Never came trouble to my house in the likeness of
> your Grace; for trouble being gone comfort should
> remain; but when you depart from me sorrow abides,
> and happiness take his leave.
>
> (I. i. 80)

Much Ado About Nothing is a play of minutely-observed social nuances; we are, therefore, at liberty to detect a certain reproof in Don Pedro's reply ('You embrace your charge too willingly') suggesting, perhaps, that this provincial official has overstepped the mark established by strict protocol.

Count Claudio is a fitting counterpart for Hero; he is the handsome *jeun premier*: colourless, conventional, lacking in individuality. The clichés of sixteenth-century sonneteers come quite naturally to him when he declares to Benedick his love for Hero—she is a jewel, a treasure, the sweetest of ladies, modest, the paragon of beauty and virtue. The ground is thus prepared for a perfectly proper and predictable marriage between a scion of the minor aristocracy and a daughter of the wealthy bourgeoisie. In this way the play's social demarcations are finely drawn, with a wry though tolerant humour. A particularly felicitous touch occurs when Claudio and Don Pedro (having rid themselves of the troublesome Benedick) are at last at liberty to discuss love and marriage in the appropriately noble form of blank verse:

> *Claudio* My liege, your Highness now may do me good.
> *Don Pedro* My love is thine to teach; teach it but how,
> And thou shalt see how apt it is to learn
> Any hard lesson that may do thee good.
> *Claudio* Hath Leonato any son, my lord?
> *Don Pedro* No child but Hero; she's his only heir.
> Dost thou affect her, Claudio?
>
> (I. i. 252)

The distinction between romantic ardour (the language of which Claudio speaks so well) and financial convenience is nicely blurred; Don Pedro readily agrees to act as emissary and marriage-broker.

But the world of this play is not merely a well-observed and humorously drawn portrait of a provincial society: the setting is an exotic Messina, the people are Latins. The magnificoes bring with them the darker aspects of the *beau-monde*: the malcontents, the people of dubious credentials and the camp-followers. Of great significance in the opening scene is Don John's silence as the other characters engage in effusive courtesy or gay banter. The implicit threat and the sinister potentialities of this brooding character are brought to the surface in I. iii. when he makes his frank self-declaration to his crony Conrade:

> I had rather be a canker in a hedge than a rose in his [Don Pedro's] grace; and it better fits my blood to be disdain'd of all than to fashion a carriage to rob love from any. In this, though I cannot be said to be a flattering honest man, it must not be denied but I am a plain-dealing villain. I am trusted with a muzzle and enfranchis'd with a clog; therefore I have decreed not to sing in my cage. If I had my mouth, I would bite; if I had my liberty, I would do my liking; in the meantime let me be that I am, and seek not to alter me.
>
> (I. iii. 22)

The rough-edged honesty of the malcontent and his grim readiness to make use of his discontent assume passionate proportions. Don John's villainy introduces an essentially fantastic element into the world of the play. The last words of his self-declaration recall Iago's chilling assertions; Messina comes to possess some of the tragic intensity of Cyprus. The decorous and courteous social world becomes the victim of deception and also begins to display frightening passions. *Much Ado About Nothing* achieves the characteristic ideal landscape of Shakespearian comedy by a devious route: it begins in a polite world of substantial city-dwellers, but the special characteristics of this city and its people at length impose themselves on the play's apparently 'normal' concerns. In this instance, the social and moral analysis familiar from the traditions of orthodox comedy serves in the depiction of one of Shakespeare's fantastic environments. In Messina, Don John is among his peers—not in social standing (for he is both above and below these people) but because of the readiness its citizens have for intrigue, eavesdropping and other 'Italian' pursuits. The depiction of bourgeois manners and morality is consequently made more flamboyant, distancing the world of the play from the audience's common experience.

As its title declares, the play is based on misunderstandings, false information, rumour and the like. Though it is unique among Shakespeare's comedies for the depth and subtlety of its ethical concerns, intrigue plays such a large part in *Much Ado About Nothing* that it becomes a determining force of considerable magnitude. Don John trades in the same goods as the native Messinans—except that his practices are much more ruthless than those of his victims and completely lacking in the benevolent intentions they claim to possess. Yet they too organize their lives through indirections; their propensity for elaborate deception comes to seem strange and exotic. For no particularly cogent reason, for example, Don Pedro acts as a marriage-broker for Claudio not only in proposing the match to Leonato but also in broaching the young man's love to Hero. In such a world of indirections, Don John's practices find a fertile field. Claudio believes slanders against Hero on two occasions: not merely when deliberately deceived on the night before his marriage, but also when Borachio, Don John's ruffian, misunderstands and repeats an overheard conversation. This volatile Italian world is dangerous and treacherous. The possibilities of intrigue and deception it embodies are far greater than the audience's 'normal' experience—for most comedies of

London life in Shakespeare's age recognized the greater restrictions encountered by middle-class characters in the conduct of their affairs. The intrigue-world of *Much Ado About Nothing* seems therefore to be directed towards social and moral examination (and the play retains this element more thoroughly than other Shakespearian comedies) yet these very elements point towards the play's essentially fantastical setting: a cloud-cuckoo-land firmly based in a deceptively substantial city-life.

Out of this emerge the well-intentioned and apparently good-humoured sports of Don John's victims (during the period of the preparation for the marriage of Hero and Claudio) in the course of which they attempt to trick the nonconformists, Beatrice and Benedick, into believing that each is hopelessly loved by the other. Hero's description at the beginning of Act III of the trap laid for Beatrice is not merely decorative—the images of a humid world of intrigue are tactfully (though memorably) registered:

> Good Margaret, run thee to the parlour;
> There shalt thou find my cousin Beatrice
> Proposing with the Prince and Claudio.
> Whisper her ear, and tell her I and Ursula
> Walk in the orchard, and our whole discourse
> Is all of her; say that thou overheard'st us;
> And bid her steal into the pleached bower,
> Where honeysuckles, ripened by the sun,
> Forbid the sun to enter—like favourites,
> Made proud by princes, that advance their pride
> Against that power that bred it. There will she hide her
> To listen our purpose. This is thy office;
> Bear thee well in it, and leave us alone.
>
> (III. i. 1)

The botanical imagery and the political *exemplum* about court-favourites point towards the moral implications of this benevolent trickery; the secretive *locus* of the pleached bower is filled with potent emotional and 'romantic' suggestions.

It is in this world that the transparent calumny against Hero is accepted without question; indeed, it is accepted eagerly by Claudio when he humiliates the jewel of all virgins at the altar. In this, the corollary of gossip and intrigue is clearly depicted: for all its decorum, provincial good-manners and joviality, this is a world of passions, and these passions grip their victims with unbridled force. Leonato's violent tirade against Hero is characteristic—the recognition of truth or the objective proof of an accusation are beyond his moral faculties. The slander is believed, and the reaction to it is as absolute and as firm in its negation of former bonds of love and care as Lear's curses against Cordelia:

> doth not every earthly thing
> Cry shame upon her? Could she here deny
> The story that is printed in her blood?
> Do not live, Hero; do not ope thine eyes;
> For, did I think thou would'st not quickly die,
> Thought I thy spirits were stronger than thy shames,
> Myself would, on the rearward of reproaches,
> Strike at thy life. Griev'd I I had but one?
> Chid I for that at frugal nature's frame?
> O, one too much by thee! Why had I one?
> Why ever wast thou lovely in my eyes?
> Why had I not, with charitable hand,
> Took up a beggar's issue at my gates,
> Who smirched thus and mir'd with infamy,
> I might have said "No part of it is mine;
> This shame derives itself from unknown loins"?
> But mine, and mine I lov'd, and mine I prais'd,
> And mine that I was proud on; mine so much
> That I myself was to myself not mine,
> Valuing of her—why, she, O, she is fall'n
> Into a pit of ink, that the wide sea
> Hath drops too few to wash her clean again,
> And salt too little which may season give
> To her foul tainted flesh!
>
> (IV. i. 120)

Finally, to add reprehensible cunning to reprehensible conduct, the Friar suggests that trickery and deceit be (once more) employed to establish Hero's innocence—if, indeed, she is innocent:

> And if it sort not well, you may conceal her,
> As best befits her wounded reputation,
> In some reclusive and religious life,
> Out of all eyes, tongues, minds, and injuries.
>
> (IV. i. 240)

In these ways the unique social and moral coherence of *Much Ado About Nothing* is contained within a fantastical world, reflected here by the emphasis on the Italian nature of the setting and the characters. Though this is Shakespeare's sole essay in the high comedy of manners and in the comedy of moral discriminations, its tendency is always towards a flamboyance that (to an extent) prevents us from pursuing these possibilities to their logical limit. The so-called subplot, the merry war of Beatrice and Benedick which ends (despite their protestations) at the altar, is an instance of the play's self-regarding mode. Criticism has, at times, exaggerated the 'wit' of this material, in order (one suspects) to compensate for the alleged tedium of the main narrative interest. The verbal sallies of the madcap pair cannot match the brilliance and elegant wit of such exchanges in some of the best comedies of the Restoration; they are no more than a felicitous repetition of some of Shakespeare's comic stock-devices. But the material does help to identify the manner in which even this play is remote from the customary moral and ethical emphases of many orthodox forms of comedy.

Beatrice and Benedick supply the play with the exuberant language that is often the spoken sign in Shakespeare of the presence of an ideal landscape; but in this play (in accordance with its characteristic manner of locating pressing social issues in such a world) these two are also the only inhabitants of Messina to demonstrate a capacity for making sure moral discriminations. Beatrice's faith in her cousin's virtue remains unshaken, despite the 'incriminating' evidence that the night before the wedding was spent by Hero (contrary to custom) alone in her bedchamber. Elsewhere, too, she penetrates the hypocrisy displayed by more conventional and more orthodox members of her community. Beatrice and Benedick are both driven into defensiveness, into a masquerade of unconventional behaviour because their world cannot tolerate this particular species of honesty in any other way. And both find that they must continue to play the rôles they have adopted because these rôles have, to an extent, been imposed on them by their fellow men. Beatrice is given the play's finest and most telling moral statement. 'Kill Claudio' seems like a demand which, the audience feels, is intolerable in a comedy. She appears to imply that the gullibility and passionate vindictiveness of all around her may only be countered by an equally extreme, though painful, attitude. Yet this outcry also suggests that it represents the testing of Benedick: ordering him to kill Claudio does not transport the play into the realm of revenge-drama; instead, we are forced to realize that she is putting Benedick upon his mettle, eliciting from him a guarantee of his moral integrity and concern. This is one of Shakespeare's finest and most subtle touches—the unspoken implications of a relationship are given dramatic substance through the careful portrayal of two fantastical but fundamentally sound people, and through their reaction to a crisis which places their personal morality in the balance.

The placement of the play's true morality in Beatrice and Benedick, the nonconformists in a stereotyped world, may suggest that *Much Ado About Nothing* is much more thoroughly concerned with the examination of social conduct than the usual run of Shakespearian comedy. It may also be taken as an implicit condemnation of the smug hypocrisies of bourgeois society and a celebration of the moral (even perhaps spiritual) worth of those whom this society sees as nothing but unruly. There is little doubt that the comedy toys with these issues, for this is, it must be stressed, closest in Shakespeare to the type of comedy we encounter much more frequently in the history of European comic theatre. But the flamboyant elements in the play invalidate such schematic or specifically moralized readings. Beatrice and Benedic are placed in a world of Italian passions; their being endowed with true moral discriminations is as much a jest as a significant statement. Messina is an extraordinary and exotic place—the apparently 'normal', sensible characters demonstrate frightening reserves of passion, the 'irregular humourists', in this topsy-turvy place, are the ones that demonstrate the greater degree of commonsense and charity.

In this way, the fantastic world of Shakespeare's ideal landscapes finally dominates this play. Shakespeare's comedies (even when dealing with social and ethical values to the extent that this play does) constantly tend to distance their concerns from those possibilities of 'realism' that are implicit in most orthodox theories of comic practice. The social decorum of the play leads to playfulness as much as the extraordinary mingling of characters and historical periods in *A Midsummer Night's Dream* leads to it. As in *Measure for Measure* (though in that instance in a much more grave manner), moral discriminations also become objects of comic flamboyance. This must not be taken to imply that the play brushes aside its finely-observed portrait of moral states; but the particular and quite characteristic flavour of Shakespearian comedy may be sensed in this play in the teasingly ambivalent way in which its moral discriminations are displayed. We are constantly reminded, through its Italian passions and intrigues, that this is much ado about nothing—its faintly bitter taste is sweetened by the delightfully exuberant sense of fun.

The single instance of a flagrant indecorum in the play is an apt illustration of this characteristic. Dogberry and his friends, that very

English group of incompetents, are gloriously inappropriate inhabitants of this Messina. Through their inappropriateness, the play
achieves that eccentricity so often to be found in Shakespeare's
comedies. But through this playful departure from the otherwise
consistently maintained social decorum, certain ethical possibilities
are able to emerge as well. The watch makes the telling (though
jesting) point that the sophistication, subtlety, deviousness and
savoir-faire of the worldly-wise Sicilians are no protection against
relatively unsubtle deviousness. They are only too easily led by the
nose, whereas poor, none-too-intelligent Englishmen are able immediately to see villainy for what it is. The comedy will not permit us to
elaborate this into a moral or even into a nationalistic assertion. The
vulnerability of the Italian world is highlighted in a playfully
flamboyant way—the propositions we may tease out of the indecorous
incursion of English law-enforcers into this Messina (fashioned from a
powerful folklore about the people of the Mediterranean) constantly
return to theatrical jests.

IV

Twelfth Night contains Shakespeare's most alluringly artificial world,
peopled by characters seemingly composed of firm flesh, yet consisting
(in reality) of the most fantastical substance. Illyria appears, at first
glance, to have something of the social solidity of Messina in *Much Ado
About Nothing*: the classical name could be no more than a fiction for
the portrayal of English prejudices about Italian people and passions.
Yet Illyria, her people and her society are insubstantial fantasies: this
is Shakespeare's most evocative creation of a cloud-cuckoo-land,
transcending even the Mediterranean fantasies of *The Merchant of
Venice* and *Much Ado About Nothing*. These earlier plays, at least,
commence their exploration of ideal worlds in terms of an apparently
coherent society displaying a reasonably 'realistic' mode of character-
portrayal; but Illyria in *Twelfth Night* proves, from the start, to be
utterly fantastical. It is only Shakespeare's remarkable invention and
his ability to sustain illusion that make us accept this extraordinary
world as a natural and normal environment. In no other play is the
dramatist's capacity to create an impossible landscape (which is
nevertheless compelling and convincing) so thoroughly employed.

Illyria is preposterous—not because it cannot be found on a map or in a history-book, or because it is impossible to conceive of a society seemingly so substantial yet possessing no recognizable structure or solidity, but because the characters, their problems and their conflicts become increasingly more remote from the emotional lives and responses of common mankind. Ordinary humanity is represented, it is true, by the venality of Sir Toby, by Sir Andrew's folly, by Maria's level-headed freedom from romantic illusions, and, to a lesser extent, by Malvolio's pompous self-love. But the very British origins of Sir Toby and Sir Andrew and the isolation of the other two from the manners and aspirations of Illyrian life serve to increase the strangeness of the curious world of ambiguities in which the other characters dwell. *Twelfth Night* indulges in a most sophisticated game of illusion. Its leading characters engage out interest, even our sympathy, yet they act without motive, reason or even without consistency. This does not prevent, however, the play from remaining strangely serene: nowhere are the quixotic behaviour and obsessions of Orsino, Olivia and even of Viola registered as anything but perfectly acceptable, proper or predictable.

Each of these characters behaves in a most extraordinary manner—not merely in the context of mundane probability, but, much more importantly, in the context of that tissue of artifices that constitutes a fictional world. Each is in the grip of a particular obsession, the origins of which remain largely obscure; but the assurance of the play ensures that we remain practically oblivious of how 'surrealistic' this life is. The wit of the comedy consists, in part, in making credible and substantial characters that exist and move in a vacuum. *Twelfth Night* anticipates in several ways some much later developments in drama; it has reminded some people of Chekov, even though the vagaries of its characters are never used (as they are in *The Seagull*, *The Cherry Orchard* or *The Three Sisters*) as symptoms of their moral or psychological dilemmas. *Twelfth Night* retains the calm confidence that the characters' oddities represent nothing unusual, nothing out of the ordinary; only when the theatrical enchantment is broken, when the last notes of Feste's sadly 'realistic' and disillusioned song have died away, do we realize what an extraordinary world this has been.

The types of questions one usually asks of a play prove, in *Twelfth Night*, to be irrelevant. Why is Orsino so given to melancholy? Why is he so reluctant to press his suit to Olivia, relying instead on emissaries? Why, conversely, does Viola accept so readily her rôle as a go-between, and (more interestingly) why does she carry out her task with such faithful dedication? Why is Olivia so absolutely intent on mourning her brother, and why is she so hostile to Orsino's suit? A number of possible answers to these questions arise, reasonably naturally, from the play, and a number have been offered, with greater or lesser conviction, by critics and commentators. But the play itself remains extremely vague about these and a number of related issues.

Actors like to impersonate Orsino as an effete epicurean. His languishing, apparent from the first speech in the play, his celebrated comment on music

> That strain again! It had a dying fall;
> O, it came o'er my ear like the sweet sound
> That breathes upon a bank of violets,
> Stealing and giving odour!
>
> (I. i. 4)

seem to imply that he has sunk into desuetude, that he thrives on disappointment and frustration, that the bitter-sweet allure of melancholy and heartache have become for him the most treasured of experiences. Against this Renaissance precursor of Proust's Marcel, critics and directors usually place an Olivia who is also half in love with easeful death, cloistering herself from the elements, walking in veils, lamenting her dead brother. Between this pair of curiously determined melancholiacs comes Viola with her vitality, courage and good-humour. Despite this impression of good health and sanity however, she too seems to succumb to the Illyrian malaise. While her persistence in acting as Orsino's advocate may be rationalized in all sorts of ways—the dangers of her situation, the demands of loyalty, the desire to ensure the happiness of the man she loves—her consistent efforts to bring about that which will cause her pain and frustration appear to outweigh other considerations.

Is the play, therefore, an essay in deviant psychology? Does it explore, through the conceits of elegant comedy, some of the murkier areas of the human personality, especially where erotic inclinations are concerned? It is hardly surprising that an age with such a penchant for the abnormal as ours should have adopted a view similar to this towards the play. It must be admitted that there are a number of passages and episodes that suggest tantalizingly a concern with the exploration of these abnormal states. Notable in this respect is the relationship between Orsino and his eunuch-page Cesario, the disguised Viola. It may represent no more than an indication that intuitively Orsino recognizes that Viola is destined to become his fancy's queen, so that his seemingly facile transferring of affection to her at the end is thereby made more acceptable. Yet several of his speeches addressed to the 'youth' exceed propriety even by the more flexible sexual standards of Shakespeare's age:

> thou art a man: Diana's lip
> Is not more smooth and rubious; thy small pipe
> Is as the maiden's organ, shrill and sound,
> And all is semblative a woman's part.
> (I. iv. 30)

> Come hither, boy. If ever thou shalt love,
> In the sweet pangs of it remember me;
> For such as I am all true lovers are . . .
> (II. iv. 14)

> Cesario, come;
> For so you shall be while you are a man;
> But when in other habits you are seen,
> Orsino's mistress, and his fancy's queen.
> (V. i. 371)

The last extract is, perhaps, the most revealing. The confusions have all been resolved, Cesario has been transformed into Viola, the lovers sort themselves into mutually satisfactory groups. Yet still, the play ends with a duke making love to his page. The actual situation is, of course, otherwise, but the last stage-image depicts a languorous duke wooing a budding youth—for Cesario's being an eunuch is forgotten very early in the play.

These features of the play have at times received too much emphasis: the attempts to enrol the characters of this comedy into the company of M. de Charlus, Swann and Odette cannot but fail.[7] Yet a jesting interest in deviant sexuality is not entirely absent from it; but this interest is contained by the play's impossible and improbable environment—the ideal world created by Shakespeare. As so often in his comedies, these aspects of *Twelfth Night* are ambivalent and not overly concerned with the moral or ethical implications of the issues raised. This ambivalence is highlighted, in the first instance, through

---

[7] Most fully stated in Jan Kott, *Shakespeare Our Contemporary* (trans. Boleslaw Taborski), rev. edn, London 1965, pp. 209 ff.

the juxtaposition of an uproariously farcical set of attitudes with the languishing melancholy and the penchant for sexual ambiguities. The people of the subplot, the drunken Sir Toby, the inept Sir Andrew and, above all, that self-loving puritan, Malvolio, provide some of Shakespeare's liveliest comic inventions. But this hilarity, registered in the case of two of them by their specifically non-Italian nature in an Italianate world, is also present (in a more muted form) among the aristocratic characters who, on the surface, seem immune from it. Not only are Orsino, Olivia and even Viola delightfully absurd in their follies and vanities, but there is a more abstract type of hilarity to be observed in those stage-images and developments of the plot (like the dual sexuality of Viola in the last moments of the play) which are not absolutely necessary for the conduct of the action or the depiction of the characters.

Chief among these are the closely allied pursuit of the pageboy (whom we know to be a girl) by that somewhat more mature and quite dedicated melancholiac, Olivia, and the attraction Orsino feels for his page, even though he himself does not know that it is based on an intuition of Cesario's true gender. The critic needs to call on considerable reserves of tact when dealing with these matters: recent commentaries have covered the spectrum from the assertion that there is no engagement with these issues in the play[8] to the insistence that they lie at the heart of Shakespeare's conception. The surface of the work is, indeed, so beautifully maintained through its elegant languor, that to stress the 'bawdy' elements seems, in truth, a failure of taste. Yet they are very much present—in a witty, lighthearted manner, at some remove from the pathological emphasis some would place upon them. Orsino's remarks about Cesario (cited above) 'thy small pipe/ Is as the maiden's organ, shrill and sound,/ And in all semblative a woman's part' is a deliberate and obscene *double-entendre*. While verbal bawdy of this sort is relatively rare in *Twelfth Night*, the exploitation of the *oddity* of the situation is less so. The play is simultaneously 'romantic' and, to a certain extent, coarse—not only in the overtly coarse ingredients of the subplot, but also in the potentialities inherent in any situation dealing with a mistake of gender. This duality, characteristic of Shakespeare's comic landscape, results from the curious environ-ment of the play. So impossible and remote from everyday reality is Illyria that its two-fold nature (composed of opposites) seems entirely

[8] E. A. M. Colman, *The Dramatic Use of Bawdy in Shakespeare*, London 1974, p. 86.

natural and predictable. Yet, beyond the tissue of illusions produced in the play, we may discern an extraordinary ambivalence: in this comedy feelings and nuances of sensibility are refined to a remarkable degree, while the play entertains a schoolboyish hilarity about the confusions of mistaken sexuality. Viola's relationship with Orsino is, simultaneously, a touching portrait of a young woman unable to speak her love (as in the case of Viola's putative sister) and a *risqué* theatrical extravaganza in which a duke *seems* to have an unhealthy regard for his favourite page, and in which a mature lady pursues a youth much younger than herself, who is her social inferior and a girl to boot.

In a different type of play this daring would have produced either disaster or a deliberately eccentric or quirky work; in *Twelfth Night* the two aspects are beautifully integrated. The reason for this is closely connected with the creation of a landscape to contain these absurdities (while registering their emotional allure) and to allow modulation from one to the other. What is most surprising about Illyria is that its coherence and unity of tone emerge from a radical indecorum. The mingling of the Italianate world with British earthiness is far more adventurous than the incursion of Dogberry and his friends into the Messina of *Much Ado About Nothing*. The presence of Sir Toby and Sir Andrew (as well as the frequent allusions to very English things) bred, in the opinion of many former commentators, from Shakespeare's ignorance, is a flamboyant display of theatrical and poetic ingenuity. So confidently is this preposterous Illyria created, and so beautifully is its essential impossibility sustained, that it comes to have the appearance of a coherent world. We need deliberately and purpose-fully to distance ourselves from the brilliant artifice to recognize the extent to which this world is composed of an extraordinary mixture of often contradictory ingredients.

In one important respect, the ideal cloud-cuckoo-land of *Twelfth Night* is different from the impossible worlds of the other comedies, this being also the reason why its presence here is more difficult to recognize. In some of the other comedies the essential ambivalence is often signalled by the playful, jesting and (at times) discomforting incorporation of apparently weighty moral or philosophical issues. These are absent from *Twelfth Night*: this play fails to imply anything beyond its particularities, apart from several rather vague propositions about a decadent society that have received some emphasis in recent criticism. The dramatist's attention seems to have been engaged in this instance merely and exclusively in 'telling his tale'. For this reason, perhaps, the extraordinary nature of its environment has been largely overlooked: the artifice of this world of illusion (able to contain so many ambiguities and incompatibilities) is so thorough that the play's serene confidence almost prevents our recognizing it. The flamboyance of *Twelfth Night* is wholly subdued—so much so that it fails to be perceived as flamboyance. In this way it anticipates that comedy where the extraction of meanings or significances from the action has proved notoriously difficult.

Critics have found *Cymbeline* a particularly irritating play.[9] It appears to be concerned with overtly historical and political events; yet its historicity proves to be merely an illusion. Cymbeline's challenge to Roman hegemony is loosely based on Holinshead's account of Kymblin's refusal to pay tribute-money; for this reason, perhaps, the editors of the 1623 Folio placed the play among the tragedies, instead of the comedies, where (by common consent) it belongs. The bulk of the play, however, is not greatly concerned with this pseudo-historical material; it consists of a set of elaborate variations on comic motifs and conventions. This extravaganza on comic devices is, moreover, located in the most complicated of Shakespeare's illusory ideal worlds. It contains a rare confusion of historical periods and their characteristics. The geographical features of the British isles are observed with some accuracy; the notion of an historical bondage to Rome is also based on fact, yet both the Britain and the Rome of the play are *mélanges* of anachronisms and inaccuracies. Cymbeline and Cloten possess suitably British-sounding names; several of the Romans are named in a properly imperial manner. But Cymbeline's abducted sons, originally given Roman-sounding names (Arviragus and Guiderius) are named by their abductor Polydore and Cadwal—one classical, the other native in its origins. Belarius, the abductor, masquerades under the arch-British name of Morgan. Among the Roman senators and citizens we find the anachronistically named Iachimo, whose Italianate name betrays the dramatic tradition from which he is drawn: the cunning intriguer and calumniator, a comic counterpart of the Machiavel.

These confusions indicate the conflation of literary and cultural modes in the play. *Cymbeline* is a curious mixture of jingoistic historical

---

[9] See, for instance, H. Granville-Barker, *Prefaces to Shakespeare* (1930), I, London 1958 (2-vol. edition), p. 461.

chronicles; folk lore material (in the motif of the wicked stepmother); the trials and tribulations of young lovers; the central concern of much Renaissance comedy, the princelings stolen from their cradles (which Jacobean tragicomedy borrowed from Roman New Comedy); and the interest in sexual calumny and treachery—an important element in the tragicomedies as well as some of the comedies of the early seventeenth century. It is, therefore, an *olla potrida*, a mish-mash of many of the more popular theatrical devices of the period, apparently thrown together without much care for coherence or consistency. It pursues half-a-dozen or more plot-strands, bringing them together in an overgrown finale in which *cognitio* follows on *cognitio* with breathless haste. This is Shakespeare's most preposterously artificial world; it seems to have very little relevance to common experience or to the probabilities of quotidian life. Nor does it seem at all apologetic about this; nothing is done to make this hybrid world more probable, or to paper over the joins in the wholly fantastical plot: the radically different conventions, traditions and motifs from which the work is constructed jostle one another in a most extraordinary manner.

This aspect of *Cymbeline* is accompanied by a characteristic it appears to share with *Pericles*, though the unsatisfactory text of the latter makes judgement difficult. It seems that in both plays the dramatist's attention has come to concentrate exclusively on a characteristic of *Twelfth Night* noted above—the immersion in the narrative and its demands, on keeping a complex story moving through a fairly long play. The endeavour of the artist is, apparently, expended on articulating a tortuous tale as elegantly and with as much flamboyance as possible: the language, the characters and the dramatic events are, on the whole, subservient to the simpler narrative impulses. Of *Pericles*, as already mentioned, it is difficult to speak with confidence, for we do not know how much of its original texture has survived. But in *Cymbeline* (where the text is reasonably satisfactory) very few of the opportunities offered by the material for the type of playing with philosophical, moral and even religious concerns that appears in some of the other comedies are taken up. The shape of the play appears to be similar to that of *The Winter's Tale* and *The Tempest* with which it is often grouped. It deals with the themes of loss and recovery, strife and reconciliation, and with intimations of mysteriously benevolent forces that bring long-sundered people together. It contains a contrast between the intrigue-ridden world of the court and the restorative qualities of nature. But compared with *The Winter's*

Tale and *The Tempest*, these matters are barely touched on in *Cymbeline*. It is only in the episodes clustering around the killing of Cloten and Imogen's supposed death that we are able to catch some of that sense of wonder, amazement, of a supernatural agency presiding over the affairs of mankind to be found in the other two plays. The celebrated dirge, that supreme expression of calm resignation transcending strife and celebrating the consolation of death—

> No exorciser harm thee!
> Nor no witchcraft charm thee!
> Ghost unlaid forbear thee! _
> Nothing ill come near thee!
> Quiet consummation have,
> And renowned be thy grave!
>
> (IV. ii. 277)

—is the chief example of this mode in the play. But complex poetic evocation and the exploration of the more mysterious potentialities inherent in its material are generally avoided in *Cymbeline*. Throughout much of it, the more complex dramatic and poetic possibilities are neglected in favour of the demands of the narrative. Characters and the language are functional; theatrical and literary attention is so much focused on incident, on the unusually large cast of characters, and on the interweaving of essentially disparate plot-strands that there is little room, in truth, for the subtleties we normally expect to find in poetic drama. Even Posthumus's dream-vision in the prison scene (V. iv) is much more functional than, for instance, the marriage-masque of *The Tempest*. A certain amount of rhetorical embellishment enters the play at this moment, but Shakespeare has avoided endowing the scene with those emblematic and emphatic details that distinguish similar episodes in a number of the comedies. The vision is solely an elaborate means of pressing the story forward, preparing the audience for the hectic unravelling of confusions in the next scene.

These characteristics of the play have led some to suspect that it represents Shakespeare's declining powers in his dotage. *Cymbeline* enjoys the reputation (in some quarters) of being a tired play, in which the dramatist is content merely to display his familiar bag of tricks without much conviction. Others, however, have argued with some force that this return to the simplicities of a less sophisticated form of drama reflects a specific artistic aim.[10] Such disputes cannot, of course,

[10] D. R. C. Marsh, *The Recurring Miracle*, Pietermaritzburg 1962, pp. 24–124.

be settled absolutely—we shall never know what were Shakespeare's actual intentions when writing *Cymbeline*, but we may sense that in this play (and, perhaps, in *Pericles*) he discovered the potentialities for deeply moving emotional and aesthetic effects to be found in an almost child-like concentration on narrative and events. He fashioned for this play a curiously alluring and memorable landscape through which the complicated events and accidents of the plot move in an elaborate but natural manner. *Cymbeline* is a virtuoso performance in plotting and theatrical construction. The characters are compelling, though simply depicted, as a result of the vividness of the events and the aptness of their (admittedly limited) personalities to the conduct of the action.

Imogen is the last in the line of heroines, beginning with Julia in *The Two Gentlemen of Verona*, who confront the world in male disguise to win satisfaction for their love, who experience all manner of difficulties, even treachery from their beloved, to find their labours rewarded at the end. She lacks Rosalind's delightful vivacity, the pious determination of Helena, or the serio-comic pathos of Viola. By comparison with these, she is a very simple character—honest, direct, lively and resilient. She is perhaps the 'healthiest' of these women, her good-nature and her courage see her through to the end. Such simplicities in other types of drama might well become crass; but in this instance they possess a sophisticated charm as well as an ability to move because we are made, imperceptibly, to feel the artist's control over these simplifications, and to sense the appropriateness of these relatively primitive theatrical devices in the dream-landscape of play. It is thus that the clichéd and the naïve come to be transformed into art, without any loss of their intrinsic qualities. The world of this play allows Imogen to express quite naturally the fundamentally stilted images of anguish when discovering what she supposes to be Posthumus's body—

> Pisanio,
> All curses madded Hecuba gave the Greeks,
> And mine to boot, be darted on thee! Thou,
> Conspir'd with that irregulous devil, Cloten,
> Hath here cut off my lord.
>   (IV. ii. 313)

—in the context of the very different diction of the earlier portion of this speech, her words on awaking from her swoon:

Yes, sir, to Milford Haven. Which is the way?
I thank you. By yond bush? Pray, how far thither?
'Ods pittikins! can it be six mile yet?
I have gone all night. Faith, I'll lie down and sleep.
But, soft! no bedfellow. O gods and goddesses!
These flow'rs are like the pleasures of the world;
This bloody man, the care on't. I hope I dream;
For so I thought I was a cave-keeper,
And cook to honest creatures.

(IV. ii. 292)

Her resolution to become a follower of Lucius strikes no discordant
note despite her sorrow for Posthumus's death. In terms of the
particular physical and emotional landscape he created in this play,
Shakespeare is able to avoid the crassness or superficiality inherent in
Imogen's determination:

I'll follow, sir. But first, an't please the gods,
I'll hide my master from the flies, as deep
As these poor pickaxes can dig; and when
With wild wood-leaves and weeds I ha' strew'd his grave,
And on it said a century of prayers,
Such as I can, twice o'er, I'll weep and sigh;
And leaving so his service, follow you,
So please you entertain me.

(IV. ii. 390)

Yet neither Imogen nor Posthumus (who is a representative of the
frequently weak-kneed youths of comedy) is able to sustain a continued
dramatic interest. What gives *Cymbeline* its strength and compulsion
are the fascination of the narrative and the array of minor characters
surrounding the lovers. This is Shakespeare's most impressive gallery
of character-rôles; none of them has much individuality and (perhaps
with the exception of Pisanio) none is drawn with any subtlety; yet
each is vivid, memorable and theatrically striking. The Queen and
Cloten are outstanding: these two come closest in Shakespeare to that
rich source of literary interest to be found in folklore which is often
employed by writers in a variety of complex and sophisticated
transformations. Their motives are simple, direct, immediately recognizable and, as in most folk-literature, psychologically invalid. As
in *Twelfth Night*, the questions we might ask about the behaviour of the
play's characters are likely to lead to unsatisfactory puzzles. Why does
Imogen suffer so patiently the Queen's malice? It is possible to

construct an answer for this 'problem' in the play: Imogen suffers patiently because of the restrictions placed upon her by her father's authority, until the opportunity and necessity of escape arise. This motif is familiar enough from certain sophisticated forms of narrative: Victorian fiction, for instance, where psychologically and socially 'convincing' reasons are often given for such endurance of the torments of a wicked stepmother or her substitute. But *Cymbeline* neither provides nor requires this type of explanation—it belongs to another order of existence, one determined by the characteristics of its own peculiar landscape. Imogen endures, the Queen persists in her machinations, Cloten enjoys privilege and the ability to pursue his intentions, while both of them retain Cymbeline's trust, because of the internal logic of the world of folk-tales. The ideal world of this play prevents our asking *why* its characters behave in a certain fashion, or *why* certain events occur. If such questions were asked, as children know well, the tale itself would cease to be. *Cymbeline*, in other words, provides a carefully fashioned environment for a collection of characters who behave according to their type. The dramatist offers no 'realism' and little 'motivation', and none is necessary, for the literary and cultural traditions on which this example of comedy draws (and which give it support and substance) are remote from such rationalism.

The species of cloud-cuckoo-land created in this play is, therefore, a world of simplicities where some of the most basic (and in that sense primitive) ingredients of literature are able freely to operate. *Cymbeline* is not confined by the types of probability to be found in much literature, even in some of Shakespeare's comedies, though nowhere as notably as in *Much Ado About Nothing*. In *Cymbeline* Shakespeare employed the freedom of following the twists and turns of a complicated narrative with sophisticated *naïveté*, of dazzling his audience with his theatrical inventiveness, and of including in the play an amazing variety of characters drawn from many societies and literary modes. Its pleasing qualities emerge from the warm enjoyment of a well-told tale; smilingly, a few possibilities of elevated meaning are dangled before us, but the play pursues these even to a lesser extent than the other comedies which flirt with such material. The flavour and the individuality of this comedy are located in the free flow of incident and adventure, not in a set of meanings and attitudes imposed by the contemplative creative artist. *Cymbeline* is finally a vehicle for nothing but its own ingenuity.

The various ideal worlds examined in this chapter often possess very different characteristics; even in those plays which scholarship has regarded as a coherent group, the last comedies, we find the extremes of variation between the simplicities of *Cymbeline* and the apparently weighty philosophical and mystical machinery of *The Winter's Tale* and *The Tempest*. Yet this aspect of Shakespearian comedy is governed by a fundamentally stable set of artistic priorities: even *Cymbeline* arrives (by a different route) at the same place to which the overt Platonism of *The Tempest* leads. Like the last play, it is also concerned with the employment of those basic ingredients of theatre which have always proved the source of great pleasure. But *The Tempest* entertains transcendental possibilities; its terminology is drawn from some of the most idealistic of Renaissance philosophical notions: there, the playful flamboyance of Shakespeare's artificial landscapes is articulated in terms of a seemingly solemn engagement with metaphysical possibilities. Prospero's isle is a true *locus amoenus*, echoing with meanings and implications of a most elevated kind. Gonzalo's account of his Utopia (drawn from Montaigne's discourse on primitive life[11]) is to some extent prompted by his intuition of the very special nature of the place where he and his fellows have been shipwrecked. Yet the apparently 'philosophical' treatment that the ideal landscape receives in *The Tempest* is as tentative, provisional and hypothetical as the presentation of such landscapes in most of the other comedies. Shakespeare's philosophical idealism in some of his later plays (examined in the following two chapters) is but another instance of the essentially jesting nature of his art of comedy.

---

[11] Shakespeare clearly derived much of Gonzalo's views from Florio's 1603 translation of Montaigne's *Essais*. (Book I, Chapter XXX, 'Of the Caniballes' in *Montaigne's Essays* (trans. John Florio) London 1910, I, pp. 215–29.)

Magic, Miracle and Providence

I

Attempts to trace a chronological evolution in Shakespeare's work are best avoided; it is not easy to regard his artistic career in terms of growth, maturity and decay. Yet it may be observed, without violating the integrity of his art, that the comedies increasingly move away from the restraints of verisimilitude, or from the necessity of depicting a decorous world. The ideal landscapes examined in the previous chapter are instances of how the reliance on the fantastical—present, admittedly, in his earlier work—came to be dominant in the later comedies. The function of these ideal landscapes in the Romances also illuminates the remoteness of these plays from the traditional literary uses of fantasy. Little allegorical or didactic purpose is to be found in them; Shakespeare seems implicitly to have denied a common Renaissance apology for poetry's engagement with 'unreal' worlds: the depiction of life in an 'ideal' state in order to present eternal and fundamental truths in vivid and striking images. His comic theatre does not depend in any thorough way on supporting moral or ideological structures; the last comedies, particularly, reveal an art almost totally involved in its own artifice, a world without extractable meanings or abstract philosophical implications.

The Romances contain, nevertheless, much material reminiscent of philosophical patterns and systems: *The Winter's Tale* and *The Tempest* seem to reflect particular details of Renaissance Platonic optimism; the transcendental convictions of this philosophy (if it may be called that) colour many incidents and episodes in both plays, as well as their structures in general. This chapter and the following examine the peculiar manner in which these ideas are employed in Shakespeare's comedies, for it is in this respect that these plays challenge most profoundly several important cultural and critical attitudes. They appear to address themselves to issues of great moment, to embody in a fictional world some of mankind's most moving suppositions about the benevolence of nature. Yet their concern with the magical, the miraculous and the providential—all potential indications of a 'Platonic' frame of mind—is playful and hypothetical. Precisely in those plays where scholarship has detected a most thorough engagement with mystical possibilities, the simplicities of comic sport prove to be dominant. Transcendental philosophies, in the last plays, are no more 'important' than foolish clowning—their presence seems to have been dictated by aesthetic not by polemical ambitions.

In recent years, historians of Renaissance culture have uncovered an impressive body of evidence about the prevalence of magical notions in the period. The practice of (or, at least, the belief in) all types of magic was widespread throughout the European nations on both sides of the great religious schism of the time. The lower classes, as Keith Thomas has shown,[1] put their faith in a variety of magical cures and conjurings as much as in orthodox religion or in limited and costly medicinal practices. The princes and monarchs consulted, or at times employed, magicians, astrologers and spirit-healers.

The most powerful current of magical theory, however, deliberately turned away from practices its exponents considered necromantic or infernal. The characteristic magic of the Renaissance is a benevolent 'white' magic, dealing with certain quasi-philosophical ideas thought to have been derived from Plato; it displays a number of providential convictions, as well as a deep faith in natural miracles. Many of the leading intellectual figures from the last quarter of the fifteenth century to well into the seventeenth obviously felt drawn to the possibilities inherent in harnessing legitimate natural forces and in practising those ancient and holy rites which would bring great benefit to mankind and demonstrate the infinite bounty of God's creation. Their writings are filled with extravagant claims about human potentiality, about the miracle of nature, and with assertions that the practice of this magic is merely an illustration of God's providential design for humanity.

It is inevitable that this intellectual movement should have come to seem naïve and childish in the light of Cartesian assertions about the limitations of human knowledge. To the post-Renaissance world,

---

[1] Keith Thomas, *Religion and the Decline of Magic* (1971), Harmondsworth 1973 (Penguin University Books), pp. 14, 179ff., 210.

white or Platonic magic appears to be so much mumbo-jumbo. The writings of the 'Platonists'—Marsilio Ficino, Pico della Mirandola, Tommaso Campanella, Giordano Bruno and Giulio Camillo in Italy, Henry Cornelius Agrippa in Germany and John Dee and Robert Fludde in England—are filled with a confusing and confused array of assertions, misrepresentations of classical authorities, errors of fact and highly coloured but vague 'rhetoric'. Their claims are often ambiguous and paradoxical. They assert that they have discovered a *prisca theologia* completely in accord with Christianity, yet very often they fall into heresy. They insist that their practices are entirely natural, but the supernatural and the spiritual are never far from the extraordinary feats they claim to have performed. Their theories are unsystematic, all too often random and chaotic, yet their assertions constantly claim to conform to a philosophically rigorous system. Platonism, Hermeticism, benevolent magic—the whole complex of Renaissance mystical optimism—is a blind-alley of European culture. That some of the 'Platonists' espoused the spirit of the new learning, thus heralding the emergence of the empirical sciences, is essentially misleading: the movement represents, fundamentally, a primitivism, a desire to return to a golden age of faith, of human dignity and of mankind's ability to converse with God.

For all this, the impact of Renaissance Platonism on the imaginative and artistic endeavours of the period is considerable. Its doctrines spread through Europe and obviously fascinated a number of significant artists and writers in the major cultures of the continent. The effect of these doctrines is to be felt not only in the high-art of the various coteries, but also in several much more popular treatises—as, for instance, in that handbook of elegant accomplishments, Castiglione's *Il Libro del Cortegiano*.[2] Their importance for the imaginative aspects of Renaissance culture is not difficult to comprehend: though 'philosophically' unreliable, they incorporate powerful and moving assertions of divine and natural benevolence, human dignity and an almost child-like optimism. Renaissance Platonism offered a means of escape from the predominantly gloomy and pessimistic view of human life implicit in most Christian orthodoxies. It became a means of stressing the miracles of life while in no manner denying the joys of heaven.

[2] Hoby's translation is available (with an illuminating Introduction by J. H. Whitfield) in Baldassare Castiglione, *The Book of the Courtier*, London 1974.

In the play traditionally accepted as his last independent work, *The Tempest*, Shakespeare painted a memorable portrait of the Magus, the culture-hero of these beliefs. Through study and contemplation, Prospero has discovered nature's infinite bounties; he employs perfectly legitimate powers which appear supernatural and extraordinary only to the common run of humanity. He employs these forces, moreover, for the benefit of others—his aims are meliorist. He is a person of great dignity, authority and dedication. But Prospero is merely the most extended instance in Shakespeare's comedies of the appearance of this figure or of these concepts. Renaissance magical or Platonic ideas have left their mark on a number of these plays with ambivalent and often paradoxical results.

The figure of dignified authority, in touch with forces and agencies apparently beyond the human, makes its first appearance in *The Comedy of Errors*. The Abbess's startling intrusion into the last act, when the action of the comedy is speeding towards its expected resolution, is accompanied by elevated diction and by the suggestion that she controls powers beyond the ordinary through the holiness and virtue conferred upon her by her 'order':

> Be patient; for I will not let him stir
> Till I have us'd the approved means I have,
> With wholesome syrups, drugs, and holy prayers,
> To make of him a formal man again.
> It is a branch and parcel of mine oath,
> A charitable duty of my order. . .
> (V. i. 102)

The vocabulary of Renaissance medicinal magic is reproduced in these lines with some fidelity. The Abbess's powers are sanctioned by religion and morality; she employs natural distillations—syrups, wholesome drugs—accompanied by prayer. The phrase 'charitable duty of mine order' suggests that we have here something other than merely practical, secular medicine; the promise to make Antipholus a 'formal man again' reinforces the particular nature of her skill. The word 'formal',[3] in the sense used here, suggesting a return to essential characteristics, was a neologism in the 1590s. It has connections with the philosophical, scientific and religious interpretation of Plato's theory of Forms by his Renaissance successors.

[3] *OED, formal*, adj. 4c.

The Abbess's special power and function come to play a major rôle in the excessive, spectacular resolution of the play's conflicts and confusions. It is here that we encounter for the first time in Shakespeare a notable duality also to be found in Renaissance Platonism's attitude to the relationship between the magical, on the one hand, and the miraculous and providential, on the other. The revelation of the Abbess's true identity and the fact that she holds the key to the unlocking of the play's many complications are stated in a passage containing a number of mystical and even specifically Christian overtones. The peculiarity of this climactic passage is that Aemilia appears to exert control over the situation—but her control is merely emotional or theatrical: it is events and circumstances that bring about the extraordinary felicity of reunion and salvation. Aemilia is only an instrument of an apparently providential design. Her control over the course of events is extremely limited.

This duality is expressed in *The Comedy of Errors* by means of certain impressive suggestions implying the operation of a mysterious miracle beyond the capacity of reason to comprehend. As the old Syracusian merchant is led to execution, the Abbess addresses the assembly in spectacular though grave and dignified terms:

> Whoever bound him, I will loose his bonds,
> And gain a husband by his liberty.
> Speak, old Aegeon, if thou be'st the man
> That hadst a wife once call'd Aemilia,
> That bore thee at a burden two fair sons.
> O, if thou be'st the same Aegeon, speak,
> And speak unto the same Aemilia!
>
> (V. i. 338)

The anticipated ending arrives, but it arrives contrary to the expectations established within the structure of the play. Aemilia's rôle exceeds her apparent function in the plot; this excess is stressed by her spectacularly elevated diction.

There is of course, no magic here: the *cognitio* is achieved through chance and happy accident. But the mysterious and magical aura of Aemilia's speeches suggests that this fortunate resolution of dangers and misunderstandings (which comes about in a perfectly natural way) could not have taken place without her intervention. A theatrical device seems to take on thematic implications in the apparently indecorous words with which Aemilia brings the action of the play to an end:

> Renowned Duke, vouchsafe to take the pains
> To go with us into the abbey here,
> And hear at large discoursed all our fortunes;
> And all that are assembled in this place
> That by this sympathized one day's error
> Have suffer'd wrong, go keep us company,
> And we shall make full satisfaction.
> Thirty-three years have I but gone in travail
> Of you, my sons; and till this present hour
> My heavy burden ne'er delivered.
> The Duke, my husband, and my children both,
> And you the calendars of their nativity,
> Go to a gossips' feast, and go with me;
> After so long grief, such nativity!
>
> (V. i. 392)

Much has been made of two aspects of this speech: the references to the Christmas-story have been regarded as indecorous[4] in a play dealing with pagan antiquity (though similar breaches of decorum elsewhere have gone by without complaint), and the age of the twins (thirty-three years) mentioned here does not tally with the other account of their age given in the play.[5] It has consequently been claimed that this speech represents an addition to the original version for purposes of the notorious performance of *The Comedy of Errors* during the Christmas festivities at Gray's Inn in 1594.

There is little evidence, however, for this supposition. Inconsistencies of this type are not uncommon in Shakespeare (Hamlet's age is a well-known instance). The indecorous reference to Christmas is by no means without analogues. Aemilia's speech makes a vivid though oblique reference to the central mysteries of Christianity: the season of the Incarnation, a new birth and promise of bliss to come (achieved here in the reunion of a long-sundered family) and the years spent on earth by Christ. If we wish to pursue the extraordinary implications of this speech to their limit, we may discover in it a complex set of correspondences between the suffering and anguish of separation (akin to mankind's separation from God) and the promise of redemption and felicity. Aemilia describes the thirty-three years as a period of gestation, playing on the dual sense of 'travail'. This period

---

[4] J. Dover Wilson (ed.), The Comedy of Errors (New Cambridge Shakespeare), rev. edn, Cambridge 1962. Note on V. i. 406 (p. 115).

[5] E. K. Chambers, *William Shakespeare: A Study of Facts and Problems*, I, Oxford 1930, p. 309.

culminates in a birth which is also a rebirth, and it occurs through the 'sympathized one day's error'. The word 'sympathized' (like 'formal') comes from the specialist vocabulary of the half-mystical, half-philosophical doctrines of Renaissance Platonism.[6] The errors and confusions of the mad day in Ephesus, though giving every appearance of being chaotic, indeed malevolent, are controlled by a shaping purpose which the Abbess, through her special wisdom, is capable of recognizing. The climax of the play brings together suggestions of therapeutic 'white' magic and the silent operation of a providential scheme manifesting itself through the workings of chance and accident. The patterns of loss and recovery, nature's remarkable bounties, the tendency towards conferring unanticipated blessings on humanity may all be encountered here. The problem, as in the later comedies, is to what extent these elevated suggestions and possibilities are meaningful within the context of the comedy. Aemilia's 'magic' remains a mere verbal supposition needing no actual enactment. The sense of a providential design resides in no more than the characters' bemused sensation that what has occurred to them is rare and extraordinary. The magical, the miraculous and the providential may be more in the spectator's (or the critic's) fancy than in the realities of the play.

The Comedy of Errors does not end with Aemilia's rapt words; the last words, as often, are given to those earthy and vulgar characters whose horizons are very remote from the rarefied heights of the denouement. In this play, the two Dromios round off the action in a passage not unlike the *buffo* finale of *Don Giovanni*:

> *Dromio S.* There is a fat friend at your master's house,
> That kitchen'd me for you to-day at dinner;
> She now shall be my sister, not my wife.
> *Dromio E.* Methinks you are my glass, and not my brother;
> I see by you I am a sweet-fac'd youth.
> Will you walk in to see their gossiping?
> *Dromio S.* Not I, sir; you are my elder.
> *Dromio E.* That's a question; how shall we try it?
> *Dromio S.* We'll draw cuts for the senior; till
> then, lead thou first.
> *Dromio E.* Nay, then, thus:

---

[6] See examples cited in *OED: sympathy*, s6. 1 and *sympathize*, v6 3c, from which, the compilers claim, Aemilia's 'sympathized' derives.

> We came into the world like brother and brother,
> And now let's go hand in hand, not one before another.
>
> (V. i. 413)

This is clearly a parody of the harmony and mystery of the play's resolution; but, to what end? Does Shakespeare represent here the conviction that happiness and contentment are available to all men in their particular kind? Or is it, on the contrary, a cheeky admonition to the audience, warning it not to make too much of a piece of blatant theatricality? A similar situation arises at the end of *Die Zauberflöte*. The action ends with the mysteries of the Temple of the Sun, but the most striking material is the rapturous venality of Papageno and Papagena, in their ecstatic anticipation of the progeny they are about to bring into being. In neither instance is it possible to adjudicate between these apparent alternatives. The type of comedy represented by Shakespeare's and Mozart's works is content to display both. The transcendental suggestions which appear to emerge from Shakespeare's Latinate farce assume a jesting, hypothetical status within the play. The Dromios' function is not to 'undermine' the absurd implications of the denouement with their sturdy common-man's insistence on the baser appetites; it is, rather, to allow Shakespeare, even in this early and in many ways immature comedy, the opportunity of embodying in the play potentialities not intrinsically connected with any suggestions or recommendations it might appear to be making.

This pattern is repeated in later comedies. Helena in *All's Well That Ends Well* shares some of the Abbess's characteristics. Although she belongs to no order or abbey which might confer extraordinary sanctions on her, she, too, seems to have access to potentialities out of the common. The religious overtones surrounding Aemilia's office are replaced here by the powerful talismanic suggestions of Gerard de Narbon's miraculous cures. Helena stresses both the legitimacy and the 'magical' qualities of her skills when she comes to offer to cure the King's fistula:

> What I can do can do no hurt to try,
> Since you set up your rest 'gainst remedy.
> He that of greatest works is finisher
> Oft does them by the weakest minister.
> So holy writ in babes hath judgment shown,

When judges have been babes. Great floods have flown
From simple sources, and great seas have dried
When miracles have by the greatest been denied.
Oft expectation fails, and most oft there
Where most it promises; and oft it hits
Where hope is coldest, and despair most fits.
                                              (II. i. 132)

After the King has refused her offer, she persists with even greater
conviction:

Inspired merit so by breath is barr'd.
It is not so with Him that all things knows,
As 'tis with us that square our guess by shows;
But most it is presumption in us when
The help of heaven we count the act of men.
Dear sir, to my endeavours give consent;
Of heaven, not me, make an experiment.
I am not an impostor, that proclaim
Myself against the level of mine aim;
But know I think, and think I know most sure,
My art is not past power nor you past cure.
                                              (II. i. 146)

The magical or miraculous nature of Helena's cures is not
specifically mentioned in these speeches. Nevertheless, they offer clear
analogues to the type of magical healing already hinted at in *The
Comedy of Errors*: the mystical and even, perhaps, the religious
overtones of Helena's plan to cure the King are stressed. At the
beginning of the play, we hear that the King, Amfortas-like, is suffering
from an incurable ulcer; the Countess and Lafew lament the death of
Gerard de Narbon, the only man who would have been able to cure
him. It is in this context that we listen to the aphoristic couplets spoken
by the high-minded maiden as she arrives with her promise of
miraculous cures. The play moves into the realm of the symbolic and
the transcendental; Helena's practices seem God-inspired and God-
sanctioned; innocence, dedication and virtue appear to be the means
of accomplishing the impossible. The magical and providential
possibilities of folk-medicine are expressed in powerfully suggestive
terms: the cure of the aged King's festering wound by the pious virgin
recalls the world of archetypes and its symbols.

It is at this point that a perplexing moral ambiguity enters into the
play. Throughout these episodes Helena's holy piety and altruism are

stressed. Yet her endeavours are a part of her campaign to become Bertram's wife. We must be on our guard against imposing modern social and moral priorities on Shakespeare's age: those that are struck by Helena's apparently callous and determined pursuit of a youth who does not reciprocate her love may, indeed, be guilty of such historical confusion.[7] In any case, until the climactic passage in II. ii., when Bertram refuses Helena, we are free to imagine that their love is mutual. Many cultures, moreover, have seen no impropriety in a chaste young woman's determination to bring a reprobate youth to the altar. Bertram's behaviour in the second part of the play could be seen as making it all the more important that his moral welfare should be placed in hands as capable as Helena's. All this notwithstanding, the combination of the high-minded claims she makes about her healing powers with her personal aims suggests a certain ambiguity, a sense of unease. Nothing in the play stresses this, or even admits it as a possibility. Only the Clown's irreverent comments provide a faint hint that the material is being displayed in more complex terms than its simple narrative preoccupations would suggest. The Clown is, however, an unreliable witness; the point of his duty in I. iii. is too obscure to provide a firm indication. The moral qualms we register about Helena's actions (if, indeed, it is proper for us to register these) emerge from our own responses to the action and the material. Yet an uneasy feeling lingers around the disjunction between holiness and self-promotion.

This aspect of the play is given further illustration in other episodes. In the opening scene, Helena is presented, in general, as a serious, pious and high-minded maiden. And yet, at the end of the scene, she takes part in a lengthy extravaganza in which she has no difficulty in comprehending or parrying Parolles's obscene innuendoes. Once more, the difference between modern social criteria and those of Shakespeare's time may be relevant. It is not uncommon, of course, to encounter in the drama of the period characters who behave, at times, uncharacteristically; nevertheless, this episode is a further indication of the play's multi-faceted nature. It cannot be retained at a single and coherent level of meaning or suggestions: Helena is simultaneously the chaste and pious young woman, dedicated to 'good works', a cousin of Patient Griselda, and the resourceful, witty maiden overcoming all

---

[7] Helena is a woman 'who practises a borrowed art, not for art's sake, not for charity, but, woman fashion, for a selfish end'. John Masefield, *William Shakespeare*, rev. edn, London 1912, p. 148.

obstacles standing in her way. The play demonstrates a similar ambivalence: it is, by turns, serious, sombre, solemn and merely another jesting comedy.

Modern criticism has not been unaware of these difficulties; its attempts to resolve them have already received some attention. *All's Well That Ends Well* demands to be regarded, in part at least, as a witty essay in exploiting and altering certain comic conventions. The apparent moral ambiguity of its heroine and of its general ethical stance is an instance of the same preoccupation. The actual potency or piety of Helena's practices is not denied; but the play is clearly not concerned with them in the manner that post-Romantic criticism would expect. The copiousness of comedy demands that the two potentialities in the story be registered simultaneously. The dividing line between the pleasant conceit of comedy and the transcendental implications that may be elicited from it is not at all distinct. In this respect, *All's Well That Ends Well* is not fundamentally different from other (and seemingly more approachable) examples of Shakespearian comedy. But in this play the contraries it contains—the number of balls kept in the air, as it were—are greater than commonly encountered.

For this reason, it may be argued, Shakespeare chose to alter the source story in some important respects and to highlight certain motifs which do not there receive major emphasis. In all surviving accounts of the story, Helena's counterpart is rich and practically Bertram's social equal.[8] Helena is, of course, poor, and her status in the Countess's household is lowly. The story of Giletta makes little of the magical or miraculous potency of her father's cures: they are merely efficacious; the girl demonstrates considerable resourcefulness in employing them. Lastly, in none of the narratives does she desist for a moment from her pursuit of her unwilling spouse. When Beltramo abandons her in Paris, she hurries back to Rossillion to attend to the county's feeble economy. Giletta is, indeed, one of the plucky young women of Italian novellas who achieve their desires through courage, cunning and determination. Some, though by no means all, of the elements of the original tale are retained in *All's Well That Ends Well*. Much, however, is altered, and where alterations occur, there appears to have been an attempt to tease out of the material quite extreme moral and even philosophical implications. Any account of the healing of a patient whose disease is

---

[8] G. Bullough, *Narrative and Dramatic Sources of Shakespeare*, II, London 1958, p. 389.

deemed to be incurable may, of course, be seen in terms of the miraculous, the providential and even the magical. The jest (or the flourish) in *All's Well That Ends Well* resides in the enactment of the basic *metaphor* in the events and developments of the play.

The French court speaks of the miraculous, providential cure of the King. Helena herself, as we have seen, states quite unambiguously that she is the instrument of divine power. All these may be no more than metaphors, essentially fanciful turns of speech, in which we are not expected to see much significance. But the play pursues these possibilities (while retaining much contradictory material) through its deliberate departures from the source-story. It is chance, for instance, that brings Helena to Florence at the same time that Bertram arrives in the city. Unlike her counterpart in the narratives, she has initially no intention of insisting upon her conjugal rights; on the contrary, when she learns earlier the extent of her husband's disdain, she determines not to stand in the way of his happiness. In a solemn speech filled with expressions of altruism and images of self-effacement, she announces her intention of leaving Rossillion, in order to permit Bertram to find contentment:

> Poor Lord! is't I
> That chase thee from thy country, and expose
> Those tender limbs of thine to the event
> Of the none-sparing war? And is it I
> That drive thee from the sportive court, where thou
> Wast shot at with fair eyes, to be the mark
> Of smoky muskets? O you leaden messengers,
> That ride upon the violent speed of fire,
> Fly with false aim; move the still-piecing air,
> That sings with piercing; do not touch my lord.
> Whoever shoots at him, I set him there;
> Whoever charges on his forward breast,
> I am the caitiff that do hold him to't;
> And though I kill him not, I am the cause
> His death was so effected. Better 'twere
> I met the ravin lion when he roar'd
> With sharp constraint of hunger; better 'twere
> That all the miseries which nature owes
> Were mine at once. No; come thou home, Rousillon,
> Whence honour but of danger wins a scar,
> As oft it loses all. I will be gone.
> My being here it is that holds thee hence.
>   (III. ii. 100)

This is a definite turning-point in the narrative. Helena's magical and miraculous practices have brought, for her, only disaster. The discovery of selflessness prepares the way for the intervention of what may be seen as providential agencies.

Thus the extraordinary meeting in Florence takes place. Helena's prospects of happiness seem to improve because she has determined to sacrifice her happiness to Bertram's well-being. The coincidence and the near impossibility of the encounter receive considerable stress. Mario Praz has reminded us that the references to St Jaques le Grand, whither Helena intends to travel on pilgrimage, may not indicate that she is travelling the wrong way from Rossillion to arrive in Florence: Shakespeare may have had in mind the sanctuary of San Giacomo d'Altopascio near Florence,[9] not the celebrated shrine at Compostella in Spain. But if the words 'St Jaques le Grand' meant anything to Shakespeare's audience, it is likely that they would have indicated the much better known place of pilgrimage: the impression is thus very much reinforced that Helena achieves the possibility of regaining Bertram because she has decided to give up her ambition of becoming his wife. It is by indirection that she finds direction out. Is this an indication of the intervention of Providence? The play, characteristically, remains silent on this issue. Yet the coincidence is remarkable, especially since it is coupled, as we have seen, with Helena's adoption of a morally commendable stance. A providential possibility, though vague and ill-defined, may not be entirely excluded; the usual coincidences of comedy may, in this instance, be organized within certain philosophical or religious implications. Again, the characteristic ambivalence of comedy colours this episode: Helena's good fortune at meeting Bertram could be taken as an aspect of a set of elevated meanings in the play; it may also be seen as an opportunity for a protracted, intrigue-filled denouement not unlike that occupying the last two and a half acts of *Measure for Measure*.

This ambivalence is nowhere more apparent than in the actual resolution of the action. After the encounter in Florence and after her discovery of Diana's virtue, Helena's spirits rise—she becomes the resourceful maiden who brings her unwilling husband to heel. The preparations for Bertram's wedding to Lafew's daughter in the last scene are interrupted by the arrival of Diana and the Widow with their startling claim that Bertram is already married. They produce his ring

---

[9] Praz discusses various theories in 'Shakespeare and Italy', *Sydney Studies in English*, 3, 1977-8, p. 5.

as their warrant. Thereupon follows the curious episode in which Diana's riddling words elicit more and more anger from the King. All this serves merely to prepare the heightened atmosphere for Helena's spectacular entrance. To the assembled company, her appearance and her apparent return from the dead are miraculous; to Bertram her assertion that she has fulfilled his impossible conditions for honouring their marriage is even more inexplicable. To the audience, of course, there is no miracle—we have seen the means whereby the poor physician's daughter has come, at last, to occupy her rightful place as Bertram's consort. But the patterns of chance or coincidence, when coupled with the nature of Helena's inherited skills and the possibility that happiness became available to her only when she adopted a suitably altruistic position, nevertheless suggest that something beyond the rational is involved. None of this receives any stress or emphasis. The reader or spectator recognizes such potentialities at his own peril; but the play's effect (its curious and peculiar flavour) depends on the boldness and daring with which it incorporates the polarities of comedy—the trivial and the jesting on the one hand, and the elevated and significance-filled on the other.

The complex suggestions of magic, miracle and providence are more obviously present in *All's Well That Ends Well* than in *The Comedy of Errors*. *All's Well That Ends Well* is far bolder and far more adventurous in its exploration of the possibilities of comic form: it appears to deal with a reasonably coherent philosophical *schema* far removed from the pleasant trivialities of ordinary comedy. But, as this account of the play has attempted to demonstrate, these issues are not entertained in any 'serious' manner—the play neither recommends nor advocates them. They occupy a considerable part of its design in order to enhance that essential comic element which reaches its fullest expression in Shakespeare in *The Winter's Tale*—the display of a remarkable variety of possibilities within a self-contained, fundamentally jesting work of art.

II

It is often thought that the Romances recommend a misty-eyed optimism about life which is reflected in the persistent patterns of growth, renewal and reconciliation to be encountered in each of them.[10] More recently, perhaps, emphasis has been laid on the

---

[10] E. Dowden, *Shakespeare: His Mind and Art*, London 1875, pp. 403ff., 406; D. R. C. Marsh, *The Recurring Miracle*, Pietermaritzburgh 1962, p. 7.

possibility that these transcendental achievements are provisional—that these plays, as a result of their cyclic concerns, represent a potentiality for the recrudescence of evil and chaos. But despite this recension of widely held opinion, criticism still views them as plays filled with serious and philosophical implications. Their apparently thorough engagement with providential, miraculous and, at times, specifically magical issues reinforces this presumption. The Romances are considered, in short, to exploit some of the traditions of Renaissance comedy for the purpose of expressing elevated notions and views of life. Their 'lastness' assumes, therefore, considerable importance. The remnants of romanticism in modern literary thought insist that the end of a great artist's career is of great significance: these plays are taken as Shakespeare's summation of his artistic and his moral and spiritual experiences; they are presumed to embody a type of wisdom which is ultimately philosophical, not literary.

Frances A. Yates has identified the spectacular last scene of *The Winter's Tale* as an instance of Renaissance Hermetic magic.[11] How Shakespeare came to have acess to this recondite material constitutes a knotty problem for scholarship. Even though the particular details of Hermetic-Platonic lore appear to be reproduced in Paulina's conjurings in the last scene, Yates's findings have met with some scepticism. The objection has been raised that Shakespeare could not have had direct access to a body of writing which, in his time, remained arcane and eclectic. But a familiarity with the contents of the Hermetic tract known as *Asclepius* is sufficient to explain the material in the last scene of the play, as well as its general philosophical tenor. Familiarity need not imply actual knowledge. The basic ingredients of *Asclepius*, the best known of the Hermetic writings and the only one to remain familiar during the Middle Ages, passed into the culture of Renaissance Europe in the same way that Freud's theories became the common cultural currency of the twentieth century.

The employment of this material in *The Tempest* has not occasioned many critical qualms. Prospero obviously fulfils the function of the Magus.[12] Early in the play, he talks of his studious, contemplative life in Milan; the powers he discovered on his island came from his perusal of 'books'—these we may safely assume to be the 'white magical' tracts of Renaissance culture. The powers he controls are not supernatural, but

[11] F. A. Yates, *Shakespeare's Last Plays*, London 1975, p. 89.
[12] D. G. James, *The Dream of Prospero*, Oxford 1967, p. 61; W. C. Curry, *Shakespeare's Philosophical Patterns*, 2nd edn, Louisiana 1959, p. 159.

the *daimones* of the cosmology of Renaissance Platonism. Ariel, as his name implies, is a spirit of the air, resident in that element and possessing its characteristics; Caliban, by contrast, is a creature of the earth. The other spirits or potentialities marshalled by Ariel at Prospero's command are the familiar lesser *daimones* of Hermetic-Platonic thought that reside in all living and inanimate objects. These forces could be employed quite legitimately by human beings, since their use represented the harnessing of natural entities, not the invocation of the supernatural: Marsilio Ficino made much of this in his writings on the occult. The masque of mythological creatures in Act IV is clearly stated to be an illusion, not the conjuring of these beings. Prospero's decision at the end of the play to abjure his magic is reminiscent of the protestations of a number of benevolent magical practitioners of the period who insisted that their skills were employed solely for the consummation of particular humanitarian tasks.

Prospero may be taken to represent the benevolent altruism of Renaissance 'white magicians'. Much has been made of his apparent change of heart when Ariel reproaches him with harshness towards his victims:

> *Ariel*   Your charm so strongly works 'em
> That if you now beheld them your affections
> Would become tender.
> *Prospero*   Dost thou think so, spirit?
> *Ariel* Mine would, sir, were I human.
> *Prospero*   And mine shall.
> Hast thou, which art but air, a touch, a feeling
> Of their afflictions, and shall not myself,
> One of their kind, that relish all as sharply,
> Passion as they, be kindlier mov'd than thou art?
> Though with their high wrongs I am struck to th' quick,
> Yet with my nobler reason 'gainst my fury
> Do I take part; the rarer action is
> In virtue than in vengeance; they being penitent,
> The sole drift of my purpose doth extend
> Not a frown further. Go release them, Ariel;
> My charms I'll break, their senses I'll restore,
> And they shall be themselves.
>   (V. i. 17)

Nothing in the speech, however, suggests that Prospero's recognition of Ariel's capacity for pity is the catalyst that brings about greater indulgence or mildness in him. Modern sensibilities, suspicious of Prospero's exercise of power and authority, welcome any suggestion that the play presents its central character in a less than favourable light. But the portion of the speech beginning at 'Though with their high wrongs . . . ' is not causally linked with its earlier section. Rather, it is a reiteration of purpose: Prospero expresses surprise that Ariel is capable of human compassion; he then states that, being himself human, he experiences pity and compassion far more strongly. He therefore declares once more that determination he had already voiced to Miranda much earlier in the play:

> Wipe thou thine eyes; have comfort.
> The direful spectacle of the wreck, which touch'd
> The very virtue of compassion in thee,
> I have with such provision in mine art
> So safely ordered that there is no soul—
> No, not so much perdition as an hair
> Betid to any creature in the vessel
> Which thou heard'st cry, which thou saw'st sink.
>
> (I. ii. 25)

It is not necessary, therefore, to presume a change of heart in Act V: throughout the play Prospero's aims are therapeutic and benevolent. The tormenting of the court-party is, for the impure ones, an emblem of penance. They are brought to recognize themselves in their essential qualities: through recognition comes contrition; from contrition proceed forgiveness and redemption.

Renaissance practitioners of benevolent magic laid much stress on their altruism, contrasting their practices with the self-absorbed egotism of necromancers. Prospero is admittedly in a somewhat ambiguous situation, for his activities culminate in the recovery of his dukedom. But behind this we may glimpse a commitment to concepts of order and legitimacy. The well-being of the commonwealth depends on the rule of the legitimate duke; though Prospero's fault in neglecting his public duties is acknowledged, the deep conservativism of the play requires his restoration once he has recognized his former errors. Otherwise, his magic is benevolent. Ferdinand and Miranda are forced to undergo a parody of a conventional comic situation: they experience the wrath of an angry father who sets barriers in the way of their love. But the audience is constantly reassured by Prospero about the benevolence of his attitude towards the young people. The task imposed on Ferdinand, the carrying of logs, though obviously demeaning to one of his status, is nevertheless merely a symbol for, or a ritual enactment of the strenuous trials and tribulations experienced by young lovers in many comedies.

Magic, then, pervades every facet of *The Tempest*. Prospero is the *metteur-en-scène* in a most exact sense, for without his conjurings, his illusions, or his sway over the creatures of his domain, no action may take place. The characters of the play lack freedom or self-determination; they are bound by Prospero's absolute control and by the strength of his illusions. Only Caliban retains a small measure of freedom, symbolized by the lyrical exactness of his descriptions of 'the qualities o' th' isle'. His freedom, though, may be no more than a product of Prospero's contempt for this 'thing of darkness'. The lack of freedom in the world of the play and the dictatorial nature of Prospero's dispensation have attracted some attention from politically-oriented theorists in our own time.[13] Opinion varies whether the play represents Shakespeare's critique of his own *ancien régime* or whether it is a regrettable lapse on the part of the ageing artist into a form of political authoritarianism and paternalism. But the extreme lack of freedom in the play is not political in emphasis, it serves a very different purpose.

The characters and their environment are totally conditioned by Prospero's power. The audience is given full knowledge of the extent and the aims of the practices he has learnt in solitude and contemplation. He presents himself as a providential force, shaping the experiences of the shipwrecked mariners (and of his daughter as well) towards a benevolent, therapeutic and restorative purpose. In this play alone among the comedies, chance and accident play no rôle; for Prospero manipulates every part of the action with an almost divine confidence and knowledge. But the play has two perspectives: one is that which the audience shares with Prospero; the other is that seen by the characters (even by Miranda herself)—this presents them with a confusing, threatening and apparently malevolent world. From the point of view of Ferdinand or Alonzo, what happens on the island is akin to a nightmare, a series of events and hallucinations beyond comprehension or reason. After their torment or testing is completed, they are privileged to receive explanations—the random illusions are

[13] Jan Kott, *Shakespeare Our Contemporary* (trans. Boleslaw Taborski), rev. edn, London 1965, pp. 245–47.

explained as parts of a benevolent purpose, exercised for the sake of justice and for the sake of the victims' moral well-being. This latter perspective is habitually encountered in comedy as the usual series of apparently accidental events moves towards its satisfying conclusion. It is here that the silent workings of a natural providence may be glimpsed in some of Shakespeare's comic plays. The optimism of the old lord Gonzalo in *The Tempest* (whose sense of the benevolence of nature remains unshaken despite his privations) may be taken as a means of registering such possibilities. In the figure of Prospero, with his mastery of the benevolent magic of Renaissance Platonism, Shakespeare may have thus been depicting a concrete example of that natural benevolence which generally characterizes the comic dispensation. The miraculous (or providential) and magic are brought into a close causal relationship in the last of the comedies, the play that spells out simply and clearly the chief aspects of the comic world.

Such a philosophical scheme may be constructed for *The Tempest* and several attempts at it have, indeed, been made in the last few decades.[14] It is possible to regard the play as a case-book for Renaissance providential ideas in conformity with the specific doctrines of the Platonists of the period. Yet the assumption that the comedy represents a coherent programme of this sort offends, somehow, against its nature and tone—its calm, almost bland serenity, its seemingly childlike delight in the simplicities of theatre and illusion. For a play that is alleged to contain such elevated philosophical material, this is a curiously straightforward theatrical entertainment.

The Tempest is a very short play, singularly free from suspense; it displays, as critics have noted, many of the devices of a masque or a pageant. Like those entertainments, it does nothing to obscure its own artifice; on the contrary, it withdraws into the abstract, the non-mimetic to an extraordinary degree; its sophisticated *naïveté* is particularly misleading. Its similarity to the masques of the seventeenth century, especially Ben Jonson's, is notable. It is known that Shakespeare's company was, at times, entrusted with the theatrical contributions to these festivities. The presence of masque-like elements in the last plays has been taken to suggest that Shakespeare may have had some part in the staging of these aristocratic entertainments; it has been claimed, for instance, that Prospero's 'great globe' is not a punning reference to the theatre (as often supposed) but to Inigo

[14] James, *The Dream of Prospero*, p. 141

Jones's *machina versatilis*, the *pièce de résistance* in many of the masques he designed. *The Tempest* itself, because of its brevity and because of its masque-like nature, is thought by some to have been performed (at least in this version) at the marriage-festivities of the Princess Elizabeth in 1613.[15]

It is not merely in its theatrical or spectacular aspects that *The Tempest* resembles the Jacobean court masques; their fundamental stance or conceit also enters the fabric of the play. The masques, too, contain an absolutely conditioned and determined world; their threats and conflicts are provisional because, no matter what images of evil, chaos or discord are presented, the issue is always a foregone conclusion. It could not have been otherwise: the masques embody an elaborately philosophical set of concerns, drawing heavily on classical learning and mythology for their emblematic personages, but their fantastical conflicts are played out without any suspense or tension. In many masques, the presence of a Prospero-like presenter ensures that the threats to order and harmony will not triumph; in others, even this figure was felt to be unnecessary, since the presence of the monarch acts as a guarantee that peace and contentment will reign. The masque-world is not drama but ceremony. As in *The Tempest*, the total reassurance given by the powerful conventional and political over-tones of the representation inevitably stresses the decorative elements of the entertainment. The conflicts and threats are hypothetical.

The forces of light, virtue and sanctity always triumph in the masques; the essential decorum of the form demands this. In *The Masque of Queens* the House of Fame is much too stoutly constructed to be threatened in any but a purely formal or ritualistic manner by the coven of grotesque witches; for all the energy and verve of their 'preposterous' rites, they vanish immediately upon the arrival of Heroic Virtue. Love is always freed from Ignorance and Folly. The four humours and the four affections do not seriously threaten the chaste marriage-ceremony in *Hymenaei*; Reason subdues them and makes them occupy their proper place in the ideal marriage-state.

In their ceremonial enactment of political and moral com-monplaces, the masques employed an elaborate allegorical and symbolic machinery often relying on the 'mysteries' of Renaissance Platonism. In Jonson's masques, particularly, the audience was

---

[15] F. Kermode (ed.), *The Tempest* (The New Arden Shakespeare), rev. edn, London 1962, Introduction, pp. xxiiff. and lxiiff.

expected (if his notes are to be trusted) to observe the numerical and geometrical disposition of the dancers; the details of the decoration and of the costumes frequently carried symbolic significance. The spectators were also required, it seems, to have some familiarity with the philosophical 'meanings' of the various members of the classical Pantheon. In all these ways, Jonson in particular, but the other masque-makers too, sought to communicate a vision of providential care and design in these entertainments. The special nature of the court, the divinity that hedges a king, allows a perfect image of the world to be incorporated in these revels. The neat resolution of conflicts, threats and dilemmas, watched over by the benign monarch as well as by the allegorized representatives of Order, Reason, Heroic Virtue and the like, is deliberately 'unreal'. The masques stress that in the world of mundane experience such easy and spectacular re-solutions are not to be expected; but the *brilliant* world of the court masques permits the potentialities of everyday life to be depicted in their essential, immutable form. The masques, as to some extent *The Tempest*, are epiphanies of providence; politically and morally they seek to demonstrate the miraculous potentialities for harmony and peace inherent in the world.

Such, at any rate, is the programme elaborated by Jonson and the other Stuart masque-makers for these royal and aristocratic *fêtes*. But these elevated aims imply something else within the conventions of the masques, and this, too, is mirrored by certain aspects of *The Tempest*. Like all highly formal ceremonies or rituals, the masques give the uncanny impression of proceeding along their predictable course with little regard for the participants or the spectators. Even from the printed texts, the modern reader senses the detachment of the court from theatrical involvement in the representation. And, again as in such highly stylized rituals, the decorative elements catered for that interest necessary to any ritual possessing a blandly formalized structure. Just as the Roman church elaborated the use of music in the Mass, so the Jacobean masque came more and more to rely on spectacle, music and dancing: there is a note of poignancy in Jonson's complaints that his elevated sermons made less impact than Jones's splendid designs. In the masques, therefore, the material often appears to be merely a vehicle (or even an excuse) for these extraneous elements.

Thus, the world of the masques not only presents an idealized scheme of providence through which all the evils and threats of life are made impotent, it also expresses these assurances in such a ceremonial manner that the emphasis comes more and more to fall on revelry and celebration. This results in a curiously complex theatrical pheno- menon: an extraordinary mingling of the elevated and the trivial, the allegorical and the diversionary. The masques address themselves simultaneously to a high-minded celebration of royal greatness and power and to the venal pleasures of the court at play. To question which of these is predominant is improper: the conceit of the masques and the artistic and social tradition they represent refuse to allow such a distinction to be drawn. *The Tempest* resembles the masques in this respect; its profundities, with which modern criticism has been so preoccupied, and its elaborate Platonic machinery are involved in a very simple, childlike play of serene, almost bland reassurance. Prospero is akin to those creatures of great potency in the masques—Mercury and Daedalus in *Pleasure Reconciled to Virtue*, Reason in *Hymenaei*—whose duty it is to propel the slight fiction towards its predictable conclusion with as much theatrical and spectacular variation as may be contrived. *The Tempest* employs Prospero's magical powers both to promote certain elevated philo- sophical ideas and to provide simple theatrical pleasure and entertain- ment. The play's most telling lines, fraught apparently with all manner of profundities, dissolve into the simplicities of the theatre. As so often in the masques, we are teased with the astonishing implications of the events depicted or of the poetry given to the characters, only to find ourselves unable to follow these possibilities to the point towards which they seem so much to beckon. The concern with magic, miracle and providence is an important aspect of the play. The problem about its use is the same as the questions that surround the use of elevated philosophical concepts in the masques. The reason for their inclusion, in both instances, appears to be as much diversionary as polemical.

Prospero's 'Farewell' is a telling instance of the play's essentially playful use of profundities. During the heyday of biographical criticisms, this speech was usually taken to be Shakespeare's sum- mation of his attitude towards the art he was about to abandon.[16] The alluring images conjured by the poetry were regarded as signs of a lingering regret that so much must be given up.

> Our revels now are ended. These our actors,
> As I foretold you, were all spirits, and

[16] See, for instance, Dowden, *Shakespeare: His Mind and Art*, p. 427.

> Are melted into air, into thin air;
> And, like the baseless fabric of this vision,
> The cloud-capp'd towers, the gorgeous palaces,
> The solemn temples, the great globe itself,
> Yea, all which it inherit, shall dissolve,
> And, like this insubstantial pageant faded,
> Leave not a rack behind. We are such stuff
> As dreams are made on; and our little life
> Is rounded with a sleep.
>
> (IV. i. 148)

Most of this speech, however, is a precise description of a courtly masque of the type staged by Prospero for the marriage-celebrations of Ferdinand and Miranda. It refers mostly to this specific situation, and there is little readily apparent reason (apart from the richness of the poetry) why we should seek after meanings beyond the immediate situation. Only the last sentence of the quoted passage hints at those generalizing tendencies so much stressed by criticism. Prospero draws a conventional philosophical analogy between the brevity of life and the insubstantial theatrical illusion he is describing. Momentarily, the play reaches beyond its preoccupation with its own theatricality, and approaches that essentially allegorical status towards which its use of magical and providential material seems to point. But the effect is only momentary—it is a grace-note in the structure; to apply it to the play as a whole is hazardous.

III

It seems safer to claim for *The Winter's Tale*, the play preceding *The Tempest*, a genuine concern with providential and miraculous schemes. *The Tempest* is notable for its concise action and for its observation of the unities of time and place. *The Winter's Tale* is prolix and episodic; it consists, basically, of two unrelated narratives: the plight of Hermione and the troubles of Perdita and Florizel. Shakespeare does nothing to obscure this hiatus in the action—rather, he draws attention to it in the Chorus of Time in IV. i. *The Tempest* contains no suspense, it proceeds smoothly to its predictable conclusion. *The Winter's Tale*, by contrast, keeps its trump-card so hidden that the restoration of Hermione has been suspected of being an artistic miscalculation.[17] Most significantly, *The Winter's Tale* lacks the easy-going decorativeness of *The Tempest*; like the earlier 'dark comedies', it gives every appearance of pushing

---

[17] S. L. Bethell, *"The Winter's Tale": A Study*, London 1947, pp. 47, 103.

the traditional material of comedy to the limits of endurance in its treatment of sensational and melodramatic incidents. It, too, has at times been thought of as a *tragedie manquée*. Finally, although it deals with a magical-providential scheme, this scheme emerges only gradually, until it comes to the surface in the last scene—in the 'miraculous' conjuring to life of Hermione's statue and the subsequent revelation that the report of her death had been false. Consequently, the play appears to be far more intimately concerned with these issues than *The Tempest*: that play resides among the simplicities of fairy tales; *The Winter's Tale* gives many instances of the emotional and even religious 'seriousness' of the world of folk-tales—the imaginative experiences suggested by its title.

The heterogeneous material of *The Winter's Tale* suggests an optimistic, quasi-providential movement from anarchy and chaos towards the revelation of a benevolent purpose working through chance and accident, and constantly tending towards great felicity. These possibilities are not stated at all explicitly in the play itself—they are left to inference and to the general state of amazement and wonder expressed by the characters (and experienced perhaps by an audience unfamiliar with it) as the elaborate pattern draws to its conclusion. Only when it is complete does the design become apparent. The audience's state of knowledge is almost exactly the same as that of the characters; this is a marked contrast to *The Tempest*, where the reassuring presence of Prospero makes the audience privy to his providential schemes.

The opening episode of *The Winter's Tale* presents a powerful image of an apparently chaotic, unjust and destructive world. The regal courtesy of the second scene (very much as in the opening scene of *King Lear*) swiftly devolves into brutality and jealous hysteria. Adherents of theatrical *verismo* are often puzzled by Leontes's sudden decline into insane jealousy—even though it may be justified in terms of an acute insight into the psychology of manic depression. But, contrary to commonly-held views, it is motivation not realism that is the issue here. Leontes's outbursts are surprising not because they strike us as 'unreal', but because his motives for suspecting Hermione's virtue are scant, despite the 'circumstantial' evidence of sorts that the play provides. When Polixenes announces at the beginning of I. ii. that he must return to Bohemia after a nine months' sojourn in Sicilia, Leontes's desire that Hermione should attempt to persuade the Bohemian King to prolong his visit prompts the lady to importune the visitor with a liveliness which, to her husband, seems less than comely. Yet despite these 'justifications' for Leontes's suspicions, his headlong rush into madness is swift and brutal. The material at the beginning of the play seems remote from the world of comedy; if an analogue were required, the melodramatic tragicomedies of Fletcher and his imitators, with their emphasis on the sensational and the salacious, would be the most appropriate. The persecution of Hermione, the plot to assassinate Polixenes, the tyrannical treatment of the new-born child all confirm the affinity between this play and the popular melodramas of the period. The early episodes depict a world so subject to irrational emotions that the sense of comedy is almost completely absent. We are given none of the signals suggesting that we should expect a comic world to unfold; the plot twists and turns into ever increasing confusion and menace: only the intolerable nature of the likely outcome gives a faint hope that events will change for the better.

It is difficult to see this element in the play as anything other than a deliberate preparation for the seemingly miraculous resolution at its end. Shakespeare's dramatic intentions are bold and sure: by banishing the recognizable signs of comedy, and by making the action far too swift to make a tragic emphasis likely, he insinuates an expectation for the well-being of the characters which resides in nothing other than the audience's dissatisfaction with the direction the play appears to be taking. This is accomplished through a most sophisticated reliance on the audience's sense of playing-time. The events of the first three acts are remarkably swift: Leontes's jealousy is born, grows and comes to have disastrous consequences in a series of economically constructed episodes. By the mid-point of the play, he has plotted against the life of his friend, his new-born child has been sent to its hideous fate, he has received the oracle's guarantee of his wife's virtue, and he has lost both her and his son. The play's narrative comes to a catastrophic and most unsatisfactory conclusion before the end of Act III is reached—unsatisfactory because few of the demands of drama and of the theatre have been fulfilled. It is no more than a sordid tale of sexual mistrust which has its unfortunate and not at all edifying conclusion. Because of these foreshortenings, the audience comes to expect a reversal of fortunes: the play is clearly too short to end at the conclusion of III. ii. ; the situation could not become more confusing or unsatisfactory. Leontes's world has been split asunder—there is no direction for the play to take but towards happiness and reconciliation.

Several aspects of the first half of the play hint at the possibility of the working of providential care: the oracle in III. ii. is an instance of a markedly oblique treatment of these possibilities. Our attention is focused firmly on Leontes when Cleomenes and Dion deliver Apollo's cryptic words, and on his sickening sense of despair when he realizes that his offence has had (as he thinks) irreversible consequences. The audience is led largely to ignore the crucial words in the oracle which point quite specifically towards the eventual resolution in the play:

> "Hermione is chaste; Polixenes blameless; Camillo a true subject; Leontes a jealous tyrant; his innocent babe truly begotten; and the King shall live without an heir, if that which is lost be not found."
>
> (III. ii. 130)

It is the intensity of the dramatic effect that deflects attention from the promise of a comic resolution these words contain. When the death of Mamillius is announced, the pessimistic, punitive implications of the oracle receive emphasis, not its suggestions of benevolence. The pattern of reassurance, protection and restoration receives silent and imperceptible establishment as the play declines into greater and greater disaster. The intimations of providence are hidden, devious and apt to be overlooked through the more immediate impact of evil and suffering. They emerge, however, in somewhat clearer terms at the play's turning-point, the discovery of Perdita in the last scene of Act III.

But before this is reached, there is an interesting episode which is so oblique in its suggestions that its promise of happiness is almost impossible to catch. Paulina tells of Hermione's death in a speech of great emotional force, with unusual stylistic implications:

> What studied torments, tyrant, hast for me?
> What wheels, racks, fires? what flaying, boiling
> In leads or oils? What old or newer torture
> Must I receive, whose every word deserves
> To taste of thy most worst? Thy tyranny
> Together working with thy jealousies,
> Fancies too weak for boys, too green and idle
> For girls of nine—O, think what they have done,
> And then run mad indeed, stark mad; for all
> Thy by-gone fooleries were but spices of it.
> That thou betray'dst Polixenes, 'twas nothing;

> That did but show thee, of a fool, inconstant,
> And damnable ingrateful. Nor was't much
> Thou woulds't have poison'd good Camillo's honour,
> To have him kill a king—poor trespasses,
> More monstrous standing by; whereof I reckon
> The casting forth to crows thy baby daughter
> To be or none or little, though a devil
> Would have shed water out of fire ere done't;
> Nor is't directly laid to thee, the death
> Of the young Prince, whose honourable thoughts—
> Thoughts high for one so tender—cleft the heart
> That could conceive a gross and foolish sire
> Blemish'd his gracious dam. This is not, no,
> Laid to thy answer; but the last—O lords,
> When I have said, cry "Woe!"—the Queen, the Queen,
> The sweet'st, dear'st creature's dead; and vengeance for't
> Not dropp'd down yet.
>
> (III. ii. 172)

This elaborate announcement of Hermione's death is the exact opposite of 'The Queen, my lord, is dead'. It is a spectacular, rather 'theatrical' statement, organized in accordance with those court-room procedures which lie at the heart of Renaissance rhetorical practices.[18] The whole speech is a carefully-fashioned example of *incrementum*: Paulina builds up her accusations through a list of Leontes's crimes to the greatest and the most startling: the announcement of the death of the queen. In the course of this, she employs the figure known as *negando* when she mockingly claims that Leontes's former enormities were as nothing compared with the revelation she is about to make. The speech as a whole has something of the flavour of a court-room address—from the opening flourish, a type of *conglobatio* (dwelling on the tyrant's 'studied torments') to the final climax of the announcement of Hermione's death.

It is unusual to find in the late Shakespeare such a sustained use of rhetorical formulae. This is the mode of an earlier period of English drama: the plays of the 1580s and the early 1590s. The possibility must be entertained, therefore, that he reverted to it for a very particular purpose. That purpose is bound up with the highly theatrical nature of this speech. There is a jarring note in this elaborate expression of a state of mind apparently numbed and defeated by the horror of Hermione's

[18] Peacham's *The Garden of Eloquence* (1593) is available in a facsimile reproduction (Gainsville 1954). See pp. 169, 35, 153; it lists the types of figures to be found in Paulina's diatribe.

fate. It is an oratorical and descriptive speech, not a *mimetic* representation of a psychological state. This suspicion is given some substance because the tone of this outburst and of what follows it is so contrary to Paulina's usual style of utterance. Elsewhere in the play, she is a 'plain speaker', an irreverent, shrewish woman, insisting on calling a spade a spade, as in her long dispute with Leontes when she tells him of Hermione's new-born child and insists upon the legitimacy of the baby. Her sharp reply, after he calls her 'A most intelligencing bawd' is characteristic:

> Not so.
> I am as ignorant in that as you
> In so entitling me; and no less honest
> Than you are mad; which is enough, I'll warrant,
> As this world goes, to pass for honest.
>
> (II. iii. 68)

The elaborate embellishment and the obvious employment of spectacular verbal effects when she announces the queen's death are in direct contrast to this mode.

This memorable speech is a means of preparation for the startling finale to the play—the revelation that Hermione lives, and the explanation that the promise of the oracle prompted the plot to hide the wronged queen until the propitious moment. Too much sophistication and too great an attention to the nuances of a text are required for the essentially false nature of Paulina's account of the queen's death to be recognized. Shakespeare relies on an audience's difficulty in discriminating between a theatrical performance and a theatrical enactment of a 'theatrical' performance. The exaggerations and hyperboles of Paulina's speech reveal her 'practices', but it is only hindsight that enables the spectator to know this. This is, then, another oblique, obscure intimation of a providential scheme relying both on circumstances and on the activity of a providential agent. Paulina's words to Leontes after she has told him of his wife's death intimate, once more, the possibility that Hermione has survived and give an indication of the penance he must undergo before she may be restored to him. But, again, hindsight is required for this to be noticed:

> I say she's dead; I'll swear't. If word nor oath
> Prevail not, go and see. If you can bring
> Tincture or lustre in her lip, her eye,

> Heat outwardly or breath within, I'll serve you
> As I would do the gods. But, O thou tyrant!
> Do not repent these things, for they are heavier
> Than all thy woes can stir; therefore betake thee
> To nothing but despair. A thousand knees
> Ten thousand years together, naked, fasting,
> Upon a barren mountain, and still winter
> In storm perpetual, could not move the gods
> To look that way thou wert.
>
> (III. ii. 200)

The excess implicit in these statements suggests—no matter how faintly—that Leontes is being duped, that Paulina's condemnation is ceremonial, part of a therapeutic torment preparing him for the unhoped-for, ecstatic restoration of the last scene. It is to indicate these possibilities that Shakespeare gives Paulina in the next moment some lines mollifying her anger:

> All faults I make, when I shall come to know them,
> I do repent. Alas, I have show'd too much
> The rashness of a woman! He is touch'd
> To th' noble heart. What's gone and what's past help
> Should be past grief.
>
> (III. ii. 216)

These words may seem like the final, cruel twist of the knife—but they may also be taken as consolation, a sign of the slow process of restoration and reunion.

These faint intimations in *The Winter's Tale* that the resolution of the narrative is to be a happy one come to possess analogies with the schemes of providence to be found in some of the Platonic writing of the period. Significantly, the outcome is brought about by a combination of natural, involuntary forces—chance and accident—and human intervention, represented by Paulina's recognizing the potentiality contained in the oracle and by her acting upon it. She stage-manages, in a very specific manner, the slow restoration of Leontes to grace. But she must hold her hand until the propitious moment arrives—sixteen years later in terms of the play's narrative chronology. This combination of activity and passive receptiveness is one of the fundamental philosophical ideas embodied in the comedy in a thoroughly committed, though still playful and 'comic' manner.

The active, planned, patient 'cure' of Leontes only becomes

apparent at the end of the play, when the sixteen years' deception is finally revealed. In this Shakespeare extends, and in one important way alters, a traditional preoccupation of comic drama. In most comedies — whether the largely playful sort Shakespeare wrote, or the more orthodox comedies of social criticism and comment — there often appears a motif which may be termed comic torment. The seemingly gratuitous tormenting of some of Shakespeare's characters has already been noted. Malvolio, Jaques, Falstaff, Lucio seem to offend against some criterion of love, and are therefore humiliated amidst the general jollity with which many comedies conclude. This comic torment has, at times, been found distasteful; it has also been considered an echo, transformed into fiction, of certain ancient practices and rituals[19] also to be encountered in the tragedies — as in the strenuous persecution of Macbeth.

But this mock-torment is meted out to another class of characters in some of the comedies. Sometimes, as in the case of Claudio in *Much Ado About Nothing*, the *jeun premier* must endure a species of punishment or purification before he may be allowed to enter the community of happiness established at the end. The peculiarity of the ending of *Love's Labour's Lost* flows in large measure from the abrupt halting of the play just as this movement begins, and from the theatrically improper prolongation of the period of purification to a year and a day. In *Much Ado About Nothing* Claudio's offence against Hero is highly reprehensible: his gullibility and his fundamental lack of trust result in his brutal humiliation of his betrothed at the altar. Don John's slanders are so contrary to the girl's character that, even though he had 'ocular proof', Claudio should not, we are made to feel, have accepted them so eagerly. Even by the standards of Shakespeare's world, his behaviour is worthy of the most stringent moral censure. Yet, once Hero's innocence is established, the other characters are only too prepared to restore him to felicity. The youth must be taught a lesson; playfully, almost with glee, he is threatened with all manner of retribution. He undertakes to marry Leonato's niece in reparation, even if she were a blackamoor. The sportive, lighthearted restoration of Hero (anticipating the return of Hermione in *The Winter's Tale*) is accomplished by means of an indulgent curative humiliation of the errant youth. The absence of moral stringency is an intrinsic part of this comic world.

Comic torment, the exaction of ceremonial penance or the en-

[19] C. L. Barber, *Shakespeare's Festive Comedy* (1959), New Jersey 1972, pp. 166-8.

durance of a symbolic testing, is a motif in other comedies. Ferdinand's purely formal trial of bondage is an instance. A fascinating, because gratuitous, example is to be found in the last act of *The Merchant of Venice*. In the genial, peaceful atmosphere of Belmont, Portia and Nerissa demand of their husbands the rings that had been extracted from the unfortunate youths by the clever 'attorney' and his clerk in payment for their saving Antonio from Shylock's knife. The deception is swiftly revealed, the young men's embarrassment is short-lived: happiness is not impeded by this momentary darkening of the play's horizons. The tormenting of Bassanio and Gratiano is not in earnest; it is offered to the audience as a sport, a jesting coda, without anything but decorative implications.

This aspect of comic drama is lengthened in *The Winter's Tale*, and it is specifically made a part of the benevolent therapeutic practices of Paulina. Most importantly, it is kept from the audience. We remain, until the end, as much ignorant of the course of events and the purpose behind them as Leontes. For the only time in the comedies, the audience's level of awareness is exactly the same as the character's on whom the deception is being practised—unless we have those unlikely powers of divination which would enable us to recognize the occult signs in the play when Paulina launches her therapeutic torment in III. ii. Through hindsight, however, after the pattern has unfolded, we come to learn of Paulina's benevolent, forward-looking care and cure of the king. She educates him into patient repentance and into a recognition of his own moral status—not merely as a transgressor (this he realizes soon enough) but also as a creature worthy of salvation. When the terms of the oracle have been fulfilled and the lost child has been restored, her deceptions reach fruition. At that moment both the audience and Leontes learn of the unhoped-for, startling felicity of Hermione's return. The conventional mock torment of comedy becomes a purposeful, philosophically consistent pattern of redemption. The comedy seems to pass into *commedia*; Paulina emerges as a figure of benevolent knowledge and authority, an optimist who fashions great good out of the chaotic, evil-oriented passions of imperfect humanity.

In this, Paulina is akin to Prospero and to the practices and aims of the exponents of Renaissance benevolent magic. Her altruistic and providential designs come to seem miraculous and magical, but they are based upon purely natural causes, the ebb and flow of life, as revealed by Apollo's oracle. It is only the absence of Prospero's magical authority that prevents our recognizing, until the last moments of the play, the essential affinity between these two characters. Like Prospero, Paulina is able to exercise only limited and confined control over the course of events. Her plans and designs could not have reached fruition had she not faith (as Hermione tells) in an impersonal pattern of benevolence manifesting itself in the apparently purposeless and random events of the play. She puts her trust, that is, in a natural providence. A great deal of what happens in the play is beyond her control or knowledge. If anything may be said to control it, it is that emblem of change and mutability, Time (the chorus in IV. i.), binding its disparate events together. Yet everything in this seemingly random progression of events contributes towards the fulfilment of the play's optimistic drive, culminating in the great reunion of the last scene. Leontes's villainy, the sad fates of Antigonus and Mamillius, Polixenes's tyrannical objection to the marriage of his son and the shepherd-maid, the ruse employed by Camillo to enable him to return to Sicilia, even Autolycus's cruel torment of the hapless old Shepherd, all these, no matter how shoddy or venal the motive behind them, tend silently and mysteriously towards the great achievement of restoration. It is this that Paulina employs—though her employment is essentially passive, a matter of faith and trust. At the end of the play, we find that her function has been largely ceremonial and consolatory; she has demonstrated the possibility of hope, the reality of benevolence; but her control has been largely illusory.

The Winter's Tale reproduces with remarkable fidelity the doctrines and the symbols of those Renaissance theories of miraculous providence which were usually claimed to be in accordance with Plato's teachings. The concern with magic, miracle and providence is extraordinarily consistent throughout the play—even if the artistic purposes behind it are curiously ambivalent. All aspects of the play represent, indeed, a meticulous working-out of an irresistible tendency towards good emerging from evil and chaos. The play incorporates an optimistic declaration of faith in a natural providence unfolding through the ordinary events of human misfortune. But these patterns are hidden from the characters and from the audience until their revelation in the last moments of the comedy. The intimations of miracle and providence are vague; Paulina's magic (which proves not to be magical at all) is confined to the last scene. Until that point the presumptions about a philosophically coherent system in the play must remain largely conjectural.

The last scene changes all this. Its ambiguous conjuring-trick provides a point of reference from the perspective of which the earlier portions of the play seem to fall into place within its elaborate pattern. The Platonic mystery in *The Winter's Tale* (no matter how playfully it employs the characteristic notions of the magical, the miraculous and the providential) is retrospective. The play itself is structured, as we come to see, through retrospect and the recognition—outside the theatre as it were—of the import of events that, at the time of their occurrence, seemed to hold no particular portent. This retrospective nature of the play and its obscured miraculous machinery echo not merely the basic tenet of Renaissance Platonism, but some of its incidental details as well. The lack of specific signs pointing towards that system of belief until the last scene is, curiously but significantly, an essential part of the play's 'Platonic argument'.

5   *The Platonic World*

I

The Winter's Tale and *The Tempest* are the only instances of a thorough engagement with Renaissance Platonic lore among Shakespeare's plays. Elsewhere, scholarship has been able to suggest some analogies with the optimistic and transcendental aspects of this mystical philosophy (or pseudo-theology), but in most cases it is not possible to discover anything other than fleeting resemblances.[1] Because comedies coventionally end in happiness and because such conclusions often come about through startling changes of fortune, these Platonic analogies may be regarded as no more than an accidental congruence between comic conventions and a body of philosophical belief. The last two plays, however, despite the reluctance of scholarship to accept the possibility that Shakespeare had access to source-material it regards as much too *recherché*, include too many instances of the specific details of Renaissance Platonism for the analogy to be merely accidental. As already suggested, these plays are thoroughly concerned with the details of the Platonic lore of the time.

The reasons why at the end of his productive life Shakespeare should have turned to a set of convictions seemingly so contrary to his preferences (as far as they may be surmised from his plays) must remain conjectural. The remnants of romantic literary theory would insist, of course, upon a conversion, or at best upon a recognition of the essential characteristics of the comic view of life. Earlier in his career, it may be observed, Shakespeare appears to have expressed a healthy scepticism about the assertions conventionally made by Renaissance Platonists. Hotspur's *bons mots* as he deflates Glendower's magni-

---

[1] Richard Cody (*The Landscape of the Mind*, Oxford 1969, pp. 81–150) argues, however, that Platonic-pastoral concepts play a most important part in several early comedies, most notably in *A Midsummer Night's Dream*.

loquent boast that he is able to summon spirits from the 'vasty deep'[2] indicate a common-sense refusal to be impressed by fashionable mumbo-jumbo. It would seem, therefore, that the incorporation of Platonic mysteries in *The Tempest* and in a more subtle (though no less significant) manner in *The Winter's Tale* must be taken to represent a recognition—in the significant last phase of an artist's creative life—of transcendental possibilities. Or else, if the portrait of the artist in old age discovering the consolations of mysticism is found unacceptable, the phenomenon may be seen as a species of senile wish-fulfilment, an escape into cloud-cuckoo-land.

The personal reasons, if any existed, for Shakespeare's employment of Platonic material in these plays cannot be discovered; but they are, also, largely irrelevant. There is no necessity to assume a commitment towards the material he used; the presence of Platonic lore in the last two plays must be examined from the point of view of its function. The previous chapter has already intimated the possible significance of this material in these plays—it is a part of the conceited, 'witty' quality characteristic of Shakespearian comedy. The elaborate philosophical machinery is a means of enhancing copiousness—that inclusiveness which delights in the flamboyant display of often contradictory possibilities, a 'serious' jesting with elevated and transcendental issues. The Platonism of the last plays indicates the boldness of Shakespeare's experiments with comic form. The confidence and panache of the last phase of his dramatic career urged or enabled him to push the familiar materials of comedy towards theatrical and aesthetic effects of extraordinary virtuosity. If these plays are valedictory, as many have thought them to be, they are so in an impersonal sense—summations of the art of comedy, not personal testaments of belief. *The Winter's Tale* and *The Tempest* do not turn their back on the world of the earlier comedies, nor do they represent a discovery of how material implicit in those plays may be employed for the recommendation of elevated philosophies. They are nothing other than extravagantly brilliant instances of comic virtuosity. They represent a form of solemn levity in which issues of great moment are stated with a lightness of touch and without any apparent didactic or persuasive purpose. The provisional and hypothetical nature of Shakespeare's comedies reaches its fullest expression in these plays. They are as ambivalent in their use of source-material as earlier comedies; it is just as difficult to confine these plays

---

[2] *1 Henry IV*, III. i. 52–55.

to a single, consistent view of the world. Their wit resides in the manner in which the complex philosophical material in each is employed in minute detail to achieve comic exuberance.

Intimations of the richness of Platonic detail in *The Winter's Tale* and *The Tempest* occur spasmodically in earlier plays. The conventional shape of the comic action, as already mentioned, offers a number of analogies with the basic tenets of Platonic optimism. Viola and Sebastian in *Twelfth Night* may offer some hints of the Platonic theory of the relationship of the sexes and of Aristophanes' account of the primordial androgynes in *Symposium*. Benedick's famous comment on music in *Much Ado About Nothing*

> Now, divine air! now is his soul ravish'd. Is it not strange
> that sheeps' guts should hale souls out of men's bodies?
>   (II. iii. 54)

may be taken as an allusion to Plato's largely magical view of the power and nature of music. But such things, we must insist, are merely analogies; too fleeting and too circumstantial to permit us to identify confidently the presence of Platonic material. We are on safer ground in assuming that the magical healing to be found in *The Comedy of Errors* and in *All's Well That Ends Well* depends to some extent on Platonic lore as understood by the Renaissance. But the most extended reminiscence of the Platonic world among the earlier plays is to be found in *The Merchant of Venice*. The last act of this comedy provides a deliberate contrast to the earlier acts. The commercial world of Venetian intrigue is replaced by the anodyne of Belmont. This may be no more than a means of restoring to the play that sense of romance which had been absent from so much of it. But several historians of culture have pointed out that its musicological material indicates a philosophical point of view,[3] while others have suggested that Belmont represents a *locus amoenus* with distinct philosophical overtones.[4]

It is certainly 'a place apart'; it represents aristocratic solitude and security, especially when compared with the busy, cut-throat world of

---

[3] Leo Spitzer, *Classical and Christian Ideas of World Harmony* (revised version prepared by Anna Granville Hatcher), Baltimore 1963, pp. 99, 133.
[4] C. L. Barber, *Shakespeare's Festive Comedy* (1959), New Jersey 1972, pp. 186–9. This passage does not identify Belmont specifically as a *locus amoenus*, but the attributes and significances of Portia's house, as described by Barber, are clearly derived from that tradition.

the Rialto. This serene security is expressed through the use of images
and symbols filled with mystical significances. At the beginning of the
fifth act, in the 'duet' of Lorenzo and Jessica—the operatic term is not
at all inappropriate here—we are given images of cruelty, treachery
and death. The young pair intones a litany of ill-starred or betrayed
lovers: Dido and Aeneas, Troilus and Cressida, Jason and Medea,
Pyramus and Thisbe. This memory of tragic and disastrous love is
celebrated in verse of serene—if somewhat cloying—loveliness:

> In such night
> Stood Dido with a willow in her hand
> Upon the wild sea-banks, and waft her love
> To come again to Carthage.
>
> (V. i. 9)

In this way, the scene suggests the security and contentment of these
lovers: Belmont is not a world of treachery; it is a place where love is
secure, where fate may be tempted without danger:

> *Lorenzo*   In such a night
> Did Jessica steal from the wealthy Jew,
> And with an unthrift love did run from Venice
> As far as Belmont.
> *Jessica*   In such a night
> Did young Lorenzo swear he lov'd her well,
> Stealing her soul with many vows of faith,
> And ne'er a true one.
> *Lorenzo*   In such a night
> Did pretty Jessica, like a little shrew,
> Slander her love, and he forgave it her.
> *Jessica* I would out-night you, did no body come;
> But, hark, I hear the footing of a man.
>
> (V. i. 14)

Such mystical playfulness serves as a reminder that Belmont is not
subject to the vicissitudes of the world outside; this is echoed, later in
the scene, by the joyful game of jealousy played by Portia and Nerissa
on their husbands. The secure felicity of the ideal world permits the
indulgence of playful fantasies which, in mundane experience, would
invite disaster.

The security of Belmont is depicted specifically in terms of the
familiar Pythagorean-Platonic doctrine of the music of the spheres. A
servant announces Portia's imminent return by way of 'holy crosses,

where she kneels and prays/For happy wedlock hours'. Lorenzo invites Jessica indoors, to prepare to welcome the mistress of the house; but he changes his mind, and summons the musicians outside. Before their arrival, he speaks those hackneyed lines about the relationship between the ideal, inaudible music of the heavenly bodies and earthly music, the faint echo of those stellar harmonies.[5] This commonplace idea is expressed in terms significantly reminiscent of the Platonic doctrine of Forms or Ideas:

> How sweet the moonlight sleeps upon this bank!
> Here will we sit and let the sounds of music
> Creep in our ears; soft stillness and the night
> Become the touches of sweet harmony.
> Sit, Jessica. Look how the floor of heaven
> Is thick inlaid with patines of bright gold;
> There's not the smallest orb which thou behold'st
> But in his motion like an angel sings,
> Still quiring to the young ey'd cherubins;
> Such harmony is in immortal souls,
> But whilst this muddy vesture of decay
> Doth grossly close it in, we cannot hear it.
>
> (V. i. 54)

The conventional doctrine of the transcendental potentialities of music is expressed here not merely in elaborately 'Pythagorean' terms, but with the significant addition of a reminiscence of Plato's allegory of the cave. Renaissance 'Platonists' often took this step when considering the nature of celestial music, and they frequently indulged in the type of moralizing Lorenzo indulges in when Jessica says that music disposes her to sadness:

> The reason is your spirits are attentive;
> For do but note a wild and wanton herd,
> Or race of youthful and unhandled colts,
> Fetching mad bounds, bellowing and neighing loud,
> Which is the hot condition of their blood—
> If they but hear perchance a trumpet sound,
> Or any air of music touch their ears,
> You shall perceive them make a mutual stand,
> Their savage eyes turn'd to a modest gaze
> By the sweet power of music. Therefore the poet
> Did feign that Orpheus drew trees, stones, and floods;

---

[5] Spitzer, *Classical and Christian Ideas of World Harmony*, p. 133.

> Since nought so stockish, hard, and full of rage,
> But music for the time doth change his nature.
> The man that hath no music in himself,
> Nor is not mov'd with concord of sweet sounds,
> Is fit for treasons, stratagems, and spoils;
> The motions of his spirit are dull as night,
> And his affections dark as Erebus.
> Let no such man be trusted. Mark the music.
>
> (V. i. 70)

Throughout the cultural phenomenon which we must describe, no matter how uncomfortably, as Renaissance Platonism, a close connection was constantly maintained between astral influences and Orphic incantations. Marsilio Ficino, Pico della Mirandola, Giordano Bruno, Henry Cornelius Agrippa, and many lesser thinkers interpreted the familiar legend of Orpheus's power to charm inanimate objects and beasts by the use of music to mean that he drew benevolent stellar influences from the truest of all music, residing in the stars and inaudible to imperfect humanity. Orphism thus became an important aspect of the benevolent white magic of Renaissance Platonists.[6] Lorenzo's lecture is an orthodox exposition of these commonplaces. Nevertheless, as in much of the 'Orphic' lore of the Renaissance, his words are ambivalent. The music of the spheres may be no more audible at Belmont than it is in Venice; the lecture is playful and hypothetical. Yet the leisure, security and happiness of this fortunate place enable mankind to recognize—no matter how fancifully—the great mysteries of nature. Portia's house, and especially her moonlit garden, is an example of contentment *sub specie aeternitatis*. At this moment, that is, the play moves to an ideal plane (or one closer, at least, to the ideal). There is a transcendence, just as a transcendence is implied by the removal of the action to Belmont after the resolution of the play's conflicts in Venice at the end of the fourth act. The muddy vesture of decay, the dog-eat-dog world of commerce and treachery are left behind in favour of the ideal, aristocratic security of Belmont.

It is in this setting, with the fanciful echoes of the great Platonic doctrines resounding through the speeches, that characteristically misty-eyed optimism and comic playfulness come together to produce the notable *ceremonies* of this act. Lorenzo and Jessica play a little game

---

[6] For detailed discussions, see F. A. Yates, *Giordano Bruno and the Hermetic Tradition*, London 1964, pp. 78ff.; and D. P. Walker, *Spiritual and Demonic Magic* (1958), London 1975, pp. 12–25.

of jealousy, just as Portia and Nerissa later practise such deceptions on their husbands. In a less happy world this would be tempting fate, inviting disaster. In Belmont, it is sport; the transcendent world not only showers blessings on its inhabitants (and those worthy enough to inhabit it), it is also a fit place and a proper occasion for jovial sport. The sharp disjunction between the first four acts of the comedy and its final act reveals, therefore, certain philosophical possibilities existing somewhat uneasily side by side with the usual characteristics of the comic world. Irrespective of the function or the *meaning* of Act V of *The Merchant of Venice*, material specifically related to the Platonic idealism of the Renaissance is unambiguously present in it. This is the strongest intimation among Shakespeare's earlier comedies of the importance and extent of Platonic lore in *The Winter's Tale*, his most thorough employment of these doctrines, despite their more obvious presence in *The Tempest*. And, as in *The Winter's Tale* itself, the 'Platonism' of *The Merchant of Venice* seems, simultaneously, deeply serious, and a pleasant flourish with which a comedy may elegantly come to an end.

The presence of certain Platonic-Hermetic patterns in *The Winter's Tale* has been discussed by Frances A. Yates in her study of Shakespeare's last plays. As previously mentioned, how Shakespeare came to have access to this arcane material has proved something of a problem for scholarship, since the more *recherché* aspects of Renaissance Platonism are not thought to have had wide currency in Shakespeare's England.[7] Despite the apparent complexity of this material, however, there is nothing in *The Winter's Tale* which could not have been gleaned from the Latin text known as *Asclepius*, or, indeed, from a circumstantial account of the contents of this celebrated account of divine revelation. The last scene of the comedy reproduces one of the most widely known passages from this tract.

Asclepius feigns to contain the revelations of the ancient sage and prophet Hermes Trismegistus about the nature of divinity. Hermes tells his disciple Asclepius about the extraordinary abilities of the priests of ancient Egypt. He recounts that these men, through pious study and the contemplation of divinity, learnt to control the *daimones* (or spirits) resident in all things. By discovering the virtues latent in all creation—plants, stones, liquids—they were able to produce specta-

---

[7] See, for instance, Ann Pasternak Slater's most unfavourable review of Yates's book in *The Sunday Times*, 18 May 1975.

cular, apparently supernatural conjurings in order to convince humanity of the greatness and benevolence of the supreme god. One feat, in particular, receives ecstatic description in *Asclepius*, and it came time and time again to be recounted in the writings of the Renaissance Platonists. Hermes tells how, in order to demonstrate to errant humanity the astonishing richness of creation, these priests summoned *daimones* to take up residence in statues of the gods and to make them move with apparent life. The passage is oblique but quite specific in its implications:

> And now that the topic of men's kinship and association with the gods has been introduced, let me tell you, Asclepius, how great is the power and might of man. Even as the Master and Father, or, to call him by his highest name, even as God is the maker of the gods of heaven, so man is the fashioner of the gods who dwell in temples and are content to have men for their neighbours. Thus man not only receives the light of divine life, but gives it also; he not only makes his way upward to God, but he even fashions gods . . . . Mankind is ever mindful of its own parentage and the source whence it has sprung, and steadfastly persists in following God's example; and consequently, just as the Father and Master made the gods of heaven eternal, that they might resemble him who made them, even so do men also fashion their gods in the likeness of their own aspect.—*Ascl*. Do you mean statues, Trismegistus?—*Trism*. Yes, Asclepius. See how even you give way to doubt! I mean statues, but statues living and conscious, filled with the breath of life, and doing many mighty works; statues which have foreknowledge, and predict future events by the drawing of lots, and by prophetic inspiration, and by dreams, and in many other ways; statues which inflict diseases and heal them, dispensing sorrow and joy according to men's deserts.[8]

(23b, 24a)

Another passage expands this account of the remarkable ability of the Egyptian holy men:

> Let us now return to the topic of man, and that divine gift of reason, in virtue of which man is called a rational animal. Marvellous is all that I have told you of man; but one thing there is, more marvellous than all the rest; for all marvels are surpassed by this, that man has been able to find out how gods can be brought into being, and to make them. Our ancestors were at first far astray from the truth about the gods; they had no belief in them, and gave no heed to worship and religion. But afterwards, they invented the art of making gods out of some material substance suited for the purpose. And to this invention they added a supernatural force whereby

---

[8] *Asclepius* in *Hermetica* (ed. and trans. W. Scott), I, Oxford 1924, p. 339.

the images might have power to work good or hurt, and combined it with the material substance; that is to say, being unable to make souls, they invoked the souls of daemons, and implanted them in the statues by means of certain holy and sacred rites.[9]

(37)

The climax of *The Winter's Tale*, the miraculous animation of Hermione's image, is not merely an analogue of these feats; it reproduces closely the basic tenets of these passages as well as the significance they came to occupy in the Platonic thought of the Renaissance.

It must be stressed, once more, that Shakespeare need not have had access to *Asclepius* and its many obscure and esoteric doctrines (though an ability to read its simple Latin was probably not beyond his powers). The material could have reached him via the extraordinary importance of these passages for Platonic thinkers for a century and a half before the play was written. There is no place in a study of this nature for a detailed analysis of the transformation of the feats reputed in *Asclepius* to have been performed by Egyptian priests and holy men. But we must take some note of how they came to be reinterpreted in the light of the philosophical and religious beliefs of those who espoused their underlying assumptions. For the resurrection of Hermione represents not an obscure incident in a minor mystical text of the early Christian era, but perhaps the single most notable and significant anecdote to have emerged from the Renaissance Platonists' fascination with Hermetic writings.

These 'conjurings' are reported by Augustine in *The City of God* (VIII. xxiii.), they are mentioned by Aquinas[10] and other scholastic writers, but they came into full prominence only after the promulgation of the other Hermetic texts in the last quarter of the fifteenth century. In the writings of Ficino, Campanella, Bruno, Agrippa and other 'Platonists', the ability to make statues seem to live and to cause them to perform miraculous acts became an important part of an optimistic mythology they derived from the Hermetic texts and from their rather strange understanding of Plato's writings. By reference to these feats, they sought to magnify the powers of humanity, to

---

[9] *Hermetica* (ed. and trans. W. Scott), p. 359.
[10] Aquinas denounced these practices in a celebrated passage in *Contra Gentiles* (III, civ–cvi).

celebrate the generally benevolent nature of the cosmos, and to reconcile these ancient teachings with the spirit of Christianity. It is significant that in Renaissance accounts of these magical practices Hermes himself is often credited with having performed them.[11] This represents an attempt to stress the holiness and legitimacy of these endeavours, since Hermes came to be thought of as a *priscus theologus* (who lived before Christ, Plato, or Moses, or even Noah, according to some enthusiasts). Consequently, the 'naturalness' of bringing statues to life is frequently emphasized in the writings of the Platonists when they insisted that there was nothing supernatural (despite certain assertions to the contrary in *Asclepius*) about these activities. Hermes and his followers (or the priests of ancient Egypt, according to those that read the original Latin carefully) employed some parts of the realm of nature which, though hidden from debased humanity, may properly be exploited by mankind through God's providential care. Thus the activity became, ultimately, a symbol for the limitless munificence of nature, a means of celebrating God's infinite bounty, and a guarantee of the benevolence of His creation.

Remarkably enough, the original Hermetic material, especially *Asclepius*, is closer to some of the basic tenets of Christianity (for all its anti-Christian bias) than are the Renaissance attempts to reconcile it with Christian revelation. *Asclepius* is informed by a strong sense of judgement and discrimination; it insists upon a rigorously moral way of life, and it regards humanity as answerable to the ethical demands of divinity. Though by no means uniform or coherent, it contains passages of deep pessimism when it deals with the imperfect and fallen state of mankind. It was a common characteristic of Renaissance Platonists to transform much of the material they adopted and championed. In their writing, consequently, the Judaeo-Christian rigour of the Hermetic texts is softened through the emphasis of those passages which suggest the availability of happiness or illumination to all mankind. The questions of morality, desert and merit came largely to be overlooked or brushed aside. The reasons for this had to do with the peculiar intellectual and emotional preferences of these writers. The impulse to give the original material markedly different emphases is also intimately bound up with certain philosophical notions that the Renaissance Platonists associated with it. Many of them were attracted towards a celebration of the infinite mysteries of the created

[11] Yates, *Giordano Bruno*, p. 67.

world. The attempt to enlarge the realm of nature (that is to say, that part of creation over which mankind has legitimate control) inevitably involved an attempt to blur the orthodox distinction between the natural and the divine realms. Thus mankind's ability to transcend the commonly accepted limits of human experience and to discover the seeds of divinity in all creation came to be seen in terms of the type of natural magic Hermes describes in *Asclepius*.

The implications of these views were widespread during the Renaissance, even where their specifically magical elements were absent. They penetrated many of the most influential writings of the period, as in the final pages of Castiglione's *Il Cortegiano*, which Englishmen could have read in Sir Thomas Hoby's 1561 translation:

> Behold the state of this great Ingin of the worlde, which God created for the health and preservation of every thing that was made. The heaven rounde besette with so many heavēly lights: and in the middle, the earth environed with the Elements, and upheld with the waight of it selfe: the sunne, that compassing about giveth light to the whole, and in winter season draweth to the lowermost signe, afterwarde by litle and litle climbeth againe to the other part: The moone, that of him taketh her light, according as she draweth nigh, or goeth farther from him: And the other five starres, that diverslye keepe the very same course.
>
> These thinges among themselves have such force by the knitting together of an order so necessarily framed, that with altering them any one jotte, they should be all lowsed, and the world would decay. They have also such beautie and comelinesse, that all the wits men have, can not imagin a more beautifull matter.
>
> Thinke now of the shape of man, which may be called a litle world: in whom every parcell of his bodie is seene to be necessarily framed by arte and not by happe, and then the forme altogether most beautifull, so that it were a hard matter to judge, whether the members, as the eyes, the nose, the mouth, the eares, the armes, yᵉ breast, and in like manner the other partes, give either more profit to the countenance and the rest of the bodie, or comelinesse.[12]

It is of the foremost significance that Castiglione's elegant but intellectually not very demanding work reproduces with some fidelity the more important assertions of Renaissance Platonism: the beauty and mystery of creation, the perfection of its order and form (thereby implicitly denying the common doctrine that at the Fall all nature became imperfect) and the centrality of man himself.

[12] Baldassare Castiglione, *The Book of the Courtier* (the Hoby translation), London 1974, p. 309.

The current of Renaissance Platonism, when it addressed itself to the miracle and magic of nature, received another most important stream of thought, as Ernst Cassirer has shown.[13] These were the views of Nicholas Cusanus about the relationship between faith and reason, as contained in his most influential work, *De docta ignorantia*. The adepts of Hermetic-Platonic magical philosophy in the Renaissance (for whom the activities described in *Asclepius* became a paradigm for 'true' philosophy) resented what they saw as the inflexible division between reason and faith, deduction and imagination in orthodox 'Aristotelian' thought. Cusanus's doctrine, that the limitations of human knowledge made it impossible for any phenomenon to be regarded as unreasonable or unacceptable, proved most alluring. The main thrust of the theory of learned ignorance, as the Renaissance Platonists saw it, is that only the crabbed and confined suspicion of mankind makes him refuse to accept the existence of aspects of creation not available to the sensory faculties. Thus it is not an act of faith, involving a suspension of reason, that should make us assent to the infinite greatness of God's realm, but reason itself should teach us that in the hands of omnipotence all is possible, and that, therefore, all should be accepted as reasonable. The miracle of nature and natural miracles became a part of the world of reason and of the intellect, even though reason and intellect could not empirically prove their existence.[14] That the thrice-renowned Hermes, whom most thinkers believed to have been a sage of fabulous antiquity, should have insisted on similar propositions when he told his fable of a natural event (the bringing of statues to life) which only *seemed* magical and miraculous to benighted humanity, ignorant of the greatness of God, appeared to be the ultimate proof of his compatibility with revealed religion.

It is against these aspects of the Platonic tradition that we must view the final scene of *The Winter's Tale*. Paulina's pretence of bringing Hermione's statue to life is superficially no more than an analogue of the matters discussed above. A similar motif is also to be encountered at the climax of *Pericles*. The reunion of Pericles and Thaisa is presented as a 'resurrection', with distinctly mystical overtones. But the particular details of Shakespeare's presentation of the return of Hermione make the connection with Platonic convictions much more intimate. Paulina's 'magic' is anticipated in the previous scene when

[13] Ernst Cassirer, *The Individual and the Cosmos in Renaissance Philosophy* (trans. Mario Domandi), Oxford 1963, pp. 7–72.
[14] Ibid., pp. 10–24 (esp. p. 13).

the Third Gentleman describes in ecstatic terms Julio Romano's great skill in making the statue of the dead queen depict her as she would look now, sixteen years after her death. Basically, this is no more than an elaborate ruse, a deliberate misleading of the audience in order to prepare it for the *coup de théâtre* in the next scene. It is, nevertheless, a thematic strand of some importance; its significance is discussed in Chapter 6.

The final scene commences with a note of serene courtesy; soon however, Paulina's words take on an air of mystery and (as we discover through hindsight) of ambiguity. Her reply to Leontes's complaint that he cannot find the statue they had come to see is teasingly paradoxical:

> As she liv'd peerless
> So her dead likeness, I do well believe,
> Excels whatever yet you look'd upon
> Or hand of man hath done; therefore I keep it
> Lonely, apart. But here it is. Prepare
> To see the life as lively mock'd as ever
> Still sleep mock'd death. Behold; and say 'tis well.
> I like your silence; it the more shows off
> Your wonder; but yet speak. First, you, my liege.
>
> (V. iii. 14)

Several important ideas are insinuated into this passage: the concept of wonder (which is to assume considerable significance a little later); the theatricality of Paulina's comments and actions; and her stress on the isolation of the statue. The last-mentioned is the first inkling of the religious overtones that dominate later portions of the scene. Finally, the blurring of the distinction between what is alive and what seems to possess life points forward to the climax of the scene some lines later.

Leontes's reply indicates that in his imagination he is already crediting vitality to the work of art, even though at this moment he is merely employing the clichés of art appreciation:

> Chide me, dear stone, that I may say indeed
> Thou art Hermione; or rather, thou art she
> In thy not chiding; for she was as tender
> As infancy and grace.
>
> (V. iii. 24)

He observes the lines and wrinkles on the face of the statue; Paulina assures him that therein lies the 'carver's excellence' in depicting the queen as she would be now, not as she was at the time of her death. This is both a reversal and a confirmation (as it turns out) of the commonly expressed Renaissance view that the function of art is to make things appear in their ideal state, not as they are in mundane reality—as, for instance, in the discussion of King Cyrus in Sidney's *Apologie*.[15] Leontes then introduces in a conventionally metaphoric way the supposition of magic—it is, perhaps, his highly-wrought imagination, which leapt on the 'signs' of Hermione's infidelity at the beginning of the play, that prompts his intuition of the direction the scene is eventually to take:

> I am asham'd. Does not the stone rebuke me
> For being more stone than it? O royal piece,
> There's magic in thy majesty, which has
> My evils conjur'd to remembrance, and
> From thy admiring daughter took the spirits,
> Standing like stone with thee!
>
> (V. iii. 37)

The statue is magical: it has truth to life, and it has a striking effect on its beholders, conjuring Leontes's guilt into his memory, and projecting Perdita into a trance-like state—the word 'admiring' carries more than its usual force here.

Perdita herself contributes to the hypothetical, fanciful and extravagant suggestion that the statue is sensible. We observe how the onlookers are propelled from this purely metaphorical 'admiration' into a realization that the metaphor represents actuality. This is accomplished, of course, by Paulina's stage-management, but it is generated, theatrically and emotionally, through the excess of praise and wonder expressed by the characters. Perdita exclaims:

> And give me leave,
> And do not say 'tis superstition that
> I kneel, and then implore her blessing. Lady,
> Dear queen, that ended when I but began,
> Give me that hand of yours to kiss.
>
> (V. iii. 42)

After this, Paulina brings about a spectacular change in the course of the scene's development. She issues a stern warning; it is practical enough, but it carries curious overtones of an injunction against

---

[15] *An Apologie for Poetrie* in O. B. Hardison Jr. (ed.), *English Literary Criticism: The Renaissance*, New York 1963, p. 105.

sacrilege: 'O, patience!/ The statue is but newly fix'd, the colour's/ Not dry'. Observing Leontes's sorrow, she twists the knife slyly, apologizing for the pain she has caused him, offering with grim solicitude to spare him from further anguish. She insists that she is the owner of the statue; what follows is of such dramatic and emotional complexity that it demands to be quoted at some length.

> *Paulina*   Indeed, my lord,
>   If I had thought the sight of my poor image
>   Would thus have wrought you—for the stone is mine—
>   I'd not have show'd it.
> *Leontes*   Do not draw the curtain.
> *Paulina* No longer shall you gaze on't, lest your fancy
>   May think anon it moves.
> *Leontes*   Let be, let be.
>   Would I were dead, but that methinks already—
>   What was he that did make it? See, my lord,
>   Would you not deem it breath'd, and that those veins
>   Did verily bear blood?
> *Polixenes*   Masterly done!
>   The very life seems warm upon her lip.
> *Leontes* The fixture of her eye has motion in't,
>   As we are mock'd with art.
> *Paulina*   I'll draw the curtain.
>   My lord's almost so far transported that
>   He'll think anon it lives.
> *Leontes*   O sweet Paulina,
>   Make me to think so twenty years together!
>   No settled senses of the world can match
>   The pleasure of that madness. Let't alone.
> *Paulina* I am sorry, sir, I have thus far stirr'd you; but
>   I could afflict you farther.
> *Leontes*   Do, Paulina;
>   For this affliction has a taste as sweet
>   As any cordial comfort. Still, methinks,
>   There is an air comes from her. What fine chisel
>   Could ever yet cut breath? Let no man mock me,
>   For I will kiss her.
> *Paulina*   Good my lord, forbear.
>   The ruddiness upon her lip is wet;
>   You'll mar it if you kiss it; stain your own
>   With oily painting. Shall I draw the curtain?
> *Leontes* No, not these twenty years.
> *Perdita*   So long could I
>   Stand by, a looker-on.
>   (V. iii. 56)

Few incidents in *The Winter's Tale* illustrate as fully as this Shakespeare's confident mastery of technique. The situation is tight and filled with suspense; its fundamental 'trickiness' is contained within the very real emotions displayed by those upon whom Paulina's grand deception is practised. Moreover, the episode also contains a series of complex suggestions (so embedded in the theatrical 'particularity' of the scene that it is difficult to extract them) comprising a mixture of awe, impatience and powerful insinuations of idolatry and sacrilege.

To this point, the 'life' of the statue is merely a metaphoric conceit: the characters are seized by their admiration of the supreme work of art and express their powerful emotions by means of this conventional conceit. Paulina then announces, absolutely without ambiguity, her pious aims and her holy powers. She speaks as a 'Magus', invoking her authority, the specifically religious location of the statue, and the piety of her activities:

> Either forbear,
> Quit presently the chapel, or resolve you
> For more amazement. If you can behold it,
> I'll make the statue move indeed, descend,
> And take you by the hand, but then you'll think—
> Which I protest against—I am assisted
> By wicked powers . . . .
>   It is requir'd
> You do awake your faith. Then all stand still;
> Or those that think it is unlawful business
> I am about, let them depart.
>   (V. iii. 85; 94)

The carefully managed preparation and the inculcation of a suitably 'amazed' sensation among the onlookers culminate in the performance of the great feat. Paulina's expression of her intentions and of her piety is couched in elevated language recalling the circumstances of 'Platonic' conjurings. The action takes place in a chapel; evil purpose is specifically disclaimed; only those able to participate in the ceremony with faith may remain in this consecrated place. Paulina states memorably and forcefully the interaction between the fanciful *wishes* of the onlookers and her own ability to bring them into actuality.

The 'conjuring' itself is effected with the significant use of music—as much an essential ingredient of Renaissance Platonic practices[16] as of theatrical conventions in such episodes:

[16] See above, note 6, p. 148.

> Music, awake her: strike.
> 'Tis time; descend; be stone no more; approach;
> Strike all that look upon with marvel. Come;
> I'll fill your grave up. Stir; nay, come away.
> Bequeath to death your numbness, for from him
> Dear life redeems you. You perceive she stirs.
> Start not; her actions shall be holy as
> You hear my spell is lawful. Do not shun her
> Until you see her die again; for then
> You kill her double.
>
> (V. iii. 98)

Leontes delivers the summation of this extraordinary scene: 'O, she's warm!/If this be magic, let it be an art/Lawful as eating'. The final scene of the comedy culminates, therefore, in the performance of a 'magical' feat; in this way it reproduces in some detail certain convictions Renaissance Platonism derived from *Asclepius* which became a cornerstone of these philosophical and mystical assertions.

There is, of course, no magic in Paulina's conjurings, no statue, no carver's excellence, merely an elaborate deception prolonged over sixteen years and practised on the deserving yet still pitiable Leontes. After the ecstatic moment when the unhoped-for miracle occurs, Hermione provides the necessary explanations:

> You gods, look down,
> And from your sacred vials pour your graces
> Upon my daughter's head! Tell me, mine own,
> Where hast thou been preserv'd? Where liv'd? How found
> Thy father's court? For thou shalt hear that I,
> Knowing by Paulina that the oracle
> Gave hope thou wast in being, have preserv'd
> Myself to see the issue.
>
> (V. iii. 121)

The powerful suggestions of magic and miracle, the elaborate 'Platonic' machinery of Paulina's trickery, dissolve into the conventional 'revelations' of Jacobean tragicomedy. In its last moments, *The Winter's Tale* retreats from its elevated climax into the orthodox clichés of popular entertainment. Yet even this 'rationalism', far from invalidating the implications of Paulina's practices, serves to confirm the intimate connection between this play and the fundamental tenets of Renaissance Platonism which (in this instance as in so many others) often employed the account of the miraculous conjuring of statues contained in *Asclepius* as a symbol or an emblem for its claims and convictions.

The tale of the remarkable powers of the sages of ancient Egypt is itself ambiguous. The text of *Asclepius* presents considerable difficulties, not only on account of its frequently confused state, but also because it is probably a Latin translation of a Greek original. Nevertheless, it seems likely that the report of the image-making powers of the ancient Egyptians contained in 37 suggests that this ability was not derived from agencies beyond the realm of nature. But our problem is somewhat remote from the conjectural reconstruction and translation of this difficult passage by modern scholars. What is at stake is how the Renaissance came to understand the significance of this passage, and what was its commonly held meaning.

The usual Renaissance attitude remained reasonably stable. Writer after writer stressed that ancient magi (or Trismegistus himself, for he came often to be credited with the actual performance of these feats) only appeared to have employed occult forces. They activated, it was insisted, forces in nature, available to all pious and learned men, for the purpose of providing striking and memorable examples for errant humanity of God's infinite bounty and of the boundless possibilities contained within the created world. Marsilio Ficino has a most revealing and often cited passage concerning these matters in his *De vita coelitus comparanda*.[17] Drawing on *Asclepius* and on Plotinus (*Ennead IV* iii. 11.), he discusses the conjuring of statues in the following manner:

> [Mercurius] goes on to say that the wise Egyptians of antiquity, who were also priests, at a time when they could not persuade the people by reason that there are gods (that is, certain spirits superior to mankind) devised that forbidden magic which by enticing demons into statues revealed them to be gods. But Iamblichus condemns the Egyptians, for they not only accepted these demons as a step towards the search for some of the higher gods, but also worshipped them in great numbers. In fact, he favours the Chaldaeans, who did not occupy themselves with demons, over the Egyptians . . . Yet we suspect that the Chaldaean as much as the Egyptian astrologers attempted in a certain manner to draw demons into their clay statues by means of celestial harmony.

Ficino continues with an elaborate refutation of the opinion of St Thomas and others concerning such astrological ceremonies, and concludes:

[17] M. Ficino, *Opera Omnia*, Basle 1576, pp. 571ff.; see also Yates, *Giordano Bruno*, pp. 66–7 and Walker, *Spiritual and Demonic Magic*, pp. 40–4.

But let us revert now to Mercurius, and indeed to Plotinus. Mercurius says that the priests took appropriate virtues from the nature of the world and mixed them together. Plotinus agrees with him, and considers all capable of being readily united in the soul of the world. This is so because it gives birth and motion to the forms of natural things through certain seminal reasons infused with its own divinity. He even calls these reasons gods, for they are never set apart from ideas in the supreme mind.

The tenor of this passage (for all its Platonizing jargon) is to insist on the essentially metaphoric and symbolic nature of these magical feats. They are in essence not at all magical, supernatural or beyond reason; they are merely discoveries of the potentialities of nature—their magical and miraculous qualities are presented by Ficino in much the same terms as the nineteenth century saw its own technological advances and inventions. Throughout the sixteenth and seventeenth centuries, and for reasons which had as much to do with political prudence as with philosophical beliefs, accounts of these acts are more often than not accompanied by similar assertions. Platonic magic claimed to accomplish the most natural and reasonable of effects; they only appear supernatural because debased humanity cannot believe the greatness and benevolence of God's creation.

It has been suggested that most of Ficino's writings and activities adhered to these convictions. Though he studied deeply in the various occult sciences—astrology, magical healing, talismanic magic, Orphism—he always insisted that nothing in these practices went beyond the realm of nature (or that part of creation which mankind may employ legitimately) or phenomena capable of rational explanation. Moreover, the accounts he gives of his remarkable achievements often seem metaphoric or symbolic; the boundary between actual events and psychological, emotional or even aesthetic states is not at all clearly defined. His employment of astrology for instance, the invoking of beneficial influences from stellar bodies through the strumming of a lyre and the intonation of suitable 'Orphic' hymns, is essentially symbolic. There is some reason to suspect that he himself recognized that the desired effects did not occur in any demonstrable sense. The importance of his practices may, indeed, have been purely psychological: the Platonic practitioner endows himself with an emotional and artistic experience of the interconnection between the world of the mind and the world of the flesh—a paradigm of magic.[18] It is here that such practices enter the realm of art.

[18] Walker, *Spiritual and Demonic Magic*, p. 44. Edgar Wind discusses the 'poetry' of Ficino's thought in his *Pagan Mysteries in the Renaissance*, London 1958, p. 110.

Paulina's conjurings in the last scene of *The Winter's Tale* mirror some of these convictions. For all her flamboyance, her apparent control over the emotions of the onlookers who have come to her chapel to view Julio Romano's masterpiece, and her insistence on the magnitude of her powers, she does nothing: her activity is merely ceremonial. She has recognized the promise of Apollo's oracle, she has learnt to trust in the benevolence of providence, and has awaited the fruition of these designs. She is a psychological practiser, inculcating in her victims—especially in Leontes who, as we see throughout the play, is most susceptible to the power of sense-impressions—a state of wonder and awe. Reason, to use Ficino's terminology, could not persuade mankind of the greatness of the gods or of the miracles of creation. The benevolent patterns of the world seem like the operation of blind chance or even as active malevolence.

A spectacular instance of sleight-of-hand is required to bring home to errant humanity the munificence of creation. But it must be stressed that the unhoped-for felicity is not achieved through the intervention of a skilled magician who is able to make the impossible happen. On the contrary, Paulina, like the sages of ancient Egypt or their Renaissance emulators, must demonstrate that this benevolence is a part of the natural pattern of things. Hence in *The Winter's Tale*, as in the writings of the Renaissance Platonists, the magical feats are presented in a significantly ambivalent manner. It is suggested, simultaneously, that a person of great skill and learning is required to bring about such happy events, and that the consummation is the product ultimately of forces over which the practitioner has little if any control.

The structure of the play is an image for these preoccupations. In none of his comedies does Shakespeare keep his audience as much 'in the dark' as he does here.[19] Most comedies give firm guarantees of the eventual happy resolution, either through insinuation or through the presentation on stage of incidents unknown to the main characters. The need to cater for theatrical suspense is usually met by the prolonged or circuitous way in which the anticipated outcome is achieved. Thus in *Much Ado About Nothing*, once the clownish watch discovers Don John's villainy, we are reasonably reassured that no great harm will come to the threatened characters; but the difficulties they experience in making their discoveries known provide the required tension.

[19] B. Evans, *Shakespeare's Comedies*, Oxford 1960, p. 145.

There is no such reassurance in *The Winter's Tale*; the return of Hermione is as unexpected for the audience as it is for Leontes. As already shown, far greater discrimination than usual is required from the spectators to enable them to recognize that Paulina's great speech in III. ii., in which she acquaints Leontes with the death of the queen, is essentially deceptive. Moreover, in Antigonus's speech in III. iii. (15ff), the audience is consciously and deliberately misled. Antigonus describes his dream-vision of Hermione's ghost interceding for the child he is about to abandon on the wild Bohemian shore. Quibbles about Shakespeare's psychological realism or the state of early seventeenth-century opinion concerning the appearance of people still living in dream-visions are somewhat beside the point. The speech is a powerful indication to the audience that it should think of Hermione as dead.

The lack of reassurance—the failure to provide the conventional guarantees of comedy—leads towards the type of sensational dependence on *coups de théâtre* characteristic of the tragicomedies of Fletcher and his imitators. Of all the Shakespearian comedies, *The Winter's Tale* gives the least appearance of a coherent design. The basically narrative progression of *Pandosto, or The Triumph of Time* has been transferred to the stage without the customary elisions or alterations (apart from Hermione's return) habitually adopted by Shakespeare when dramatizing such sprawling chronicle-material. The form of the play seems primitive when compared with his mature works; the introduction of a practically fresh set of characters in the last scene of Act III and in Act IV is accomplished in an apparently nonchalant manner. Nothing seems to have been done, moreover, to provide a smoother stylistic transition between the two sections of the comedy.

But viewed from the perspective of the denouement, this apparently purposeless progression and artless construction may be seen to fall into a coherently organized pattern. Jacobean tragicomedy, too, is a form of drama in which the finale provides explanations—by way of sudden changes of heart or revelations of mistaken identity. But *The Winter's Tale* contains a far more *organic* retrospect in its last moments; it reveals a chain of causality wherein Leontes's initial offence leads to blessings of unimagined extent. The tortuous paths of misadventure, cruelty, ill-fortune, treachery and greed produce, at the end, the forging of a new commonwealth of happiness for almost all the characters. The tendency in the play, as we may see from the vantage-point of Hermione's explanations, is towards the habitual aims of comedy. But the effect of this achievement is very different in this case largely because we have been *discouraged* from anticipating the return of Hermione as a part of the desired conclusion. Far more radically than at the end of *The Comedy of Errors*, where the return of Aemilia has a somewhat similar theatrical effect, Shakespeare relies on the audience's expectation that the restoration of Perdita is all that may be hoped for (in accordance, too, with the denouement of the source-story) for the startling effect of his finale.

There is a remarkable ambivalence, therefore, in the structure of the play, just as there is an ambivalence in Paulina's magical conjurings. The progression of the plot may be seen, on the one hand, as a coherently articulated design with philosophical implications suggest-ing that the most random and chaotic events of life are shaped by a benevolent purpose. On the other hand, though, the narrative material of the play may be seen as no more than the usual sensational clichés of Fletcherian tragicomedy. The magical moment when the statue comes to life is channelled into the 'rationalism' of anti-climactic explanations. It is a deliberate (and provocative) facet of the play's design that it should constantly suggest the polar opposites of profound significance and generally undemanding entertainment. It looks constantly in two directions; yet the magical, providential world of Platonic optimism (as the Renaissance understood it, at any rate) may not be overlooked. It is persistently confirmed by quite minute aspects of the play's structure and language. The critical task is not merely to acknowledge the presence of these lofty notions in *The Winter's Tale*, but to examine their status within its total aesthetic effect. This comedy, like *The Tempest*, is concerned with a Platonic scheme of providence; but that is not to say that it recommends in any active, polemical way the implications of the scheme it employs.

II

Everyone in Shakespeare's world, it has been said, believed in Providence.[20] This is undoubtedly true if we heed the endless reports of the punishment of sinners, the discovery of foul crimes or, as in certain accounts of English history, the saga of the elaborate exaction of divine

---

[20] See the section on Providence in Keith Thomas, *Religion and the Decline of Magic* (1971), Harmondsworth 1973 (Penguin University Books), esp. pp. 96ff.

vengeance for crimes committed by the kings and princes of the realm. But this notion of Providence becomes so ubiquitous and so indiscriminately applicable that it proves, ultimately, of little use in an attempt to understand the beliefs of an age. Since God's ways are mysterious, and since his essential purpose defies discovery, every chance or accident may be regarded as part of a coherent providential pattern.

The potential absurdity and intellectual dishonesty of such an attitude to mundane events did not escape certain independent-minded spirits of the Renaissance, and we find, from time to time, instances of rationalistic scorn poured on the bland acceptance of every trivial event as a demonstration of the hand of God. Giordano Bruno, that fiery spirit who met a terrible end at the hands of the Inquisition in 1600, and whose brief sojourn in England seems to have had some impact on the intellectual life of that country, subjected such beliefs to satiric and comic parody.[21] *Lo spaccio de la bestia trionfante* was written during Bruno's English exile. It contains an hilarious account by the god Mercury of Jove's benign care over every facet of life.

We first learn of certain dispensations concerning a melon patch and the fruit of a nearby jujube tree. Next, provisions are made for a woman curling her hair with hot irons, for a colony of maggots breeding in the dung of an ox, and for another woman, who is combing her hair. Precise schedules are given for a cuckoo's song and flight, and it is decided that a tailor should spoil a garment. Then more serious matters are broached. It is decided that:

> twelve bedbugs should crawl out of the board of Costantino's bed and make for the pillow: seven of these being very large, four quite small, and one of medium size—and what will become of them this evening at candlelight, we will provide. That at the fifteenth minute of the same hour, through the fourth circuit of her tongue around her palate, the old woman of Fiurulo will lose the third molar of her right lower-jaw; this loss will be without bleeding or pain because the said molar has reached the end of its trepidation (which has endured exactly seventeen annual revolutions of the moon). That Ambruoggio will interrupt his transaction with his wife after the hundred-and-twelfth thrust, and that he will not impregnate her on this occasion, but at some other time with the semen produced by the leek-stew which he is now eating with millet bread. Pubic hair will begin to grow around the private parts of Martinello's son, and his voice will begin its gradual breaking at the same time. That, as he is trying to retrieve a broken needle

[21] See A. D. Imerti's Introduction to his translation of Giordano Bruno's *Lo Spaccio de la bestia trionfante*, New Jersey 1964, esp. pp. 22ff.

from the ground, the red lace of Paolino's breeches will break through his exertions; if he should swear on account of this, I wish him to be punished in the following manner: this evening, his soup should be too salty and taste of smoke. If this should cause him to swear, we will provide [punishment] later. That of the seven moles which began their journey from the deep earth towards the air four days ago by diverse routes, two should surface in the same hour, one at noon exactly, the other fifteen minutes and nineteen seconds later, in Antonio Faivano's orchard at a distance of three paces, one foot and one half finger's length. Concerning the others, we will decree time and place later on.[22]

It is mistake, however, to concentrate exclusively on the reductive, Voltairian tenor of this passage. The hilarity and the comic burlesque of providential schemes serve another purpose. *Lo spaccio de la bestia trionfante* is not concerned with the proposition that chance rules all, and that schemes of providence are so much moonshine. Rather, it seeks to show and persuade, by means of a characteristic mixture of passionate idealism and exuberant hilarity, that the universe is constructed in an essentially benevolent manner by a spirit of *joviality*. This account of Jove's providence is, therefore, an instance of that Renaissance optimism which became so closely allied to systems of thought derived from Plato, or at least from the understanding of Plato and his works by Bruno and his contemporaries.

He attacks, in essence, the solemnity and vengeful bias of conventional providential schemes. Though he could never be described as an orthodox Christian, his writings seem often to be informed by a general sense of *caritas*. Instead of dour accounts of church-roofs falling on the heads of blasphemers, or of glasses remaining miraculously unbroken when hurled to the ground by desperate females insisting that as sure as the glass will break there is no hell, [23] Bruno gives an account of providence in which all tends towards the good, and in which all may be accepted as parts of a benevolent design. The literary means of expression for this becomes 'comic', an outrageousness relegating divine vengeance to the domain of the prat-fall. The result is a cheerful acceptance of the world and its ways; without the terrible irony intended by his creator, Dr Pangloss's conviction that all is for the best in this best of all possible worlds is not too distant from Bruno's intellectual stance. Most importantly, providence of this sort operates

[22] Translated from Giordano Bruno, *Lo Spaccio de la bestia trionfante* in *Dialoghi Italiani* (ed. G. Gentile, rev. G. Aquilecchia), Florence 1958, pp. 635–7.
[23] Thomas, *Religion and the Decline of Magic*, p. 145.

through the trivial and the mundane as well as the seemingly accidental. Orthodox views of Christian Providence insist theoretically on the truth of this proposition; but in practice the Platonic providence envisaged in *Lo spaccio de la bestia trionfante* gives concrete examples of what, in conventional Christianity, usually remains notional.

There is, of course, something potentially dishonest in this bland refusal to give a place to suffering, misery and distress in the divine plan for the world. But such accounts of providence were probably intended as a corrective to what was regarded as an overly punitive and pessimistic view of the operation of divine purpose. The tendency is to find delight in the created world and in the purposes of its creator, and to deny the conventional and orthodox (even though theologically difficult) belief that some aspects of life are far too trivial for the Almighty's attention. The beautiful and stirring words with which Mercury concludes his *bravura* account of Jove's providence demonstrate this intention—they also show that while Bruno's views were obviously unacceptable to religious orthodoxy they were, nevertheless, merely an extrapolation of the conventional pieties of such orthodoxies.

> Everything, no matter how insignificant, is subject to a providence of infinite magnitude; the smallest things, no matter how humble, are of the greatest account in the order of totality and of the universe, because great things are composed of lesser, the small from even smaller, and these last of indivisible, minute [particles].[24]

This attitude is similar to the stance adopted by many of the Renaissance writers and thinkers who claimed to be following Plato's precepts. Their predilections, moreover, were often joined, as in Bruno's case, to an interest in 'natural magic' in order to make powerful claims about the wonder and goodness of creation. It is, significantly, in the context of a celebration of Jove's infinite bounty (which extends to the least aspects of creation) that Bruno makes reference in *Lo spaccio de la bestia trionfante* to the god-creating passage in *Asclepius*. He is intent on differentiating it from dark idolatry:

> These priests, in order to petition blessings and gifts from the gods by means of their familiarity with profound magic, penetrated certain natural states

[24] Bruno, *Lo Spaccio* in *Dialoghi Italiani*, p. 643.

in which (in such a way) divinity was latent and through which it had the power and the ability to make itself apparent. These rites, therefore, were not vain fantasies, but living voices which touched the very ears of the gods . . .[25]

The narrative indirections of *The Winter's Tale*, culminating in ceremonial mock-magic, reflect these convictions. There is no need to presume that Shakespeare had access to Bruno's work, as some have done; the passages cited from *Lo spaccio de la bestia trionfante* represent the commonplaces of an exotic but fashionable system of belief in the Renaissance world. The powerful tendency towards happiness and reconciliation revealed by the action of the play operates through all manner of things: innocence, in the love of Perdita and Florizel; chicanery, in Autolycus; self-interest when Camillo betrays the young lovers in order to indulge his desire to see Sicilia once more. It is manifest at all levels of the moral and social scale, encompassing shepherds and kings, and extending from the virtue of Hermione to the terrible guilt of Leontes. The apparently rambling progression of the plot—so dependent on chance and accident—is analogous to Bruno's list of the trivia occupying Jove's will. The ordinary accidents of life, even its disasters, like the death of Mamillius, or the hideous fate of Antigonus, come finally to be 'reconciled' in that benevolence for which the comic celebration is an appropriate image. The structure of the play is a paradigm for these concerns. In order to stress the miraculousness of nature's bounty and the irresistible bias towards happiness in creation, it lacks, quite specifically and deliberately, those sign-posts we find in the earlier comedies pointing towards the eventual resolution. The sense of wonder and amazement expressed by the characters when the pattern has unfolded, and shared by the audience too, depends on the apparently purposeless progression of event and incident. The breaking of the fairly minimal decorum of English Renaissance drama in the extraordinary time-span and geographical dislocations of the plot serves as a telling emblem of the silent workings of this natural providence. The action of the play is so filled with random events that there seems to be no purpose, no causality behind it. Yet when the unhoped-for miracle arrives, we may see, through retrospect, how these events, superficially so disconnected and random, all contribute towards the achievement of bliss. The material of this comedy represents no new departure for Shakespeare.

[25] Ibid., pp. 778.

The culmination of *The Winter's Tale* is merely an intensification of the usual peripeties of Renaissance comedy; where the play is distinguished is in the thorough working out of its providential scheme, even though this is retained within the usual formulae of diversionary comic drama.

There is indeed, as already suggested, a profound and characteristic ambiguity in this play—it points towards the most elevated of mysteries while dealing with the trivialities of conventional entertainment. That stance is fundamental to the play's aesthetic effect, for *The Winter's Tale* is not, it must be stressed again, a Platonic tract, but an employment of some of the basic tenets of Renaissance Platonism in a seriously jesting manner. The comedy remains within the bounds of its kind, it does not stray into the area of persuasion or of polemics; it is abstract, self-regarding in the manner of Shakespeare's other comedies. The elevated philosophical and mystical material is employed for emotional and purely aesthetic purposes—to make the play richer in its implications, to heighten the conventional ingredients of comedy and to cater for that inclusiveness which is so fundamental to Shakespeare's comic endeavours. *The Winter's Tale* is also a particularly bold instance of Shakespeare's experiments with comic form and conventions; the thoroughness of its Platonic machinery is an aspect of its profound conceitedness.

So thorough, indeed, is the play's use of Platonic notions that it embodies certain emblems or symbols of Platonic lore which could not possibly be noticed in the theatre. It is necessary, therefore, to consider some purely *literary* aspects of this comedy, and to suggest that, for some reason or another, Shakespeare included within his play fundamentally anti-theatrical effects and flourishes. Renaissance Platonism revelled in mysteries. In its attempts to find a justification for and a confirmation of its beliefs, it stressed the Egyptian location of those Hermetic mysteries which became such an intrinsic part of its system. Egypt was renowned for the invention and cultivation of all sorts of secret writing: the hieroglyphs were supposed to preserve occult and inscrutable divine lore known only to its priests and sages. Through the study and contemplation of these secrets, it was believed, mankind could have access to the great miracles of nature. The interest evinced by some Platonists like Pico della Mirandola in the rabbinical Cabala was yet another instance of their penchant towards the mysterious.[26] Hence the close connection between Renaissance

[26] Yates, *Giordano Bruno*, pp. 84ff.; Wind, *Pagan Mysteries in the Renaissance*, p. 137.

Platonism and the other great contemporary preoccupation or pastime, numerology, and the allied interest in cryptograms, emblems, *imprese*, and the other means of discovering the magical writings of eternity. God (or the supreme god) reveals his secrets to the initiate through eternally valid symbols; the Magus, Prospero-like, must study deep and long, he must subject himself to moral and spiritual discipline, and thus he becomes able to discover for himself nature's most secret mysteries. But this divine knowledge must be protected from the commonality, lest it fall into improper hands (the Stephanos and Trinculos of the world): for the pious and the holy, however, nature's secrets reveal a world of infinite possibilities. So, in the words of Pico della Mirandola's *Oration on the Dignity of Man*, men become gods.[27]

Much Renaissance writing (as scholarship has been gradually discovering) is filled with portentous symbols; *The Winter's Tale* echoes a number of the more familiar ones, clustering around the concept of time and its computation, around change and alteration, and around the properties of numbers themselves.[28] Time appears as the emblematic chorous linking the two parts of the play, and the concept of time colours much of the language and imagery. From Polixenes's first words in the play—

> Nine changes of the wat'ry star hath been
> The shepherd's note since we have left our throne
> Without a burden.
>
> (I. ii. i)

to the words of Leontes at the end—

> Lead us from hence where we may leisurely
> Each one demand and answer to his part
> Perform'd in this wide gap of time since first
> We were dissever'd. Hastily lead away.
>
> (V. iii. 152)

---

[27] See E. L. Forbes's translation in Cassirer, Kristeller, Randall (eds), *The Renaissance Philosophy of Man* (1948), Chicago 1956, p. 225.

[28] Since the discussion that follows was written, the numerical symbolism in *The Winter's Tale* has been examined (with rather different emphases) by Alastair Fowler in 'Leontes' Contrition and the Repair of Nature', *Essays and Studies of the English Association*, New Series, 31, 1978, pp. 36–63.

—time remains a fundamental concept within the plot, rhetoric and imagery. The clue for this was provided by the subtitle of the source-story, *Pandosto, or the Triumph of Time*; but in Greene's novella, the concern with time does not get much beyond the illustration of such commonplaces as 'Time reveals all' or 'Time cures everything'. In Shakespeare's hand, this material came to be articulated in a complex symbolic and numerological manner. This is, perhaps, surprising for a poet so renowned for his commonsense antipathy to fashionable mysteries. But the frequency with which tell-tale signs of these concerns appear in this comedy makes it difficult not to regard their use as purposive.

In his chapter on the iconology of Father Time, Erwin Panofsky discusses the transformations of the antique image of Time in post-classical culture, coming finally to be fused with the image of Saturn/Kronos, and thus acquiring the familiar sickle and elderly aspect. Time destroys, but Time also reveals; it is a figure of threat and awe, but it is also dignified and curiously serene, since time is eternal and outwears all. Panofsky further mentions that the Renaissance Platonists reinterpreted this image, as they reinterpreted so much else, to transform Time into a symbol for the eternal *nous*, the representative of the highest, immortal, immutable divine principle of mind.[29]

It was from this recension of the imagery of Time that the allied concern with numbers and their significance grew. Where the arcane, and to modern minds often childish, concern with the magical properties of numbers appears in Renaissance writing and art, it is usually a sign of a 'Platonic' cast of mind. That it should be so is hardly surprising, for, from *Timaeus* onwards, the immutable world of numbers came to be recognized as the building-blocks of the universe, the ultimate verities, and humanity's only access to the transcendental world of Ideas. Time is, of course, intrinsically related to numerical relationships, for through its variations the processes of measurement come to be revealed. Time, in a sense, is subservient to numbers, but in another, numbers are the servants of Time.

The Winter's Tale draws on a commonly recognized numerological symbolism which, in the treatises of the period, was often expressed in a temporal sense.[30] The particular numbers are twenty-three and sixteen. At the conclusion of II. iii., the return of Cleomenes and Dion

[29] Erwin Panofsky, *Studies in Iconology*, Corr. edn, New York and Evanston 1962, p. 80.
[30] G. Qvanstrom, *The Enchanted Palace*, Stockholm 1967, p. 106; A. Fowler, *Spenser and the Numbers of Time*, London 1964, p. 282n.

from their truth-seeking mission to the oracle at Delphos is reported in the following manner:

> *Servant*   Please your Highness, posts
> From those you sent to th' oracle are come
> An hour since. Cleomenes and Dion,
> Being well arriv'd from Delphos, are both landed,
> Hasting to th' court.
> *A Lord*   So please you, sir, their speed
> Hath been beyond account.
> *Leontes*   Twenty-three days
> They have been absent; 'tis good speed; foretells
> The great Apollo suddenly will have
> The truth of this appear.
>
> (II. iii. 192)

This is a remarkably specific amplification of the account of this incident in the source. In *Pandosto*, the time taken to accomplish the journey is described much more vaguely. Greene first describes the outward voyage:

> Pandosto . . . chose out six of his Nobility . . . and providing all things fit for their journey, sent them to Delphos. They willing to fulfill the King's command, and desirous to see the situation and custom of the Island, dispatched their affairs with as much speed as might be and embarked themselves to this voyage, which (the wind and weather serving fit for their purpose) was soon ended. For within three weeks they arrived at Delphos . . .[31]

Greene then recounts the manner of the Bohemians' reception and the delivery of the oracle, and continues:

> The Bohemian Lords, carefully obeying his command, taking their leave of the Priest, with great reverence departed out of the Temple, and went to their ships, and as soon as wind would permit them, sailed toward Bohemia, whither in short time they safely arrived.[32]

From this account, contrary to his normal practices, Shakespeare concocted a precise schedule of twenty-three days for the mission of the courtiers. That number possesses, indeed, curious implications in Renaissance numerology.[33]

---

[31] G. Bullough, *Narrative and Dramatic Sources of Shakespeare*, VIII, London 1975, p. 169.

[32] Ibid., p. 170.

[33] Fowler, *Spenser and the Numbers of Time*, p. 247n., pp. 66–73; Qvanstrom, *The Enchanted Palace*, p. 106.

Exodus xxxii. 28. in the Vulgate claims that the Levites slaughtered 23,000 of the unfaithful at Moses's command. Biblical scholars are of the opinion that this error may have been caused by 1 Corinthians x. 8. 'We must never fall into sexual immorality; some of them did, and twenty-three thousand met their downfall in one day'. This itself seems to have been based on a passage in Numbers xxv. 1–9. In this rather vague and complicated manner, then, numerologists came to associate the number twenty-three with God's vengeance on sinners. That Cleomenes and Dion complete their truth-seeking mission in twenty-three days has, therefore, a numerological decorum. The audience entertains no doubts, of course, about Hermione's virtue. But in this way we are given a sign that the events of the play, apparently heading towards disaster as a result of Leontes's mad folly, are under the observation, as it were, of divinity, destiny or providence. The symbol gives a guarantee that Leontes's crime will not go unnoticed. This number possessed, moreover, another set of significances, drawn not from biblical lore but from astronomical data. The maximum angle of the sun's declination from the equator is (in round figures) twenty-three degrees. When it reaches this point in its perambulations around the heavens, its seemingly uncontrolled motion is checked; it returns on its former path. This astronomical fact possesses, therefore, important possibilities of symbolic interpretation. It shows, primarily, that events of the most disastrous potential—the disappearance of the sun in winter, its uncontrolled ascent in summer, thereby threatening to parch the earth—are neither random nor chaotic, but governed by inflexible laws. God has set definite limits to the potentialities in nature for uncertainty, misrule and disaster. There is also a promise of restoration, for as the sun continues its career towards extinction in the winter months, miraculously but predictably it halts in its path and commences the return journey towards spring. The same is true for the sun at its height in the burning season of summer. Twenty-three became, therefore, a number symbolic of providence *par excellence*, especially through its connection with the concept of the sun as the Eye of God, *sol iustitiae*,[34] thereby joining together the discrete elements in its numerology. It is at the same time a guarantee of God's vengeful awareness of evil and a promise of restoration, of a protective benevolence towards the human species and an earnest of justice towards individual men.

[34] See above, note 28, p. 170.

The return of Cleomenes and Dion is one of the turning-points in the complex narrative of *The Winter's Tale*. The lyrical beauty of the messengers' description of their experiences at Delphos is an aesthetic token for the promise of restitution contained in the oracle.

> *Cleomenes* The climate's delicate, the air most sweet,
>   Fertile the isle, the temple much surpassing
>   The common praise it bears.
> *Dion*   I shall report,
>   For most it caught me, the celestial habits—
>   Methinks I so should term them—and the reverence
>   Of the grave wearers. O, the sacrifice!
>   How ceremonious, solemn, and unearthly,
>   It was i' th' off'ring!
> *Cleomenes*   But of all, the burst
>   And the ear-deaf'ning voice o' th' oracle,
>   Kin to Jove's thunder, so surpris'd my sense
>   That I was nothing.
> *Dion*   If th' event o' th' journey
>   Prove as successful to the Queen—O, be't so!—
>   As it hath been to us rare, pleasant, speedy,
>   The time is worth the use on't.
> *Cleomenes*   Great Apollo
>   Turn all to th' best! These proclamations,
>   So forcing faults upon Hermione,
>   I little like.
> *Dion*   The violent carriage of it
>   Will clear or end the business. When the oracle—
>   Thus by Apollo's great divine seal'd up—
>   Shall the contents discover, something rare
>   Even then will rush to knowledge.
>
>   (III. i. 1)

Subtly and tactfully, the overtones of the explicit symbolism of the number twenty-three (stated in the following scene, where the exact length of the journey is mentioned) are embodied in this memorably lyrical passage. The 'qualities o' th' isle', the celestial habits of the priests (with a possible pun on the term 'habits'), the ceremony, the conviction that the oracle will produce something rare—a rush of knowledge—all these intimate the possibility of restitution which is stated emblematically through the biblical and astronomical implications of the time needed for the journey.

The oracle brings no fruit. This turning-point in the play, for all its lyrical promise and the hieratic significance of its number symbolism, culminates in disaster, the death of Hermione, the quashing of all hope. But the impasse is merely apparent; for the oracle declares, as it turns out, the promise of blessings beyond comprehension—but this promise is not to be fulfilled in the dramatic present-time: it is to come in a future which is, once more, determined by numerical symbolism.

The emblematic figure of 'Time as Chorus' informs us that sixteen years elapse between the two parts of this quite disjointed play. In this instance Shakespeare adopted Greene's account of Fawnia's fortunes in *Pandosto*, for there, too, the denouement occurs at the time when the foundling is sixteen years of age. But, whereas in Greene there is no suggestion that sixteen is anything but a convenient age of nubility (though a little late perhaps by the standards of the age), Shakespeare seems to have taken some pains to stress the 'sixteenness' of the time elapsing between the two halves of the play. Time's choric address contains a surprising flourish or grace-note which plays most elegantly with numerological notions.

Shakespeare had inherited from Greene an awkward plot. The long passage of time before the narrative may reach completion is a theatrical liability. Earlier in his career, Shakespeare might have indicated the passing of sixteen years through the dialogue of IV. ii. But in this late work, he seems to have chosen a deliberately theatrical, quite 'unrealistic', almost baroque and extravagant way of communicating the necessary information. Time's speech contains thirty-two lines: it consists of sixteen regularly rhymed couplets, but the enjambment is so extreme that the ear does not catch the presence of a rhyme-scheme until the final couplet.

> I, that please some, try all, both joy and terror
> Of good and bad, that makes and unfolds error,
> Now take upon me, in the name of Time,
> To use my wings. Impute it not a crime
> To me or my swift passage that I slide
> O'er sixteen years, and leave the growth untried
> Of that wide gap, since it is in my pow'r
> To o'erthrow law, and in one self-born hour
> To plant and o'erwhelm custom. Let me pass
> The same I am, ere ancient'st order was
> Or what is now receiv'd. I witness to
> The times that brought them in; so shall I do
> To th' freshest things now reigning, and make stale
> The glistering of this present, as my tale

Now seems to it. Your patience this allowing,
I turn my glass, and give my scene such growing
As you had slept between. Leontes leaving—
Th' effects of his fond jealousies so grieving
That he shuts up himself—imagine me,
Gentle spectators, that I now may be
In fair Bohemia; and remember well
I mention'd a son o' th' King's, which Florizel
I now name to you; and with speed so pace
To speak of Perdita, now grown in grace
Equal with wond'ring. What of her ensues
I list not prophesy; but let Time's news
Be known when 'tis brought forth. A shepherd's daughter,
And what to her adheres, which follows after,
Is th' argument of Time. Of this allow,
If ever you have spent time worse ere now;
If never, yet that Time himself doth say
He wishes earnestly you never may.

(IV. i. 1)

This speech contains a 'literary' wit not usually encountered in drama. The sixteen couplets are obscured, as already mentioned, by the heavy enjambment; the sixteenth line, marking the end of the first half of the speech (or, basing our computation on couplets, the end of the first *octave*) represents a witty play on 'turning' and on the growth of the scene. This is emphasized because the last couplet of the first part of the speech and the first couplet of the second (i.e. lines 15 and 16; 17 and 18) combine feminine rhymes with the grammatical suspension inherent in the use of present participles or gerunds in each case (allowing/growing; leaving/grieving). Time's speech is, therefore, an emblem for the structure of the play. Its pattern, the sixteen rhymed couplets, is obscured by the apparently random progression of its metrical devices. Only at its end (as at the end of *The Winter's Tale* itself) may we glimpse the symmetrical pattern which has been unfolding.

But there is more involved here than mere playing on Perdita's age—though playfulness of a sort becomes, ultimately, the justification for these complications. Sixteen, according to Renaissance numerologists, is a potent symbol for perfection, harmony, human greatness and divine providence.[35] The list reads as a jumble, and the significances drawn from the mysterious properties inherent in this

[35] Qvanstrom, *The Enchanted Palace*, p. 111, p. 159.

number are, indeed, often baffling, and at times (to put it bluntly)
inane. But these possibilities seemed, nevertheless, to have fascinated
men of Shakespeare's world—the usual arguments about the number
must, therefore, be set out as fully as tolerable.

Sixteen was thought to have many properties. Since it is four raised
to its first power, it is the quadrate of the great tetraktys or quaternion
$(1 + 2 + 3 + 4 = 10)$, here represented by its last term. The tetraktys
was considered, after the example of 'Pythagoras', to contain the
building-blocks of the universe, that is to say, all possible arithmetical
proportions. As ten was commonly considered to denote the return of
the conventional method of computation to its inception—the monad,
unity, the number one—the tetraktys was often thought to be circular:
thus sixteen could be regarded as the squaring of the circle. But
another quality of sixteen is that it is the sum of seven and nine.[36] Seven
is the sum of the first even numbers $(1 + 2 + 4 = 7)$ one being both odd
and even, nine is the sum of the first odd numbers in the sequence of
numeration $(1 + 3 + 5 = 9)$. Even numbers, according to a curious
mystico-physiological belief, represent femininity and instability (because they are capable of being divided into two equal parts), odd
numbers, on the other hand, because of their indivisibility, are
masculine and stable. Seven, moreover, represents *regnum naturae*,
because of the seven planetary bodies, the seven-fold division of the
human body, the seven ages of man. Nine denotes the divine, since this
is the number of the spheres beyond which God dwells, and it is also the
last number, since ten (as mentioned above) returns to the inception of
computation. The sum of seven and nine, then, represents the
marriage of the divine and natural; the total complex of creation, the
fabulously difficult task of squaring the circle.

This list does not exhaust the possibilities Renaissance numerologists saw in the number sixteen. It is also the sum of eight and eight.
In this instance, we must take into account Renaissance musico-
astronomical (or astrological) lore. Eight represents the diapason, the
full system of the seven intervals (eight notes) of the octave scale. It is
well known that this naturally occurring harmony was thought to
correspond to the distances between the heavenly bodies in the
Ptolemaic universe; it is less well known that attempts were made in
the Renaissance to equate this scheme with the proportions of the
human body. Sixteen represents the double diapason which, for no

[36] Ibid., p. 93.

particularly cogent musicological reason, received some attention in Renaissance numerological treatises. Thus man came to be seen as standing at the mid-point of the union of divine and worldly, nine and seven, and on either side of him stretched, as it were, the two octaves of harmony: the fabled, inaudible music of the spheres, and the echo of these celestial Ideas, the everyday music of the world. These views are merely numerological sophistications of the commonplace notions that appear in Lorenzo's discourse in the last scene of *The Merchant of Venice*.

The Folio text of *The Winter's Tale* is divided into fifteen scenes. The mid-point of the structure is, therefore, III. ii. It has seven scenes on either side of it, and may thus be regarded as completing the octave commenced in I. i. and commencing the one that ends with V. iii. This central scene represents the major turning-point of the action—after the false turning-points of the earlier scenes of the act. In this scene, the worlds of Bohemia and Sicily, of death and rebirth, of suffering and joy meet: Antigonus is torn apart by a bear, but Perdita is rescued. The change, which occurs more or less in the middle of the scene, is indicated by a particularly striking change of style. The first part of the scene comes to an end with Antigonus's verse monologue, culminating in the grim words:

> The day frowns more and more. Thou'rt like to have
> A lullaby too rough; I never saw
> The heavens so dim by day. A savage clamour!
> Well may I get aboard! This is the chase;
> I am gone forever.
>
> *Exit, pursued by a bear.*
> (III. iii. 54)

For a moment, the stage remains empty; then, with the entrance of the old Shepherd, the tonality undergoes a notable change, in an almost musical manner:

> I would there were no age between ten and three and
> twenty, or that youth would sleep out the rest; for there is
> nothing in the between but getting wenches with child,
> wronging the ancientry, stealing, fighting. . .
>
> (III. iii. 59)

The latter passage is recognizably *comic*; the matter, for all its jocularity, raises the great issues of fertility and vitality; the images of life replace the images of death. It is almost exactly at the mid-point of the scene that the child is discovered, and some few lines later, the Shepherd speaks those words which have come to assume major significance in many modern discussions of the play: 'Now bless thyself; thou met'st with things dying, I with things new born'.

The change in the play, therefore, is not merely a fortuitous event; it seems to have been designed with some care and with some attention to structural symmetry. Moreover, there are two other changing-points in *The Winter's Tale*, both of which may be placed within its structure with reference to the numerical scheme of seven and nine. In III. ii., the seventh scene of the play, Apollo's oracle is delivered. But it arrives in vain: Hermione seems to die, and the subsequent remorse of Leontes is of no avail. But this partial turning-point, symbolized by the earthly, mutable significance of the number seven, is followed by the episode of the eighth scene where the actual physical rescue of Perdita takes place. The mundane peripety in the play (the delivery of the oracle, with its unrecognized promise of restitution) is followed by the human (the rescue of the child) to be replaced by the turning-point in the *ninth* scene of the play—the revelation of the true supernatural force which directs the play's events towards bliss: Time.

The vague sense of a natural, benevolent providence inherent in the play's action is thus filled out through the incorporation of certain mystic, symbol-laden number-games in the movement towards the supreme 'natural miracle' of Hermione's restoration. The numerological scheme gives a recognizable though *occult* flesh to the sense of a benign providence working through natural processes. In *The Winter's Tale*, the use of this conceit extends to the other major feature of the comedy, its pastoral episode.

III

The complex notions constituting Renaissance Platonism found their intellectual and emotional inspiration in images of the antique world. The authority of the Egyptian priests, invoked by most adherents of the mystique, is no more than a symbol for the habituation of the pagan world to the requirements of modern idealism. But the Platonic thinkers sought after a means of invoking classical antiquity without having to assent to the philosophical rigours of those aspects of ancient culture that passed into the fabric of orthodox, scholastic thought. Egypt proved ancient enough and sufficiently exotic to permit an escape from the absolute authority of Aristotle and Cicero;

Renaissance Platonism developed in this way an alternate vision of the classical world.

It discovered, at times, another potent symbol for such ambitions in the company of the pagan gods, living a life somehow anterior to the social and intellectual structures of Greece and Rome; the pastoral world, in consequence, made its appearance in the writings of some of these thinkers. The radically displaced version of the pastoral conceit in the fourth act of *The Winter's Tale* is, perhaps intentionally, perhaps as a result of one of those extraordinary coincidences we may encounter in art, a repository for the concerns and possibilities flowing out of Shakespeare's employment of Platonic ideas in his most complex comedy. The pastoral scenes in *The Winter's Tale* become the emotional and intellectual centre of the play, not merely through the elevated notions they embody, but also through the characteristic playfulness of the pastoral mode. The fourth act of the play presents a version of the pastoral which, in feeling at least, is very close to its classical and 'learned' prototype. And yet, with a curious flourish, the pastoral world is displaced into an alien environment in a way that highlights the play's artifice—thereby suggesting that the pastoral, itself a 'poetic' fancy, is to be placed in a truly imaginary, fictional context.

One of the more persistently irritating puzzles of literary scholarship has been Shakespeare's apparently perverse or careless reversal of the settings provided by his source for the two parts of the action. Greene locates the court of Pandosto, Leontes's counterpart, in Bohemia; the place where the foundling child is reared is the pastoral landscape of Sicily.[37] In *The Winter's Tale*, these locations are reversed. Moreover, there is some evidence to suggest that these countries are presented in climatically inappropriate terms—though scholarship and criticism have, at times, exaggerated this reversal. It is not entirely accurate to say that Leontes's Sicilia is a cold, wintry land; but it possesses strong moral and spiritual implications of a winter world. Mamillius speaks of a tale fit for winter; Leontes's gnarled verse, when expressing his jealousy in the first act, suggests solstitial tempests; Hermione's memorable exclamation during her trial—

> The Emperor of Russia was my father;
> O that he were alive, and here beholding
> His daughter's trial!
>
> (III. ii. 117)

[37] Bullough, *Narrative and Dramatic Sources of Shakespeare*, VIII, p. 157.

—plays significantly with images of winter in an associative and an emotional sense.

The contrast between the two realms—Sicilia and Bohemia— establishes a winter/spring context in the play. This is achieved with telling effect in the modulation from Antigonus's *Sturm und Drang* verse to the recognizably comic and genial prose of the old Shepherd in III. iii. The Bohemia where these events take place, by contrast to the icy and crabbed world of Sicilia, is an ideal landscape wherein the various seasons of fertility, spring and autumn, are artfully mixed. At its centre stand the figures of Perdita and Florizel, proper inhabitants of this landscape, who (in their speech and in their deportment) lead us into the cultural roots and significances of the pastoral mode. But the presentation of the great emblems of this *displaced* pastoral in IV. iv. emerges through a series of carefully established gradations.

The conversation between Polixenes and Camillo in IV. ii. serves as a reminder of Leontes's crime, while promising, in an altered key, a repetition of the jealousy, mistrust and tyranny that sped the events of the first part of the play towards their apparently disastrous con- clusion. The new beginning evokes old disasters; yet Polixenes's tyranny is milder and, in a most specific sense, more prosaic than Leontes's outrage. Here is one intimation of the direction the play is about to take. In the next scene, the extraordinary figure of Autolycus invades the play, and with him comes an image of the antique world in its truly elemental, pagan quality. He is a transformation of the clowns of comedy: a *farceur*, an image of misrule, a theatrical invention of boundless vivacity threatening to swamp other aspects of the scenes in which he appears. But this vitality is held in a representational or emblematic framework. He is not merely an embodiment of uncon- trolled amoral energy; rather, he is an essentially *witty* allusion to his namesake, the son of Hermes, grandfather of Odysseus, master of disguises, the most cunning of thieves. Shakespeare's invention goes beyond this ancient image of misrule to establish an even more 'primitive' rôle for Autolycus: he is a priapic figure *par excellence*, and, at his first appearance, the various threads of these antique memo- ries are woven together in the stylized artifice of his song. That he pos- sesses such a venerable pedigree may be difficult to recognize be- cause of the freshness and spontaneity demonstrated by much of his rôle; the pedigree is, nevertheless, strongly implied by the song:

When daffodils begin to peer,
  With heigh! the doxy over the dale,
Why, then comes in the sweet o' the year,
  For the red blood reigns in the winter's pale.
                                          (IV. iii. 1)

Autolycus's credentials are thus established when he first appears;
the passing of winter is registered through the burgeoning of this
roguish energy. That we must view him against the background
suggested by his name is acknowledged, with a jesting earnestness, in
the speech following his song:

> My traffic is sheets; when the kite builds, look to lesser
> linen. My father nam'd me Autolycus; who, being, as I
> am, litter'd under Mercury, was likewise a snapper-up of
> unconsidered trifles. With die and drab I purchas'd this
> caparison; and my revenue is the silly-cheat. Gallows and
> knock are too powerful on the highway; beating and
> hanging are terrors to me; for the life to come, I sleep out
> the thought of it.
>   (IV. iii. 23)

These words make no claim that Autolycus *is* his mythological
namesake; he remains too much a specific figure of the Jacobean
underworld for that. But the alignment of Autolycus with the half-god
whose name he fears allows for the transformation of villainy. The
ideal pastoral world, as it emerges in these scenes of Act IV, makes it
possible for the emotional and ethical responses of the everyday world
to be suspended. Autolycus, the rogue and highwayman, fit for the
gallows or the lash, becomes a source of theatrical joy; Polixenes,
though repeating Leontes's sickening jealousy, is a figure of some
mellowness; the danger encountered by Perdita and Florizel, though
reminiscent of Hermione's tribulations, is nevertheless ceremonial.
The pastoral world transforms the common features of mundane life.

The apotheosis of Perdita in the fourth scene is a most memorable
instance of this feature of the play; it is closely bound up with its
Platonic idealism. The ecstatic transformation of the shepherdess
(and, to an extent, of her princely swain) into stellar beings is among
the most exquisite and moving passages in all drama. Yet to put it as
bluntly as this is to misrepresent the richness and complexity of the
episode. In no sense whatever is Perdita transformed into anything but
herself; the play avoids the type of hyperbole implicit in the term

apotheosis. Yet in the characteristically playful though deeply moving manner of Shakespeare's comic art, an apotheosis occurs in terms of the special qualities of the pastoral world—an antique society of rural folk for whom the gods are ever-present. From the moment when Perdita first appears, this curious but significant note is struck; the simplicity of the harvest festival suggests, easily and naturally, transcendental overtones. There is nothing jarring in the conceits with which Florizel addresses Perdita because their context has been so carefully established in the previous two scenes:

> These your unusual weeds to each part of you
> Do give a life—no shepherdess, but Flora
> Peering in April's front. This your sheep-shearing
> Is as a meeting of the petty gods,
> And you the Queen on't.
> (IV. iv. 1)

The language is fundamentally the same as the artificial mode of the Renaissance court-pastoral; its impact, however, is of the most natural simplicity and appropriateness, for the creation of this landscape gives freedom and imaginative conviction to a convention which, in *Il pastor fido* for instance, is merely tiresome. Shakespeare's version of pastoral mythology adheres to the agricultural and *pastoral* vocabulary of the tradition; the meeting of the mythological and the homely produces, as in Virgil, a striking effect. This is most evident in another of Florizel's addresses to 'the queen of curds and cream':

> The gods themselves,
> Humbling their deities to love, have taken
> The shapes of beasts upon them: Jupiter
> Became a bull and bellow'd; the green Neptune
> A ram and bleated; and the fire-rob'd god,
> Golden Apollo, a poor humble swain,
> As I seem now. Their transformations
> Were never for a piece of beauty rarer,
> Nor in a way so chaste . . .
> (IV. iv. 25)

As the scene continues, these delightfully playful suggestions of a transcendental world merge into the shearing-festivities: the songs and the dancing take on seemingly philosophical overtones. Yet, as always, simple, almost hedonistic, notes dominate:

> Lawn as white as driven snow;
> Cypress black as e'er was crow;
> Gloves as sweet as damask roses;
> Masks for faces and for noses;
> Bugle bracelet, necklace amber,
> Perfume for a lady's chamber . . .
>
> (IV. iv. 215)

At one of the climaxes of this rich scene, the princess reared as a farm-lass and the disguised king engage in a debate about nature and artifice; shortly afterwards, lest we take this instance of the pastoral cloud-cuckoo-land as merely decorative, deeper and sadder notes are sounded in Perdita's catalogue of flowers:

> O Proserpina,
> For the flowers now that, frighted, thou let'st fall
> From Dis's waggon!—daffodils,
> That come before the swallow dares, and take
> The winds of March with beauty; violets, dim
> But sweeter than the lids of Juno's eyes
> Or Cytherea's breath; pale primroses,
> That die unmarried ere they can behold
> Bright Phoebus in his strength—a malady
> Most incident to maids; bold oxlips, and
> The crown-imperial; lillies of all kinds,
> The flow'r-de-luce being one. O, these I lack
> To make you garlands of, and my sweet friend
> To strew him o'er and o'er!
>
> (IV. iv. 116)

The decorative and the moving are held in fine balance; the commonplace members of an old English herbal are translated into these incandescent presences. Consequently, Florizel's litany to Perdita becomes deeply affecting, escaping all the absurdity implicit in such utterances when they lack this manner of careful preparation:

> What you do
> Still betters what is done. When you speak, sweet,
> I'd have you do it ever. When you sing,
> I'd have you buy and sell so; so give alms;
> Pray so; and, for the ord'ring your affairs,
> To sing them too. When you do dance, I wish you
> A wave o' th' sea, that you might ever do
> Nothing but that; move still, still so,

And own no other function. Each your doing,
So singular in each particular,
Crowns what you are doing in the present deeds,
That all your acts are queens.

(IV. iv. 135)

Disaster threatens towards the end of the scene; the harsh events of the
first part of the play promise to repeat themselves. Yet the potent
suggestions of benevolence and peace are so richly established in this
complex episode that even these threats are transformed into serenity.
This, too, results from the evocation of this pastoral landscape.

The pastoral world of *The Winter's Tale* is thus heightened in
accordance with the mode of this remarkable comedy; in comparison
with the forest scenes of *As You Like It* (or the ideal worlds to be found in
other comedies) there seems to be some justification for suspecting that
the philosophical or mystical implications of the material and of the
setting are also exploited in it. The fourth act reverberates with echoes
of the pagan mysteries of the Renaissance. Even the clown figure, the
amoral Autolycus, assumes some of the characteristics of the great god
Pan. It is here that the pastoral scenes of *The Winter's Tale* confirm the
play's immersion in Renaissance Platonic thought. Historians of
culture have for long insisted that the combination of high-flown
idealism with an employment of the venal affairs of the Greco-Roman
gods in the writings of Ficino and the other Platonists may be
explained through the generally allegorical tendency to be found in
their works. The truth of this cannot be denied: Ficino, principally,
seems to have made popular (if, indeed, he did not initiate) the
transformation of Venus into the two philosophical principles of *Venus
volgaris* and *Venus coelestis*. But to claim that this interest in the amours
and deeds of the ancient gods was allegorical is merely to claim half the
truth, for these 'allegories' are among the least decorous of Renaissance
writings. Constantly, whether in a philosophical tract or in a work of
art influenced by Platonist thought (as in Titian's painting usually
known as 'Sacred and Profane Love') there is an ambivalence between
the treatment of elevated notions and the exploitation of the sensuous,
the pagan and the amoral. The petty gods became, it is true,
repositories of transcendental possibilities; but in the stream of thought
and art flowing out of the works of Ficino, Campanella, Bruno and the
other champions of Plato, the spirit of a hedonistic return to the
freedom of pagan antiquity may be as clearly discerned.

Shakespeare reproduced in the pastoral scenes of *The Winter's Tale* some of the overtones, if not the actual main material, of the often fanciful habituation of the ancient gods by the Platonists of the Renaissance to philosophical and idealistic convictions. The incidents and the language of the sheep-shearing festivities suggest that the characters and their environment assume emblematic proportions. What these are may not be clearly identified, just as many of the assertions of the Platonists of the Renaissance remained poetic and emotive; but the implications of benevolence and optimism are continually felt. Yet Shakespeare ignored, it seems, a fundamental aspect of the employment of the pastoral for philosophical or mystical purposes: the identification of the stamping-ground of the petty gods which, from the time of Theocritus, has been by convention the Sicilian landscape. The great wave of benevolence which drives the events of the play towards their elevated conclusion rises in the fourth act where a number of instances are to be found of the traditional and 'learned' uses and implications of the pastoral mode. The natural providence watching over the fates of the characters is given emotional and poetic substance by the images of the pastoral world.

Yet in *The Winter's Tale*, as already noted, the pastoral scenes, seemingly so close to the antique Sicilian prototype, are located in Bohemia, while the Sicilia of the play is the repository of the world of northern nightmares. The reasons for this curious reversal will never be recovered absolutely—we will never know whether it is the product of purpose, carelessness or ignorance. But it is possible to suggest, tentatively, that this transference (whatever the reasons behind it) is curiously appropriate, given the strikingly ambiguous status within the play occupied by its profound possibilities. *The Winter's Tale* is not Platonic propaganda; its employment of these mysteries and doctrines is playful, directed towards poetic, emotional and theatrical (not didactic) ends. One of the uses of these mysteries is to transform and heighten a routine melodramatic narrative into a play of outstanding richness and variety; the play, however, seeks neither to preach nor to persuade: its Platonism is a conceit, worked out with thoroughness and surprising invention, but stopping short of anything that might seem like a recommendation of these views. Any attempt to see the play as a persuasive or didactic document is bound to be frustrated—it dissolves into the simplicities of fairy-tale. For a play to retain this jesting, hypothetical relationship with profundities which are given their emotional weight but not their intellectual or philosophical implications, it is essential for it to rearrange its environment into an ideal landscape. In other comedies, as in *The Winter's Tale*, the familiar geographical and historical aspects of the real world are so altered and transformed that the audience receives a powerful (though not consciously registered) impression that what it sees on the stage is an impossibility which echoes faintly the mundane environment, but has no existence beyond the theatre. It is therefore appropriate that *The Winter's Tale* should go one better—it registers its essentially playful employment of transcendental mysteries by translating the artifice of the pastoral from the traditional Sicilian landscape to the northern world of Bohemia, where the ancient gods never walked.

IV

The elaboration of these conceits in *The Winter's Tale*, as presented in a work so obviously theatrical and so little concerned with stressing its profundities, challenges some fundamental notions of literary decorum. The play's numerological and philosophical material may be encountered elsewhere in Renaissance literature, but such material is usually found in works with a specific and declared allegorical intent. *The Faerie Queene* furnishes the prime example. Evidence uncovered by patient (though at times apparently fanciful) research indicates that Spenser's contemporary readers were required to attend to details in the poem which are not usually taken into account in modern reading habits. The minute detail with which numerological relationships are worked out suggests a literary perspective no longer recognized except by specialist scholarship. Other works of the Renaissance are also said to show similar characteristics, though not to the degree of complexity to be found in *The Faerie Queene*.

Nevertheless, while modern readers may not be fully conditioned to perceive these nuances, the notion itself is not usually found to be indecorous, for most readers and critics of *The Faerie Queene*, of *Orchestra* and of a significant number of literary works from the sixteenth and seventeenth centuries will readily admit that these poems are basically allegorical or emblematic in intent. A comparison between such works and a play like *The Winter's Tale* involves a number of important factors. Primarily, it must be stressed that *The Faerie Queene, Paradise Lost* and other 'numerological' or 'cryptogrammatic' poems belong firmly to a book-culture. The physical shape given by Herbert to a number of the poems in *The Temple* could not exist beyond the confines of the printed page. The wealth of material in Spenser and Milton depends on the liberation of the work of art from the passage of time, on the reader's ability, that is, to possess a text 'synchronously', to exercise the privilege of being able to turn back the pages.

In recent criticism, the concept of a Shakespearian play as a poem has been, with some justice, challenged. Earlier critics habitually maintained that while these works found their inception in a theatrical representation, and are therefore subject to the progression of a text through time (thereby making each moment passing and irrecoverable), they nevertheless rise to the status of 'literature'. These emphases have been replaced by an insistence on the theatricality of Shakespeare's plays — the assertion that they depend on the possibilities and limitations of performance. The supposition of the presence of certain nuances in *The Winter's Tale*, especially such a flagrant instance of book-culture as Time's sixteen rhymed couplets or its 'philosophical' employment of the pastoral, runs counter to the sensible and prudent insistence among recent critics that we should be wary of elaborating Shakespeare and his colleagues into fully 'literary' artists. Moreover, we may no longer take refuge in the once common contention that in his last plays Shakespeare abandoned theatricality in favour of the use of drama as a poetic vehicle: the last plays obviously return to and exploit the basic sources of theatrical pleasure — the interest in incident and spectacle.

Dogma is the enemy of judiciousness. Admittedly, it is generally preferable to regard Shakespeare as a theatrical rather than a literary artist. But in truth he is both. Throughout his plays, not only in the comedies, there is evidence of a fashioning care which produces effects transcending the limitations of oral art, no matter how much more finely attuned Renaissance ears might have been to catch nuances inaudible to us. The commonly-held belief that Shakespeare did not intend his plays to be published might be seen as a denial of this aspect of his work, but such a contention is, once more, based on romantic notions of art as communication which did not necessarily apply in earlier periods. From the statuary of a Gothic cathedral placed far from the beholder's eye to Bach's 'sight music' in the two Passions and *The Art of the Fugue*, pre-romantic culture offers a number of instances of art and of the devices of art not capable of being perceived. A groundling cannot see the sculpture of a cathedral; a listener cannot hear the numerological elaboration of *The Passion According to St Matthew*.

The fact that *The Winter's Tale* is a play need not therefore urge us to insist that these complexities are more in the researcher's fancy than in the realities of the text. But a more difficult and more persuasive argument may be made against the acceptance of these 'subtleties'. This is the indecorum of such material in a comedy. In the allegorical poems of the Renaissance, the surprising elaboration of the 'machinery' is merely a means of repeating a work's central concerns and convictions at a microcosmic level. Thus, Christ's two twenty-three line speeches clustering around the central line of *Paradise Lost* are fully decorous, for the poem deals with the twin concepts of divine justice and divine mercy. The emblematic ascent of the Son of God at the mid-point of the poem is an appropriate *icon* for Milton's theological and philosophical preoccupations. The same may be said for the hidden details in Gothic architecture and the inaudible symbolism of baroque music. Though the representations of some of the biblical figures on the great cathedrals may not be seen from the perspective of an 'ordinary' beholder, and though the three-part harmony in some of the 'trinitarian' passages of the *St Matthew Passion* may not be heard as such, both features are consistent and justified aspects of these structures: they are drawn from the two-part symmetry of the Bible and its doctrinal implications. The house of God and the act of musical worship contain minute details which are fully decorous with their basic intent and design.

Many would regard as offensive, however, the claim that *The Winter's Tale* possesses a similar status. The conversion of this example of stage-comedy into a *commedia* or even into an English precursor of Calderon's *autos* represents an apparent failure of critical tact. It is contrary to our received notion of Shakespearian drama or of the temper of his age to view theatrical art in these terms. It must be insisted, indeed, that *The Winter's Tale* and *The Tempest* are significantly different from the allegorical poems of the Renaissance or from the architectural and musical monuments of pre-romantic culture. Nevertheless, the numerological and 'Platonic' material discussed in this chapter plays a significant and important part in these plays: it is their *status*, as already intimated, that requires some examination.

It might be tempting to regard this aspect of Shakespeare's last comedies as an instance of a widely-held belief about Renaissance literature by claiming that they make their appeal on a multiplicity of levels. *The Winter's Tale*, especially, may be taken as appealing, on one level, to purely theatrical criteria, while it may be seen, on another, as a 'dark conceit', a set of transcendental suggestions available only to the *cognoscenti*. But *The Winter's Tale* (in common with other comedies) does not possess the intellectual or philosophical consistency of reference to be found in allegorical or symbolic works. Its reliance on the images and emblems of Renaissance Platonism is an aspect of the hypothetical, abstract wit of comedy, whereby a variety of issues is displayed and entertained in a consistently ambivalent manner. For, it must be stressed again, this play is not merely Shakespeare's most thorough essay in the employment of the mystical optimism of Renaissance Platonic thought in all his drama, it is also a most accomplished instance of that thoroughly *diversionary* theatrical form, Jacobean tragicomedy. It fulfils the requirements of the sub-genre through its provision of a sensational plot and a succession of startling revelations. But with an essentially decorative wit (that may not be fully communicable in performance) this example of tragicomedy incorporates a series of analogies drawn from a remote philosophical system. The conventional devices of popular entertainment are thereby enriched; they are made to reverberate with the emotional possibilities inherent in the presentation of unexpected revelations and coincidences in terms of an elevated mystical system. The world of Platonic optimism becomes a source of rich theatrical effectiveness; it is also a flamboyant and in a way outrageous instance of the daring extension of the normal boundaries of comic drama.

The Winter's Tale is a richly suggestive play. The slow, seemingly random progression towards the restoration of Hermione finds its theatrical and emotional effectiveness through its employment of a number of transcendental notions which, when joined to the particularities of a theatrical narrative, become deeply moving and prove to be the source of a grave aesthetic pleasure. The mode is essentially eclectic. The material is not organized into a consistently argumentative or illustrative unity; rather, it displays a variety of devices, themes and styles; these are employed for the sake of enriching the essentially non-referential beauty of the work of art. Yet its connections with Renaissance Platonism are significant on another, perhaps more remote, level. The grave playfulness of this work mirrors a similar ambivalence and spirit of play in those philosophical writings from which Shakespeare (no matter how circuitously) drew his images and emblems. In Ficino, in Bruno, indeed in the whole complex of Platonic-Hermetic thought in the Renaissance, there is a constant interplay between the actual and the fanciful, between statement and metaphor. No other philosophical movement in the history of

European culture had such close connections with the world of the imagination. For the practitioners themselves, their writings and their predilections constantly tended towards that emotional area which is, strictly speaking, antithetical to the ratiocinative world of 'philosophy'. This was, perhaps, inevitable in the context of a set of beliefs so committed to the mystical, the transcendental and the idealistic. Consequently, on reading their works, it becomes apparent that the assertions of the Renaissance Platonists were recognized even by them to exist in the provisional world of the imagination and, therefore, of art.

There may be no special significance in the fact that these convictions made their most notable impression on Shakespeare's final plays. Moreover, on the surface at least, the 'Platonism' of *The Winter's Tale* and of *The Tempest* are markedly different. In the last play it is decorative, readily apparent, and a part of its masque-like complex of extravagance and simplicity. In the earlier play, it is far more 'mysterious', emotionally more surprising and moving. But each play, in addition, possesses some of the characteristics of the other—in each case, the employment of such transcendental ideas is both earnest and playful: both plays demonstrate the intrinsic ambivalence of Shakespeare's comic art. Earlier plays, too, demonstrate this quality; and the precursors of the Platonic 'themes' in the late plays to be encountered among their predecessors answer similar requirements. The extraordinary turns of good fortune, the vague sense that the sympathetic characters dwell under a benevolent, protective dispensation, the faint intimations of magic and providence, are all intrinsically pertinent to the particular flavour of Shakespeare's comedies which mingle the profound and profane, the grave and the jesting in a complex and almost indefinable manner. That *The Winter's Tale* and *The Tempest* present these conventional ingredients of Shakespearian comedy in the light of mystical and philosophical convictions does not necessarily imply, as already stated, a conversion on the part of the poet towards the assertions contained in these systems. It may represent, however, an aesthetic and perhaps even unconscious recognition that both the type of comedy he practised and the philosophical phenomenon on which he drew tend towards the same state—the creation of certain moving, richly satisfying hypotheses (existing only in the imagination) in the *unreal* world of the theatre.

It is for this reason that Shakespeare's comedies are simultaneously filled with 'significances' and are yet retained at the level of theatrical entertainment. The Platonism of the last plays is merely the logical extension of the mode and manner of the earlier comedies in which a variety of possibilities is displayed for the delectation of the beholder. The supreme moment in *The Winter's Tale* takes place in Paulina's gallery. It is not too fanciful to see in this an image for comedy itself. Shakespeare's comedies are galleries in which a variety of beautiful objects is displayed. We enjoy these delights in our progress through the few hours' traffic of the stage, but, as in most galleries, the objects are not selected in accordance with any predetermined programme: they are there for the sake of their own beauty. It is thus that Shakespeare's comedies, especially the epitome of his art of comedy, *The Winter's Tale*, with its richness of implication and its generosity of inclusion, achieve a true *discordia concors*.

I

Several of Shakespeare's comedies seem to contain passages which may be taken as complex commentaries on the nature and effect of art.[1] This concern with the power of illusion is frequently expressed dramatically in terms of vivid, often threatening sense-impressions which cause the characters to feel that they are victims of irrational visitations or sinister practices. They are cast into alarm and they fear the loss of their identity. The images of art scattered throughout the comedies are emblems of these transformations; they colour many important episodes: the characters' sensations and experiences seem to mirror in a most beguiling manner the effect that these works of art have on the spectators themselves. Bertram, when confronted by the living Helena, and Angelo, when he finds Claudio alive and his former liaison with Mariana revealed, both display a numbing disbelief, a sudden sense of the irrational. Each character is, significantly, silent, for silence is the most eloquent witness to the heightened state of consciousness produced by the presence of vivid illusions, the *trompe l'oeil* effects with which these events are filled. In *All's Well That Ends Well* the King interprets for us Bertram's stunned incredulity:

> Is there no exorcist
> Beguiles the truer office of mine eyes?
> Is't real that I see?
>   (V. iii. 298)

Such effects—often concentrated in the closing moments of these plays—reveal the manner in which the complex associations of illusion

[1] Stanley Wells in 'Shakespeare Without Sources' (*Shakespearian Comedy, Stratford-upon-Avon Studies*, No. 14, London 1972, pp. 58–74) gives a detailed discussion of this topic. Note particularly his view that 'In *The Tempest* Shakespeare wrote not only about his own art, but about that of all who work through the mind' (p. 72).

are employed in the comedies. Art, as it comes to be displayed in these jesting fables, is usually presented in terms of its ability to transform the familiar through vivid sense-impressions. Though these experiences are almost always strange and very often sinister and threatening, we are made to feel that their victims nevertheless live most intensely when under their spell. In almost every case, of course, the audience is prevented from *sharing* these emotional states for, as in the case of Helena's 'resurrection', it has been privy to the practices that have brought about such extraordinary developments. But these isolated and 'contained' incidents within the comic works of art are images for the effect they exert on the spectators themselves: Shakespeare's comedies impose on their beholders that remarkable sensation which many of the characters experience when the world of illusion takes hold of them.

The concern with the illusory power of art in these plays is, therefore, most complex. We may not find in them intellectual programmes or schematic demonstrations, yet the combination of sensuous experiences with illusions (and the practices that bring such illusions into being) ultimately confers on these comedies an engagement with the function of their own artifice. As in a number of other ways, *The Comedy of Errors* proves in this matter too to be a promise of things to come. The whole of this play comes to stress the implications of those vivid sense-impressions (implicit in its plot) which are integral to the conventions of farcical comedy. Shakespeare obviously exploited certain possibilities inherent in theatrical confusions and misunderstandings: the comic *imbroglio* suggests to the characters that they are victims of irrational, perhaps malevolent practices. Significantly, Shakespeare altered the setting he found in *Menaechmi* from Epidamnum to Ephesus; whatever his motive, he obviously seized the opportunity to make his characters feel that they are in the grip of the city's notorious sorcerers. For Antipholus of Syracuse, the impact of the confusions caused by his presence in Ephesus clearly emerges from such practices:

> They say this town is full of cozenage;
> As, nimble jugglers that deceive the eye,
> Dark-working sorcerers that change the mind,
> Soul-killing witches that deform the body,
> Disguised cheaters, prating mountebanks,
> And many such-like liberties of sin . . .
>
> (I. ii. 97)

In such lines, even this early comedy (that follows relatively faithfully the conventions of Latinate farce) begins to deal with issues beyond the normal confines of comic theatre. The characteristic combination of 'magic' and transformation is here potentially present. As the situation becomes more and more perplexing, and as an increasingly greater number of the characters is caught up in the multiplying confusions, the play comes to stress the consequences of this perplexing situation. The characters are lost in a nightmare-world: we, the audience, with our serene knowledge that this is all caused by a perfectly explicable (and, indeed, happy) coincidence, are able to derive amusement from their perplexity, but their experiences serve to transport them beyond the rational and human limits of existence. Although in a relatively rudimentary manner, the play begins to address itself to an examination of the nature of that loss of identity that most of the major characters experience. This results in a type of transformation: the stranger appears to possess social obligations in a city where he had arrived only a few hours before; the respected citizen finds that the structures of his existence begin to dissolve. It seems to both that they are the victims of a transforming manipulation: they stare into a chasm which, in the characteristic manner of farce, promises chaos and destruction, even though, to the audience, it is merely a source of mirth.

Nothing in the play suggests that this exploitation of the elements of farcical comedy and of certain suggestions implied by its source have anything to do with the nature of artifice. But *The Comedy of Errors* provides a framework for at least one later comedy where similar experiences lead to the possibility that the incidents of a play are being used to comment obliquely (and in a not-at-all-solemn way) on artifice itself. *A Midsummer Night's Dream* hints at a suggestion that its transformations stand for something more than their purely narrative function. But where it differs from the earlier play is that these nightmarish adventures are followed not by a spectacular theatrical trick (Aemilia's intervention in the action and her startling revelations) which merely implies an interest in the function of artifice, but by much more explicit comments on the significance of the vivid sense-impressions the four young Athenians receive from their night of amorous misunderstandings.

Theseus's much-anthologized speech on lovers, madmen and poets states very clearly certain Renaissance commonplaces about the nature and effect of illusion:

> I never may believe
> These antique fables, nor these fairy toys.
> Lovers and madmen have such seething brains,
> Such shaping fantasies, that apprehend
> More than cool reason ever comprehends.
> The lunatic, the lover, and the poet,
> Are of imagination all compact.
> One sees more devils than vast hell can hold;
> That is the madman. The lover, all as frantic,
> Sees Helen's beauty in a brow of Egypt.
> The poet's eye, in a fine frenzy rolling,
> Doth glance from heaven to earth, from earth to heaven;
> And as imagination bodies forth
> The forms of things unknown, the poet's pen
> Turns them to shapes, and gives to airy nothing
> A local habitation and a name.
> Such tricks hath strong imagination
> That, if it would but apprehend some joy,
> It comprehends some bringer of that joy;
> Or in the night, imagining some fear,
> How easy is a bush suppos'd a bear?
>
> (V. i. 2)

To extract such a passage from a play and to endow it with thematic significance is often dangerous; here the danger is increased because elsewhere Theseus is shown as having a particularly pragmatic and business-like cast of mind. But this speech resembles a set passage, and its latter portion, at any rate, despite its overtly censorious tone, sounds rather remote from Theseus's generally unsympathetic view of what he regards as a cock-and-bull story told by four love-struck youngsters.

The speech is, furthermore, a collection of commonplaces. It deals with the conventional idea of *furor poeticus*:[2] what Theseus says about poetry would have been recognized by an Elizabethan grammar-school pupil as a most orthodox point of view. But these truisms are here intensified by their more than usually analytic manner of presentation. When Theseus speaks of the imagination bodying forth 'The forms of things unknown', he is doing no more than repeating the familiar Renaissance notion that the power of poetry resides in its ability to create new heaven and new earth. But when he continues by speaking about the poet's pen giving these things a shape, 'A local habitation and a name', more is involved than the mere discovery of an

---

[2] For a discussion of *furor poeticus* in post-classical literature, see E. R. Curtius, *European Literature and the Latin Middle Ages* (trans. Willard R. Trask), London 1953, pp. 474–5.

apt and vivid expression for a commonplace idea. A variety of
Renaissance clichés about the potency of the poet's art are emphasized
and, in a way, transformed through this insistence on the conjunction
between the shapeless, indistinct, incorporeal on the one hand, and on
the other the concrete, specific and individual. This is an admirably
concise definition of poetic creativity. But Theseus also credits poetry
with another ability—its capacity to transform common experience.
The imagination alters the appearance of quite ordinary objects so
that they come to resemble things entirely unlike themselves. This,
again, operates by way of the sensuous, the vivid apprehension of
unreal states that seem, nevertheless, to be more meaningful than
mundane reality. It is true that these comments do not refer
specifically to the poet's craft: they are concerned with the more
general topic of the imagination, especially the kind displayed by the
young lovers when they told of their strange experiences. Yet these
words are a natural consequence of the preoccupation with poetry
expressed earlier in the speech. Moreover, Hippolyta's remark in
answer to her husband's strictures adds another significant term to this
series of statements about the nature of the imagination:

> But all the story of the night told over,
> And all their minds transfigur'd so together,
> More witnesseth than fancy's images,
> And grows to something of great constancy,
> But howsoever strange and admirable.
>
> (V. i. 23)

A pattern of significances may therefore be seen to emerge from
Theseus's speech and from Hippolyta's rejoinder. Poetry creates a
world from nothing, giving substance to what has no existence in the
'real' world. It is able to transform the characteristics of mundane
experience into strange (often threatening) yet 'admirable' shapes,
thereby producing 'something of great constancy'. Despite the
possibility that this passage represents no more than a fancifully
expressed discussion between a peremptory monarch and his new
consort about a strange tale of nocturnal adventures, their words,
nevertheless, reverberate in a curiously fascinating way. Construing
them as an embodiment of Shakespeare's concern with the sense-
experiences generated by comedy, where essentially artificial structures are constructed out of the commonplace aspects of the everyday
world, may be no more than a barely legitimate employment of certain

tentative possibilities. But we may regard this passage in *A Midsummer Night's Dream* as a more specific discussion of the nature of artistic illusion because it comments on those aspects of the comedy for which *The Comedy of Errors* (in its treatment of the impact its confusions make on the characters) provides a framework. In the later play, the errors and misunderstandings, the dangerous transformation of common experience, do not merely seem to be produced by deliberate and possibly malevolent practices; they are very much the results of certain actions within the play carried out in sight of the audience. In this way, the play brings together its central intrigue and a discussion on the nature of poetry and imagination in a most specific way. The conversation between Theseus and Hippolyta marks the beginning of the play's finale: the threats and conflicts have been resolved, the marriage-revels are to follow. This statement about the power of art, stands, therefore, between Oberon's practices, an emblem of art, and the play's concluding example of art's ability to transform the commonplace and the inept.

Transformation is a basic conceit in *A Midsummer Night's Dream*. Bottom's translation is derived, of course, from Apuleius, no matter how remotely. But the play involves other instances of transformation besides the change of the weaver into the consort (for the night) of the Queen of the Fairies. Most notable is the case of the four Athenians. These transformations are effected by use of a device which may be taken as a symbol for the transforming potentialities of art.[3]

The transformations and confusions in the play arise from Oberon's practices and from Puck's misapplication of the flower of the purple dye. The device of the flower itself does not carry specific overtones of a concern with the artist's capacity of changing quotidian experience into a nightmare, or into a dream-world of shadows. Yet Oberon's description of how he came to find the flower contains some intimations of its significance. The account relies, remotely, on the tale of the metamorphosis of Adonis which Shakespeare had already told in *Venus and Adonis*; but the decorative and emotional detail in the speech

---

[3] For a discussion, see David P. Young, *Something of Great Constancy*, New Haven 1966, pp. 155 ff. Young concludes that the play is Shakespeare's 'ars poetica', and must therefore 'be regarded as one of his most important plays and a touchstone for the understanding and interpretation of others' (pp. 179–80). Earlier criticism was largely preoccupied with the political allegory Rowe claimed (in his *Life of Shakespear*) to have discovered in Oberon's speech cited below. The *New Variorum* edition of *A Midsummer Night's Dream* (ed. H. H. Furness), New York 1895, gives a comprehensive account of eighteenth- and nineteenth-century speculation in its gloss to II. i. 153–75.

implies certain suggestions in excess of a strictly conventional function. He tells how he once saw Cupid take aim:

> At a fair vestal, throned by the west,
> And loos'd his love-shaft smartly from his bow,
> As it should pierce a hundred thousand hearts;
> But I might see young Cupid's fiery shaft
> Quench'd in the chaste beams of the wat'ry moon;
> And the imperial vot'ress passed on,
> In maiden meditation, fancy-free.
> Yet mark'd I where the bolt of Cupid fell.
> It fell upon a little western flower,
> Before milk-white, now purple with love's wound,
> And maidens call it Love-in-idleness.
> Fetch me that flow'r, the herb I showed thee once.
> The juice of it on sleeping eyelids laid
> Will make or man or woman madly dote
> Upon the next live creature that it sees.
>
> (II. i. 158)

There is no specific coupling in this speech of the powers of the herb with the potentialities of poetry. Yet the description of this fairly ordinary plant—which is to assume emblematic significance in the play's action—is achieved in terms of an elaborate rhetorical display depending, to a great extent, on the imagery and subject-matter of much Renaissance poetry. Oberon's description, while serving the basic function of introducing an important element of the plot, has the secondary effect of evoking an art-world—the decorative, artificial and stylized landscape of poetical description. This is, admittedly, not sufficient warrant for our equating the flower of the purple dye with the concept of art and imagination, yet Oberon's fanciful device (employed for the gulling of Titania) comes to represent an emblem of the transforming powers of poetry and of art.

As a result of Puck's ineptitude (or, perhaps, because he is 'puckish') the juice of the flower has an unfortunate effect upon its victims. In Titania it brings about the transformation her husband desires; but with the young Athenians it has disastrous results, until Oberon, a Prospero-like manipulator, takes matters in hand. The emblem of art represented by this magical herb refers, moreover, not merely to the potency of illusion and the strength of sense-impressions. It also glances at the traditional aims of comedy, though it comes, ultimately, to deny the often voiced ethical and moral justifications for comic drama. The apparently trivial symbol serves, therefore, as a complex device in the play's treatment of art's transforming capacity.

We may, if we wish, regard Oberon's revenge on Titania, his humiliating her through the strength of his might, as an analogue for the common Renaissance definition and defence of the art of comedy. By subjecting representative social and moral types to ridicule, especially of the sort that emerges from humiliation, comedy fulfilled its fundamental therapeutic function. The clearest, and at the same time a characteristically extreme, instance of this is to be found in the last scene of Jonson's *Poetaster*; Horace, a true poet, applies a quantity of pills to Crispinus, the poetaster, thereby making him vomit out all the vile and inartistic neologisms with which he defiled the poet's honourable craft. Shakespeare's way is different; yet Titania is subjected to similar therapy: her night of bestial love teaches her her proper rôle and status in the fairy world. Puck's misuse of the drug also has certain analogies with Renaissance attitudes towards the function of art—he is the improper practitioner, that figure of insufficient ability, command, authority or benevolence in whose hands the powerful tools of the artist become dangerous.

It must be stressed, once more, that the concern with the potency of art in *A Midsummer Night's Dream* is not stated explicitly; it remains one among a number of suggestions the play seems to explore or embody. Yet these aspects of the play possess an insinuating quality—somewhere beyond the rationally (or academically) demonstrable—that constantly implies the presence of a concern with these largely abstract issues. The effects of Oberon's practices on his victims provide, however, some less ambiguous or shadowy instances of an engagement with these themes. The therapeutic practices in Renaissance comedy usually have benevolent effects, and these effects usually receive due praise. The comedy of the period is filled with a succession of fools and knaves who are exposed and humiliated, and who become, thus, once more fit members of the society from which they have strayed. Shakespeare employs this device in the least characteristic of his comedies, *The Merry Wives of Windsor*; after his humiliation and mock-torment by 'elves' and 'fairies', Falstaff, for all his bluster, admits defeat: 'use me as you will'. Ford insists that restitution must be made to 'Master Brook', while Page indicates that, having been purged, Falstaff may once more be received into the community of Windsor-folk: 'Yet be cheerful knight; thou shalt eat a posset tonight at my house' (V. v. 164). Jonson, in the 'purging'

episode of *Poetaster*, characteristically sharpens the moral implications
of this familiar comic device. After Chrispinus has vomited out all his
words, Virgil comments:

> These pills can but restore him for a time;
> Not cure him quite of such a malady,
> Caught by so many surfeits; which have fill'd
> His blood, and brain, thus full of crudities:
> 'Tis necessary, therefore, he observe
> A strict and wholesome diet.[4]
>
> (V. iii. 531)

He continues by prescribing a strict literary regimen to effect the
complete cure of the false poet. Jonson indicates that the point of these
comic fancies is of real social relevance; the deviant member of society
must not only be shocked out of his errant ways, but his cure must
continue in order to maintain the swiftly-achieved moral health.

Shakespeare's use of this familiar material in *A Midsummer Night's
Dream* is quite different. Superficially, the deception of Titania fulfils its
purpose; but the reasons behind this deception are typically ambivalent, even perhaps disturbing. She is deceived and humiliated not in
order to achieve a cure of social errors, but to allow Oberon to seize the
prize, the foundling Indian boy, the cause of the strife in fairy-land.
Even allowing for the late sixteenth century's rather crass social
standards, Oberon's practices on his queen are petty; more important,
however, are their effects on Titania while she is under Oberon's spell
and on her unwitting partner, Bottom the Weaver. The curiously
ambivalent beauty of the scenes between the Fairy Queen and the
translated Bottom have already been noted: the whimsy, hilarity and
pathos of this strange night of love produce a thing of beauty. It is
grotesque and, at times, farcical; it has little truck with romantic
notions of the beautiful; yet none of this prevents the episode from
having a curious allure of its own. Titania's tenderness towards her
ass-eared lover is of a moving, childlike gentleness:

> Be kind and courteous to this gentleman;
> Hop in his walks and gambol in his eyes;
> Feed him with apricocks and dewberries,
> With purple grapes, green figs, and mulberries;

---

[4] Quoted from Jonson's *Works* (eds C. H. Herford and P. Simpson), IV, Oxford 1932,
p. 314.

> The honey bags steal from the humble-bees,
> And for night-tapers crop their waxen thighs,
> And light them at the fiery glow-worm's eyes,
> To have my love to bed and to arise;
> And pluck the wings from painted butterflies,
> To fan the moonbeams from his sleeping eyes.
> Nod to him, elves, and do him courtesies.
>
> (III. i. 150)

Even Bottom's attempts to emulate the gallantry of love are transformed into something, if not beautiful, then certainly of a higher order than his former strutting and buffoonery:

> Mounsieur Cobweb; good mounsieur, get you your weapons in your hand and kill me a red-hipp'd humble-bee on the top of a thistle; and, good mounsieur, bring me the honey-bag. Do not fret yourself too much in the action, mounsieur; and, good mounsieur, have a care the honey-bag break not; I would be loath to have you overflowen with a honey-bag, signior.
>
> (IV. l. 10)

These episodes in the play explore the artistic possibilities of illusion, trickery and of the use of agencies—whether magical flowers or poetry—capable of transforming our normal perceptions. Even though the night of love has something nightmarish about it, these nocturnal experiences possess their own particular values. Titania expresses loathing and humiliation when the spell is broken:

> My Oberon! What visions have I seen!
> Methought I was enamour'd of an ass.
> . . . How came these things to pass?
> O, how mine eyes do loathe his visage now!
>
> (IV. i. 73)

but the audience, the privileged onlookers, cannot agree with this insistence on the strict supremacy of waking reality over the illusions of the night. Bottom, on waking from his dream, carries away a more suggestive reminiscence—for him the experience has become 'something of great constancy': inexplicable, strange, even perhaps alarming, but also curiously satisfying:

> I have had a most rare vision. I have had a dream, past the wit of man to say what dream it was. Man is but an ass if he

go about to expound this dream . . . . The eye of man hath
not heard, the ear of man hath not seen, man's hand is not
able to taste, his tongue to conceive, nor his heart to report,
what my dream was. I will get Peter Quince to write a
ballad of this dream. It shall be call'd "Bottom's Dream",
because it hath no bottom . . .

(IV. i. 202)

The transformation of the madness of the night into poetry is
expressed as a joke; the ballad entitled 'Bottom's Dream' cannot
entirely claim artistic integrity. Yet this jesting statement of important
and significant propositions is characteristic of Shakespeare's comic
practices—solemnities are guyed, but the jokes often suggest possibilities of some importance. The agency bringing this transformation
about is Oberon the manipulator, and beyond that, the flower of the
purple dye, possibly an emblem of the power of art and illusion. Such
practices are capable of engendering a notably ambivalent experience
mingling emotional satisfaction with the recognition of the impossibility (in terms of mundane reality) of what has occurred or what
has been experienced. The associations of the world of poetry clustering around the means employed by Oberon to bring about a result in
some ways analogous to the aims of conventional comedy may not
be reduced to consistent moral or ethical significances; their effect
is emotional rather than (as in the climax of *Poetaster*) social or rational. The magical herb produces illusions, it transmutes common
experience into extraordinary states. The deception of Titania, in
consequence, is not merely a transient, socially justifiable humiliation
or tormenting as such deceptions are in conventional comedy, but the
unintended conferring of an experience which has its own peculiar
value and excellence. Through this emblem of art and through the
associated enactment of an altered version of conventional comic
practising, the play moves close to making a statement about the
nature and function of that world of illusions we normally call art.
Illusion and the kind of wares purveyed by poetry are capable of
transmuting common experiences into extraordinary states. These
states, though often discarded through the demands of everyday
reality, are still capable of haunting us, and (at times) they assume a
greater importance than our waking lives. The play establishes this
suggestion through the complex and shadowy possibilities it evokes
from Oberon's flower and its uses: we laugh at Bottom as he wakes
from his enchantment, and we observe that he reverts soon enough to

his former blustering as 'Bully Bottom', yet his reminiscences persuade us that (in some ways) he is a privileged being—he had heard the mermaids singing. The play makes no moral or social comment or promise about this achievement; it leads to no greater knowledge or amelioration; this is no conventionally therapeutic comedy, but it indicates—always within the jesting decorum of comedy—the type of transitory and tentative emotional satisfaction the world of art and of illusions is able to produce.

The case of the four young Athenians when they wake from what seems to them a hideous nightmare is similar. The effects of their experiences—or more precisely, their rapt recollections—are strange and wonderful. Even though they have been the victims of the misapplication of art, that dangerous bugbear to many Renaissance moralists, they have gained something of value:

> *Demetrius*   These things seem small and undistinguishable,
>   Like far-off mountains turned into clouds.
> *Hermia*   Methinks I see these things with parted eye,
>   When every thing seems double.
> *Helena*   So methinks;
>   And I have found Demetrius like a jewel,
>   Mine own, and not mine own.
> *Demetrius*   Are you sure
>   That we are awake? It seems to me
>   That yet we sleep, we dream.
>   (IV. i. 184)

The play goes beyond its concern with levels of reality, forcing us to examine the clear-cut relationship we presume to exist between daylight reality and night-time fantasy; it also suggests that the manipulation of this fantasy, whether proper or misapplied, may have results and significances that are among the most vivid and most important of our experiences. The play is constantly ambivalent about its suggestions concerning the potency of art; characteristically, these relatively elevated possibilities are contained within a theatrical structure wholly intent on its own theatricality—an elaborate and sophisticated version of the usual comic preoccupation with the difficulties of young lovers. Nevertheless, insistently (and almost insidiously) it insinuates a concern with illusions and the results of these illusions into our consciousness: we may not elaborate it into a theory, but, by the same token, we feel unable to ignore it.

These vague, almost impressionistic suggestions of an engagement
with the potentialities of art and illusion come into a curious but
fascinating focus in the play's other instance of the transforming power
of art and illusion: the mechanicals' play performed as a part of the
finale. This episode occupies the same structural position as the last act
in *The Merchant of Venice*: the strife and conflict have ended; the play
concludes with a revel, a period of relaxation for the characters and for
the audience. The last act of *The Merchant of Venice* is a celebration of
the good fortune which has brought the play's problems to a happy
resolution; the finale of *A Midsummer Night's Dream* celebrates the joy
and exhilaration of poetry, but it does so in a peculiar and characteristically 'comic' manner. The 'very tragical mirth' enacted by Bottom
and his friends in honour of Theseus's nuptials is, both as a literary and
as a theatrical performance, a total disaster. The actors are inept, the
author is ignorant: their efforts to achieve gravity and tragic grandeur
misfire in the shower of doggerel, tautology, and mixed metaphors
with which they attempt to amuse and impress the courtly audience.
The effect of this theatrical debacle within *A Midsummer Night's Dream*
is, of course, quite the contrary—it produces delight and peculiar joy.
This is partly a result of Shakespeare's consummate skill as a parodist;
but it also emerges from the gaiety the performance produces among
the courtiers, and, most of all, from the appropriate position occupied
by this uproarious hilarity in the design of the play as a whole. The
comedy of the half-lit world, always hovering on the edge of the
sinister, is replaced by the open, sunny comedy of ineptitude. The
'tedious brief scene' appeals to the vulgarian in us all; and it appeals
also to that holiday liberty which allows us to mock not only the inept
tragedians, but also the craft they had attempted, with such poor
success, to master.

This transformation through art is, therefore, a spectacular conjuring feat. Poor art assumes the status of legitimate art, not because of its
intrinsic or absolute qualities, but through Shakespeare's ingenuity
and through the structural position occupied by this divertissement. In
order to be effective, the sad tale of Pyramus and Thisbe should be told
with a degree of gravity and pathos. But this version of the tale of these
unfortunate lovers lacks all such qualities; yet it produces a legitimate
and artistically justified effect. Deftly, Shakespeare shatters the
doctrine of decorum; sows' ears are turned into silk purses. But this
may only be brought about within the fabric of *A Midsummer Night's
Dream*; there would be no other legitimate way of enjoying the

mechanicals' attempts at high tragedy. In this comedy, the inartistic is transformed into art, and it is the playwright's brilliance and his manipulation of artifice that allow this transformation to occur.

No unified aesthetic theory may be culled from this comedy; but it seems to indicate a concern with the nature of poetry, of illusion, as well as a statement about the speciality of the world created by the dramatist's conjuring powers. The play comes to emphasize that transforming potential within illusion which allows a bush to be supposed a bear. It celebrates poetry's freedom from the constraints of probability, and even from the most basic emotional decorum that demands the fit expression for a chosen subject. Thus, the silly tragedy, which in actuality would breed merely boredom or hostility in an audience, acquires the opposite effect. Yet here, as elsewhere, Shakespeare does not allow us confidently to extrapolate these possibilities from the play, since, as in the case of other comic episodes seemingly filled with potentially elevated meanings, the contrary possibility is also embodied in this scene. The loutish behaviour of the courtiers during the performance of the tragedy (probably more acceptable to Shakespeare's age than to ours, but appealing, nevertheless, to the philistine in all of us) serves constantly to stress the ineptitude of the performance. Even this embodiment of a corrective to the over-emphasis of the episode's philosophical implications is, characteristically, countered by a further possibility in the scene. Through that typically sly refusal to allow the play to be pinned down to a consistent set of meanings, Shakespeare makes Theseus's final words to the actors contain an amount of grudging magnanimity, even though this instance of *noblesse oblige* is heavily qualified by the aristocratic connoisseur's disdain:

> No epilogue, I pray you; for your play needs no excuse.
> Never excuse; for when the players are all dead there need
> none to be blamed. Marry, if he that writ it had played
> Pyramus, and hang'd himself in Thisby's garter, it would
> have been a fine tragedy. And so it is, truly; and very
> notably discharg'd.
>
> (V. i. 345)

This half-hearted compliment suggests that the transforming power of art is recognized within the fiction of the comedy itself—that for a moment, tentatively, the characters themselves stand in the same relation to the world in which they exist as does the audience.

Shakespeare goes as far, perhaps, as possible (without shattering the artifice and the illusion of the theatre) to register the essential nature of the world created by art: *A Midsummer Night's Dream* itself, like Oberon's magic herb, has the uncanny ability of translating qualities into their contraries. It is, possibly, a sign that this should be acknowledged that we find in Theseus's courteous commendation of the actor's effort. Significantly, the Princess in *Love's Labour's Lost* expresses a similar sentiment (though, as befits her nature, more generously) when she rebukes the King of Navarre and his courtiers for their uncharitable mockery of the pageant of the Nine Worthies:

> Nay, my good lord, let me o'errule you now.
> That sport best pleases that doth least know how;
> Where zeal strives to content, and the contents
> Dies in the zeal of that which it presents.
> Their form confounded makes most form in mirth,
> When great things labouring perish in their birth.
>
> (V. ii. 513)

II

Typically, *The Winter's Tale* contains the most detailed and sustained treatment of the function and nature of art. As with the other aspects of its comic structure, the employment of this concern is relevant to the depiction of a natural benevolence colouring most facets of this play. The play's treatment of this topic is more extensive than that found in *A Midsummer Night's Dream*: it extends to a concern with the duality of art and nature, reality and illusion. Two passages deal directly with this theme: the 'Arcadian' dispute on natural and cultivated flowers in IV. iv. and the account given in V. ii. of Julio Romano's skill as a sculptor. Each passage seems pregnant with meaning, and there are signs in both of an engagement with the nature of artistic creation and with the subversion of the natural. Yet each passage is so surrounded by problems of interpretation, ironies, difficulties of intention and of purpose, that once more no absolutely consistent intellectual pattern may be extracted from either. All we may do is to stress that these topics enter into the play's complex web of ideas and possibilities.

The passage dealing with Julio Romano's art is the more ambiguous. It contains an apparently serious statement concerning the power of art to create true immortality:

> The Princess hearing of her mother's statue, which is in the
> keeping of Paulina—a piece many years in doing and now
> newly perform'd by that rare Italian master, Julio
> Romano, who, had he himself eternity and could put
> breath into his work, would beguile nature of her custom,
> so perfectly he is her ape. He so near to Hermione hath
> done Hermione that they say one would speak to her and
> stand in hope of answer . . .
>
> (V. ii. 91)

The notes struck in this speech are familiar from a number of sources.
It is another instance of the common Renaissance preoccupation with
the idealizing power of art; it also raises the notion (heard insistently in
Shakespeare's sonnets) that the work of art represents the most
substantial reality.[5] But the speech also glances at the world of
Hermetic-Platonic beliefs, for the Third Gentleman seems to allude to
one interesting interpretation of the statue-conjuring feats of the priests
of ancient Egypt. Giulio Camillo, who is said to have been renowned in
the sixteenth and seventeenth centuries for a mysterious 'theatre' he
had constructed, reinterpreted the passage in *Asclepius* dealing with the
creation of gods in such a way that the magical properties of the feat
were entirely excluded, being replaced by the psychological and
emotive power of a work of art to suggest a *vitality* which is a copy of life
itself. The key statement of this idea in Camillo's writing is the
following:

> I have read, I believe in Mercurius Trismegistus, that in Egypt there were
> such excellent makers of statues that when they had brought some statue to
> the perfect proportions it was found to be animated with an angelic spirit: for
> such perfection could not be without a soul. Similar to such statues, I find a
> composition of words, the office of which is to hold all the words in a
> proportion grateful to the ear. . . . Which words as soon as they are put into
> their proportion are found when pronounced to be as it were animated by a
> harmony.[6]

The first part of this statement accords well with what the Third
Gentleman has to say about Julio Romano's skill. It is echoed,
furthermore, in the following scene when Paulina's 'conjurings'

---

[5] As in Sidney's *Apologie for Poetry* in O. B. Hardison Jr (ed.), *English Literary Criticism: The Renaissance*, New York 1963, especially p. 104.
[6] Quoted in F. A. Yates, *The Art of Memory*, London 1966, p. 156.

proceed by way of a series of elaborate suggestions that Hermione's statue is so lifelike that it might indeed be thought to possess a life of its own. Camillo's statement, reflected (no doubt unconsciously) by Shakespeare, is the final confirmation of an important tendency in much Renaissance Platonic thought concerning this god-making feat. There is, as we have seen, a frequent ambivalence in these writings: it is often suggested that the actual bringing of statues to life is not of the foremost importance; what is of greater moment is mankind's ability, through the divine gift of artistic genius, to create works of art possessing a more meaningful and certainly a more lasting vitality than ordinary existence offers. Julio Romano's statue of the dead queen, as it is described by the Third Gentleman, is of such perfection that it challenges nature: this is a Hermione somehow greater and more significant than the queen who had lived and died.

But these matters are complicated by their treatment within the play. We learn that this genius is able not merely to capture physical reality, but that it transcends such reality and the tyranny of chance through its ability to depict Hermione as she would appear now—sixteen years after her death—literally wrinkled and aged. The aesthetic possibilities contained in this feat are complex: it represents the antithesis of Keats's eternally frozen youth, it glances at the critical assertion often encountered in the Renaissance that poetry (or art) is able to depict the world as it should be—not as it is. These suggestions hover tantalizingly on the threshold of intimating that art may, indeed, produce the impossible, the non-existent, or the unreal, while, through its curious magic, being able to fashion that impossibility into a higher reality. Julio Romano, though he is Nature's Ape (an emblem of the mimetic and the representational) copying the phenomena of the observable world, nevertheless beguiles nature of her custom, usurps her by appropriating her function to himself. The proof of this seems to reside (until the startling revelation of Hermione's survival) in the statue that gains so much admiration in the last scene of the play.

The topic of the relationship between nature and artifice has, however, already appeared in the play before this episode, in the discussion in IV. iv. between Perdita and Polixenes about natural and cultivated flowers. The presence of these two passages in significant parts of the play's action might well be fortuitous, but their effect cannot be overlooked. The Bohemian King, disguised as a visitor to the rural festivities, addresses a number of veiled but potentially sinister remarks to the country-lass (in reality the Sicilian princess) about the impropriety of a liaison based on social inequality. He does this in a curiously complicated and circuitous way, through the use of a botanical metaphor, and by apparently advocating the marriage of 'A gentler scion to the wildest stock'. Despite this apparent egalitarianism, however, his words assume a threatening import. Perdita, for her part, though in love with the youth she knows to be of much higher status that her own, expresses (even if unwittingly) the impropriety of transcending natural distinctions. The sustained botanical and horticultural metaphor gives an intimation of both social and artistic implications.

Perdita initiates this discussion, which comes to have such threatening overtones, through her insistence that her guests may receive only natural flowers:

> the fairest flow'rs o' th' season
> Are our carnations and streak'd gillyvors,
> Which some call nature's bastards. Of that kind
> Our rustic garden's barren; and I care not
> To get slips of them.
>
> (IV. iv. 81)

She gives a curious answer when Polixenes asks her why she neglects these—it sounds like an ecstatic celebration of the power of human ingenuity and skill, yet it is, fundamentally, an expression of caution:

> For I have heard it said
> There is an art which in their piedness shares
> With great creating nature.
>
> (IV. iv. 86)

Polixenes when urging the validity of such cultivation, claims (in language of great complexity) that an art which transcends nature is, in truth, a gift of nature, since all human activities flow out of her dispensation; he concludes with some sinister, threatening words:

> nature is made better by no mean
> But nature makes that mean; so over that art,
> Which you say adds to nature, is an art
> That nature makes. You see, sweet maid, we marry
> A gentler scion to the wildest stock,
> And make conceive a bark of baser kind
> By bud of nobler race. This is an art

Which does mend nature—change it rather; but
The art itself is nature.

(IV. iv. 89)

This apparently significant debate between the natural and the artificial assumes, consequently, a curiously ambivalent character. It would not be unreasonable to encounter in a play of such artifice as *The Winter's Tale* a recommendation of the artificial—yet this recommendation is given to a character who has acquired unpleasant and sinister potentialities, and who may be using it in a cruel game to trap the unwitting lovers into making their love known. The claims of nature, on the other hand, are spoken by Perdita, whom we know to be something other than the simple farm-lass she seems to be.

It is therefore difficult to extract a clear line of argument from the play's discussion of the nature and effect of art. Nevertheless, some of Polixenes's words as well as Perdita's significant comment seem to echo the ecstatic description of Julio Romano's masterpiece in the last act. Two possibilities arise: that these passages stand in the play as independent expressions of Shakespeare's artistic *credo*, irrespective of the circumstances in which they are delivered, or else that the particular circumstances transform the implications of these statements concerning the nature of art. The former possibility is by no means unusual in the drama of the period; the latter, however, offers several interesting possibilities. The Third Gentleman's lovely words about Hermione's statue are, in strict terms, nonsensical. There is no statue, the materpiece is nature's work, for it is the queen herself, long thought dead, who has reached maturity in the intervening years. We have little brief, therefore, to regard these words as anything but a function of the play's narrative progression. The second scene of Act V is a ruse, a means of suggesting to the audience that a fresh development is to be anticipated, yet blocking the recognition of the actual event, the revelation of Hermione's survival. It is a species of jesting, the characteristic teasing of comedy. The dramatist tells, yet he fails to tell. The Second Gentleman, in truth, gives the game away (unwittingly, we may presume), but, as in the case of Paulina's speeches announcing Hermione's death in III. ii., hindsight is required to recognize the import of what is being said:

> I thought she had some great matter there in hand; for she
> hath privately twice or thrice a day, ever since the death of
> Hermione, visited that removed house.

(V.ii.101)

The rich suggestions of this passage dissolve, it would seem, into the exigencies of the theatre; the discussion of the 'carver's excellence' ('many years in doing') is merely a flourish to advance the cunning game being conducted here with the audience's expectations.Similar possibilities arise in the debate concerning natural and cultivated plants in the previous act: it serves the function of allowing the disguised Polixenes to indicate to the audience that his intentions towards the farm-lass are not entirely benevolent. In the characteristic manner of Shakespeare's comedies, we find, when we come upon these apparently significant and meaningful passages, that their significance begins to vanish into theatrical trickery—the playwright continually reminds us that this is entertainment, not philosophy.

Nevertheless, both of these passages are insinuating: they will not allow their potentialities to be overlooked—their ambivalence, more-over, may indicate that they possess yet another significance within the play's intellectual design. In both, as we have seen, nature and art enter into a curiously complex and circular relationship. The art of the sculptor or of the horticulturist seems, at first glance, to improve upon nature, but this improvement of the natural proves to be an entirely natural activity, since it is nature itself that provides mankind with the intellectual equipment enabling it to bring about these feats. The terms natural and artificial, while kept, to some extent, distinct from each other in these passages, begin to merge. This relationship is not stated explicitly—perhaps it is incapable of being so stated—but the suggestion emerges that it is impossible to depart ultimately from nature: the more humanity strives to transform the characteristics of the natural world, so the supremacy of nature comes to be confirmed. Nature cannot be escaped—whatever is done, whatever comes into being is her gift: the ability to claim that certain things represent the natural, while others are beyond or contrary to nature, may no longer exist. Whatever man creates, nature sanctions. The connections between these possibilities and the philosophical convictions discussed in Chapter 5 are clear enough; the function of this material in *The Winter's Tale* remains, nevertheless, problematical. The only certainty to emerge is that the basic narrative grounds for both of these discourses come to be invalidated—and therein, possibly, lies their ultimate significance. The restoration of Hermione reveals, so to speak, the artistry of nature: the metaphor for this is the totally imaginary statue that Julio Romano is supposed to have carved. The com-memoration and the apotheosis allegedly achieved by the supreme masterpiece have come about through Hermione's endurance and Paulina's patient dedication. The concept of a natural miracle is thus wedded to the concept of nature's artifice. But there is a further step in the progression of ideas suggested by the comedy: the play itself stands in an ambiguous relationship to the 'natural'—that is, to that theatrical tact it seems so flagrantly to violate.

One cannot appeal to any standard of dramatic correctness in sixteenth- and seventeenth-century England. There was no theory of 'naturalness' of the type that dominated French theatre of the latter part of the seventeenth century in which the rigid prescriptions about dramatic construction were supposed to ensure naturalness and credibility. But the theatre of Shakespeare's age possessed a few implicit conventions beyond which the drama of the time rarely strayed. They were neither stringent nor rigorously observed, yet most playwrights strove to fulfil two requirements: that their plays should have, at least, the appearance of narrative continuity, and that the audience should be neither misled nor surprised beyond a certain limit. *The Winter's Tale* violates radically both of these requirements. No attempt is made to obscure the hiatus in the middle of the action, and, despite certain signs embedded in the plot, the restoration of Hermione and the manner of her survival come as complete theatrical surprises. At least circumstantial evidence is available that one of Shakespeare's contemporaries found such things too preposterous, too much straining at the credible and the natural. In the Induction to *Bartholomew Fair*, the Scrivener gives the following undertaking on behalf of the playwright (and here Jonson is clearly speaking *in propria persona*) about the play that is to follow:

> If there be never a servant-monster i' the fair; who can help it? he says; nor a nest of antics? He is loth to make Nature afraid in his plays, like those that beget Tales, Tempests, and such like drolleries, to mix his head with other men's heels. . .[7]

> (Ind. 127)

The Winter's Tale offends against commonsense and propriety. It is an outrageous manipulation of dramatic conventions and possibilities; the audience is led by the nose through a maze of complications to a conclusion where it could have some reason to feel cozened. The poet seems to have abandoned himself completely to his fancy, violating all

[7] Quoted from Jonson's *Works* (eds, C. H. Herford and E. Simpson), VI, Oxford 1938, p.16.

canons of probability and dramatic tact. This list of accusations could be further extended: the play is extraordinarily artificial, a threat to nature—as Jonson seems indeed, to have claimed.

Yet *The Winter's Tale* fits together like a beautiful and intricate toy. Though it violates the requirements of theatrical tact, it produces a great pleasure, providing an emotional and aesthetic experience which is memorable and individual. Within the enchanted world of the play, Shakespeare has fashioned a moving, amusing and, at times, pathos-filled work of art. The serenity and beauty of the artifice contain and justify the extravagance. May we, therefore, identify the effect of the play with the principle that 'over that art,/ Which you say adds to nature, is an art/ That nature makes'? Whether this connection was ever consciously intended by Shakespeare will never be known; but the comedy itself illustrates the subtle and complex relationship between illusion and probability. Because it is capable of giving pleasure and of engendering a significant emotional experience, it may be thought to represent, for all its apparent lack of 'naturalism', legitimate art. How to characterize this legitimacy is ultimately unimportant—whether we see in the play a moral consistency or one of poetical textures, the consistency and the poise remain. And within the play, the carefully worked out series of analogies with the great stream of Platonic optimism is a sign that its artifice is founded in nature, that is to say, in the dramatist's ability to fashion a world which is consistent and compelling for all its strangeness.

In *The Winter's Tale*, therefore, the concern with the two types of artifice—sculpture and the cultivation of plants—enters into a subtle set of relationships with the effect and the nature of the play itself. The duality and ambivalence in the two key instances of this theme—the horticultural dispute in IV. iv. and the concluding scenes of Act V—serve to reinforce the play's status and character. Our inability to pursue the debate between Polixenes and Perdita to its logical conclusion (because each of these characters adopts a position somewhat contrary to his or her function) mirrors the manner in which the *plot* demonstrates the naturalness of its extraordinary, seemingly miraculous events. The confusions caused by Julio Romano's non-existent statue, on the other hand, are in harmony with the *effect* of the play in which the most stylized artifice becomes 'natural' and justified through the poise, confidence and beauty of the structure and the language. *The Winter's Tale* includes (among other things) a demonstration—rather than a statement—of the artistic integrity of

Shakespeare's comic theatre: an art impossible to account for or to be experienced in terms of external intellectual or philosophical structures, yet an art able to incorporate such elevated and weighty material while retaining, all along, its concentration on the particularities of plot, incident and character.

The Tempest covers similar ground, though not with the rigour or complexity of the earlier comedy. It, too, contains a dispute between art and artifice, expressed here in terms of representative characters—Caliban, the natural creature, Miranda, the product of Prospero's careful pedagogic nurture. It deals, also, with illusion and its transforming power, and this comes to assume greater importance than the aesthetic dilemma (if we may call it that) so thoroughly explored in *The Winter's Tale*. Prospero, the master-illusionist, presides over a series of transformations in the experiences and perceptions of the court-party which, to the victims, seem like the visitations of irrational or malevolent forces. The familiar world dissolves into the vagaries of nightmares. The transformations are known, of course, to be neither random nor malevolent: *The Tempest*, of all the comedies, is most intimately engaged with therapeutic notions; Prospero's machinations are designed to bring about his enemies' moral regeneration.

We have his assurances for this. It is also demonstrated by the immunity from suffering enjoyed by the one innocent member of the court-party, the old lord Gonzalo, whose simple trust in a benevolent purpose behind these apparently malignant torments earns him the scorn of his fellow-sufferers. But the value and significance of these illusions and transformations are indicated more powerfully and, perhaps, more subtly (in a play not distinguished for subtlety) in Ariel's haunting, though mocking, song to Ferdinand:

> Full fathom five thy father lies;
>   Of his bones are coral made;
> Those are pearls that were his eyes;
>   Nothing of him that doth fade
> But doth suffer a sea-change
> Into something rich and strange . . . .
> (I. ii. 396)

The play strives to present this rich strangeness through its transformation of the known world into the simplicities of the fairy-tale. Its conceit appears to transcend the therapeutic illusions suffered by the errant or by those who are guilty through association—like Gonzalo and Ferdinand—in order to deal with the transforming power of the dramatic illusion itself, which is able to evoke curious sonorities from a theatrical fable of utter simplicity. At times, the play succeeds superbly in this; the naïve and the simple, while remaining naïve and simple, assume rich overtones without specific or inevitable meanings, but suggesting a variety of experiences and emotional possibilities. The loveliest of these is a masterful combination of the visual and the poetic, Prospero's 'discovery' at the climax of the play of 'Ferdinand and Miranda playing at chess':

> *Miranda*   Sweet lord, you play me false.
> *Ferdinand*   No, my dearest love,
>   I would not for the world.
> *Miranda*   Yes, for a score of kingdoms you should wrangle,
>   And I would call it fair play.
> *Alonzo*   If this prove
>   A vision of the island, one dear son
>   Shall I twice lose.
> *Sebastian*   A most high miracle!
>   (V. i. 172)

Yet the play cannot escape entirely a certain piety, making its concern with transformation a matter of intent rather than achievement. We are meant to feel that in this totally impossible world the poet reflects, through the use of certain powerful emblems of art, the natural condition of man and the natural state of the world; but somehow, perhaps because of the play's blandness, the powerful and enthralling undercurrents of some of the earlier comedies have become suppressed.

Nevertheless, *The Tempest* illustrates quite clearly the individual characteristics of Shakespeare's comic world. We may no longer take Prospero as a self-portrait of the poet as confidently as the last century thought him to be.[8] But in his manipulation and in his use of the 'art' of illusion, he represents a stance consistently to be found in the comic plays. These works deny, as surely as any of the literary documents of the English Renaissance, the supposition that the world we know—which must, finally, form the basis for any art—should be transmitted in its own terms. Literary and cultural theory has always

---

[8] David William in '*The Tempest* on Stage', *Jacobean Theatre, Stratford-upon-Avon Studies*, I, London, 1960, pp. 133–57, is a relatively recent commentator seeing in Prospero's abdication some hint of Shakespeare's farewell to creative life.

had some concern with verisimilitude; the theory of tragedy current in Shakespeare's lifetime fancied that tragedies reflect, as in Hamlet's mirror, the permanent and essential qualities of life in a memorably heightened manner. Many comedies of the time are content to mirror faithfully, one might almost say journalistically, the trivia of common life. But the type of comedy Shakespeare wrote transforms the reality of everyday experience into the artificial and the stylized. The pattern, in most of them, is rearranged into an aesthetic experience which seems to possess no external reference, no matter how much it might seem to consist of the common features of our daily life.

The province of this form of comedy becomes, in consequence, the world of certain potentialities inherent in mankind's ability to imagine that which falls outside of ordinary probabilities. These comedies explore the fanciful and the wonderful, the sinister and the threatening; they engage with madness and fantasy, and with the most childlike of fears and desires. They do not deny 'ordinary' life, nor do they turn their back on the profound or the trivial preoccupations of men and women; but in these privileged emblems of art, such preoccupations take on rich and strange qualities. This comic world is unique because we encounter in it the fabric of our experience as we may not meet it elsewhere. Almost every one of the comedies presents a self-contained world; its relationship with the world outside is playful and hypothetical. These plays neither demonstrate nor persuade; their creator seems to have been content merely to allow them to exist; and their artifice guarantees their coherence.

7   *Last Words*

We should not be surprised, given the richness of Shakespeare's comic world, that persistent attempts have been made to impose various orders on it. These plays provide a glittering compendium of the preoccupations of an age particularly wealthy in intellectual and emotional daring. Comedy after comedy, in the marvellous series of works stretching from *The Comedy of Errors* and *The Two Gentlemen of Verona* to *The Tempest*, displays a range of interests which evoke most powerfully and memorably that complex of ideas, possibilities and associations we recognize as constituting 'The Renaissance'. Their copiousness is remarkable: the intense Platonic optimism of the last comedies is matched by the moral and even specifically Christian concerns of *Measure for Measure* and *All's Well That Ends Well*; the subtle psychological discriminations of *As You Like It* and *Twelfth Night* are contained in environments resounding with the cultural overtones of the Renaissance world—pastoral fancy and the sunny, languishing climate of the fabulous Mediterranean countryside. In *The Merchant of Venice* and *Much Ado About Nothing*, the pressures of the social realm—the busy world of cities—are artfully mixed with moral probings of considerable force. Much more than the tragedies—which have, on the whole, dominated critical thought in the last century and a half—the comedies exemplify the rich complexity of the intellectual and artistic heritage of Renaissance culture. Thereby, comedy seems to be led from the trivial and the diversionary into the region of high art, enriched with moral and even philosophical implications.

Literary criticism, since the commencement of the systematic study of Shakespearian drama at the end of the eighteenth century, has generally viewed these plays in terms of their 'intellectual' possibilities. Such possibilities are usually expressed in terms of certain points of view or propositions concerning the interpretation of human life to be culled from these plays. It is true that modern criticism has by and large avoided the imposition of specific programmes in the manner of

Rymer's famous burlesque of the 'moral' of *Othello*, yet in most discussions of Shakespearian drama (and, thus, of the comedies as well as the tragedies and other 'serious' plays) emphases of this type are almost always to be discerned. The moral order of Shakespeare's comic world becomes, therefore, a critical preoccupation; the various strands of meaning and significance—some of which are explored in the previous chapters of this study—are woven together into a consistent (though intricate) fabric. Such a fabric must, it is presumed, be moral in its fundamental intentions even if moralizing of a particularly obvious sort is strenuously avoided. A serious and committed artist cannot be deemed to have looked at life without reaching some conclusions in a serious and committed manner about the questions any contemplation of life inevitably causes us to ask.

It would be perverse to claim that Shakespeare's comic drama does not address itself to the implications of its material. A particular insensitivity is required to argue that these brilliant works of the imagination are free of intellectual content or of artistic and poetic discriminations about the variety of emotional and spiritual states displayed in them. Leontes's jealousy, the strength of innocence in Imogen, Angelo's moral corruption are firm realities within the plays in which these characters appear; it is wrongheaded to assert that the questions of insane jealousy, innocence and deep corruption are remote from their moral horizons. Similarly, the freshness of the natural world, in *As You Like It*, and its dangers, in *A Midsummer Night's Dream*, are not merely subsumed within a flamboyant artifice which proves to be its own justification. The view of Shakespeare's comedies offered in these pages does not attempt to deny their engagement with those issues that patient and skilful scholarship has illuminated; but the status occupied by such important and subtle preoccupations requires to be considered. A consistent order may not be imposed on the comedies without violence to their individual characteristics, nor may an order be imposed on individual works without ignoring significant aspects of their structure. The mixture of modes and interests to be encountered in these plays suggests that their poise and coherence—quite obvious to the reader or the spectator—are to be discovered in an area other than the orthodox emphases and themes mapped out by literary criticism: the isolation and elucidation of meanings contained within the particular details of a text.

The most revealing characteristic of Shakespeare's comic method in this respect is his apparent refusal to endorse or to stress the discoveries contained within his plays. Frequently, the last word is a jest. The two Dromios conclude *The Comedy of Errors* with a buffo duet. The irreverent Gratiano ends *The Merchant of Venice* with some gratuitous obscenity:

> Well, while I live, I'll fear no other thing
> So sore as keeping safe Nerissa's ring.
>
> (V. i. 306)

Though the Duke in *As You Like It* is given the absolutely final line, Touchstone and Jaques provide its concluding cadence. Feste's grim little song brings *Twelfth Night* to an end. *Measure for Measure* and *All's Well That Ends Well* both focus some attention on their figures of misrule, Lucio and Parolles, while the other characters are celebrating the happy resolution of threats and conflicts. Even where the last moments of a comedy do not display such jesting, irreverent or even iconoclastic motifs, few end with the solemnity and seriousness of *The Tempest*: there Prospero sums up the experience and the significance of the play in a manner avoided by most of the other comedies. As Northrop Frye noted, many of these plays embody in their last few moments the characters' bemusement as they contemplate (but do not comment on) the extraordinary stroke of good fortune that has brought about the happy ending.[1] The intention behind such an effect may be the enhancement of that sense of wonder and amazement with which several comedies are concerned. But it is also similar to the jokes and jests standing at the end in a number of these plays: each is an instance of tact, protecting the audience from having to attend too carefully to what it already knows, and avoiding the undue emphasis on these rare and wonderful turns of events.

Another variant of the device must be noted. Some of the comedies end with a song or with a theatrical analogue of songs. These have received some critical attention, because they give every appearance of spelling out the fundamental ideas, themes and attitudes of the plays they formally bring to an end.[2] Quite obviously, the songs of spring and winter at the end of *Love's Labour's Lost* have a close metaphoric

---

[1] Northrop Frye, 'Recognition in *The Winter's Tale*' in *Fables of Identity*, New York 1963, p. 114. (This article was first published in *Essays on Shakespeare and Elizabethan Drama : In Honour of Hardin Craig*, 1962.)

[2] For a full discussion see Richmond Noble, *Shakespeare's Use of Song*, Oxford 1923, and J. H. Long, *Shakespeare's Use of Music*, Gainesville 1955.

connection with the play's main preoccupation—the necessity of achieving maturity after the follies of youth. Similarly, Feste's song at the end of *Twelfth Night* may be taken as a commentary on the play's fantastic convolutions. But the function of these concluding songs, as well as of certain analogous incidents, is more complex and more ambivalent. The two songs at the end of *Love's Labour's Lost* do not comment specifically on or refer to the play they follow. They represent, as well as a signal that the play is about to end, a curiously plangent attempt to prolong the comedy itself: to prevent, for a moment or two, the closing of the theatrical illusion. Berowne is made specifically to employ the language of the theatre when he finds that the play's 'comic' expectations are to be frustrated: thus, with the pathos of parting and penance, *Love's Labour's Lost* appears to be ending, but Armado comes forward to beg indulgence for 'the dialogue that the two learned men have compiled in praise of the owl and the cuckoo'. For a moment, the comic illusion is allowed to continue, though the King's words, 'Call them forth quickly', possess a deliberate urgency. Then follows the pair of contrasted songs, seemingly so rich in reference to the play itself.

The spring song is filled with decorative imagery:

> When daisies pied and violets blue
> And lady-smocks all silver-white
> And cuckoo-buds of yellow hue
> Do paint the meadows with delight . . .
> (V. ii. 881)

Winter's song, by contrast, is very much in the 'plain style' of Elizabethan verse:

> When icicles hang by the wall,
> And Dick the shepherd blows his nail,
> And Tom bears logs into the hall,
> And milk comes frozen home in pail,
> When blood is nipp'd, and ways be foul . . .
> (V. ii. 899)

Each of these songs has its own presiding emblems as Armado says: the cuckoo and the owl, representing, on the one hand, treachery, and on the other, wisdom and experience. The spring-world of gaiety, beauty and delight harbours the treacherous cuckoo, the terror of married men, the usurping bird. Winter, on the other hand, for all its rawness and lack of romantic colouring, seems to embody the reality of experience; its vividly precise images

> When all aloud the wind doth blow,
>   And coughing drowns the parson's saw,
> And birds sit brooding in the snow,
>   And Marian's nose looks red and raw . . .
>   (V. ii. 908)

are contrasted against the pastoral conceits of the spring song

> When shepherds pipe on oaten straws,
>   And merry larks are ploughmen's clocks;
> When turtles tread, and rooks and daws,
>   And maidens bleach their summer smocks . . .
>   (V. ii. 890)

But, with the arrival of these songs, the play has moved into a different, in a way non-dramatic, dimension. These songs are truly ambivalent; they look beyond the common confines of comedy to the hard but necessary lessons of maturity, yet, precisely because they are songs, they also refer back to the comic world—to the singing, music and dancing which are the appropriate and traditional accompaniments of the comic finale. The last moments of *Love's Labour's Lost*, like Berowne's earlier comments, stress the play's theatrical artifice.

Feste's song in *Twelfth Night* has a similar function; it caps Orsino's loving words to Viola/Cesario with the sadly disillusioned insistence that 'the rain it raineth every day'. This mocking song catalogues the world's imperfections—hostility among men, the disappointments of marriage, the short-lived solace of drunkenness. It, too, ends on a deliberately theatrical note:

> A great while ago the world begun,
>   With hey, ho the wind and the rain,
> But that's all one, our play is done,
>   And we'll strive to please your every day.
>   (V. i. 391)

Whatever ironic criticism of the hopeful delusions of the main characters might be found in this song (and some have thought that Shakespeare uses it to indicate quite unambiguously the hollowness of

Illyria)[3] the play concludes with a deliberate reminder of the artifice of the theatre. For this is a song, and at its conclusion it reminds us that a play is only a play.

The song at the end of *Twelfth Night* is merely a kind of epilogue. The epilogues to the comedies (and the other plays) are frequently overlooked because their authorship is often in doubt. But, irrespective of whether Shakespeare wrote or sanctioned them, a number of these epilogues represent a significant theatrical device. They break the dramatic illusion through a character's stepping forward to beg for applause. The distinctions between the pretence of reality and the actual circumstances of a performance are completely blurred: Puck, Rosalind, the King of France are characters in a play as well as actors on the stage. We must not make too much of this Pirandello-like device—it is no more than a convenient way of bringing a play to an end. But precisely because such flourishes are often needed, we may point to the epilogues as confirmation of the fundamental artificiality of comedy, for they stress a consistent characteristic of these plays. Comedy insists on its artifice to the very end, even where (as in the songs at the end of *Love's Labour's Lost* and *Twelfth Night*) the last words seem to deliver moral and thematic comments on the plays they conclude. These often abrupt reminders of the artificiality of the comic world stood Shakespeare in good stead at the end of *Troilus and Cressida*, when Pandarus makes a bequest of his disease to the audience: though the play is not a comedy, it employs in this instance (as in some other places) a recognizably comic device in order to restrain too thorough an involvement in the potentialities for disillusionment and pathos contained in its material. Pandarus's epilogue is a bitter one; but in a sense he is no longer Pandarus, but an actor—the cynicism and near-despair are contained within a theatrical jest.

Two comedies offer interesting examples of an extended epilogue; both display elements which shatter the dramatic illusion and retreat, at the same time, into a deliberate artifice akin to the songs that bring some comedies to a conclusion. The last act of *The Merchant of Venice* resembles an extended coda. The potential for deeply mystical meanings is embedded in some of its sections; it offers a picture of serenity which is firmly contrasted with the often bitter world of Venetian commerce and intrigue. Yet the act is highly artificial. In its

---

[3] Jan Kott, *Shakespeare Our Contemporary* (trans. Boleslaw Taborski), rev. edn, London 1967, pp. 228–30.

diction, in the 'sport' of the ring-tokens, and in the wholly unexpected restoration of Antonio's wealth, we are presented with the antithesis of the main portion of the comedy, a world governed by ordinary, mundane probabilities. The language of the first four acts, though at times fanciful and romantic, is much closer to the language of social transactions than the patterned and decorative diction of the last act. This disjunction may be taken as a sign that Belmont (and all it represents) transcends the mundane world; it is also a reinforcement of the artifice of comedy, a refusal to insist upon the moral and social issues raised by the presentation of the animosity between Jew and Christian and of the world of commercial transactions.

The end of *A Midsummer Night's Dream* is dominated by fairy-folk. Theseus's final words seem to bring the comedy to a strikingly sonorous close; his speech evokes those half-sinister suggestions which frequently lie under the surface of the play:

> The iron tongue of midnight hath told twelve.
> Lovers, to bed; 'tis almost fairy time.
> I fear we shall out-sleep the coming morn,
> As much as we this night have overwatch'd.
>
> (V. i. 352)

But this is followed by a second conclusion, as solemn and as dignified as Theseus's speech, though in a different mode. The King of the Fairies intones a ritual-like blessing of marriage; the perspective of the play shifts from the fictive marriage in the court of Athens to a much more general celebration of marriage itself. But the last notes are sounded by Puck's jesting (and, once again, overtly theatrical) epilogue:[4]

> If we shadows have offended,
> Think but this, and all is mended,
> That you have but slumb'red here
> While these visions did appear . . .
>
> (V. i. 412)

The play ends with a youthful actor beseeching applause; the last moments of the play—after the resolution of all the necessary plot-

---

[4] Puck's epilogue has, at times, been taken as evidence that the text of the play preserves alternative endings, one for a private, the other for a public performance. For a succinct resumé, see W. W. Greg, *The Editorial Problems in Shakespeare*, 3rd edn, Oxford 1954, pp. 124–5.

strands—consist of the constant alteration of the perspective, through which the fundamental artificiality of the theatre imposes itself on the consciousness of the audience. The play withdraws from an engagement with its material—the plot, the characters—to stress, instead, its own nature as a play.

The clownish, the artificial and the overtly theatrical dominate, therefore, the endings of many comedies. The holiday world of entertainment, the refusal to be entirely solemn or starry-eyed, claims its right to be heard. At those moments when the comedies approach the mystical solemnity of *commedia*, clownish lack of respect frequently engages our attention. Every Touchstone, Feste and Autolycus in this comic dispensation refuses to be impressed by that which seems so impressive. Touchstone makes pertinent gibes about the pastoral charade played by the other characters; Feste's melancholy realism is contrasted against the fashionable languor of his superiors, as well as against the hedonistic priorities of Sir Toby, and Maria's practical materialism. Thus the world of these plays is a many-sided one, often displaying an array of frequently contradictory possibilities. The heights of mysticism are accompanied by the voice of reductive commonsense. Helena's virtue must confront the irreverence of Parolles—not (we feel) for any moral reason, but for the more abstract theatrical pleasure to be experienced when contradictory possibilities are simultaneously displayed. Autolycus hovers around the rapt conversation of the three Gentlemen in the penultimate scene of *The Winter's Tale*; the account of the miraculous restoration of Perdita and of Julio Romano's rare masterpiece is accompanied by the comments of the rogue with ambitions to become a gallant. No discriminations are involved, nor are any intended: the emphasis falls on the artistic brilliance with which the poet is able to keep these seeming incompatibilities current without strain or loss of artistic harmony.

Shakespeare's comedies mirror, therefore, a glittering, playful world which displays an amazing variety of issues while suggesting, constantly, the presence of contradictory possibilities in the events and personalities represented. The plays consistently adopt a hypothetical attitude towards the material they incorporate: their themes and emphases are more often than not ambivalent—profundities are, at times, suggested, but almost always they are treated playfully. Comedy is sport; to go beyond that statement is to risk preverting the essentially *meaningless* nature of these plays: but through this sport, and through this refusal to preach, recommend or persuade, they are able to display a variety of issues and possibilities. These issues and possibilities, as this study has sought to demonstrate, do not stand in a demonstrative relationship with the plays in which they appear; we cannot extract from them rules of conduct or coherently stated views of the world. The function of the profundities and significances contained in them is almost always abstract and 'aesthetic', not polemical.

The closest these plays come to making statements or assertions is in their jesting, ambivalent intimations that they are concerned with the nature of artistic illusion discussed in the previous chapter. They are not late-romantic fables about the centrality of art; but so thoroughly artificial is the world depicted in many of them, and so flamboyant is their artifice, that they become mirrors of their own ingenuity and brilliance. 'Serious' drama constantly reaches beyond its own structures to establish connections with the world outside the theatre. The satiric scorn of many orthodox comedies and the generalizing tendency in classical tragedy both insist, fundamentally, that the work of art is an object of use. But Shakespeare's comedies are, for the most part, self-regarding; they recognize nothing outside of the confines of their own and very individual artifice. It is thus, and in a very limited sense, that they are concerned with their status as works of art. They deny implicitly the ancient conviction that the value of poetry is to be measured by its social, moral or philosophical efficacy. Instead, by turning inwards on themselves, by celebrating their own self-sufficiency, they demand to be valued in this non-referential way. But their terms of reference to the issues with which they sport so extravagantly are so varied and so comprehensive that the notion of a concern with art inevitably enters into some of them. Excessive importance must not be placed on this; yet the concern seems, marginally, to be more focal than, for instance, the elaborate Platonic games of *The Winter's Tale*. The relative importance of artifice in the intellectual fabric of several major comedies is significantly two-sided. On the one hand, the elaborate examination of sense-impressions and their relation to art in *A Midsummer Night's Dream*, the sustained exploration of the relationship between nature and artifice in *The Winter's Tale* (as well as lesser instances of the same preoccupation, like the various comments in the plays on the nature of songs and music) offer tentative intellectual categories within which these plays may be regarded. But on the other, they serve also to insist that any thematic or notional significances these plays might offer are so much a part of a flamboyantly hypothetical art-world that it is improper to extract them. Benedick's celebrated comment on the ability of music to produce, literally, a state of ecstasy is, after all, the bemused, part-cynical jest of the confirmed bachelor who is, himself, about to be snared in the nets of love.

Shakespeare's comedies are, thus, hybrid works, constantly occupied with the transformation of the known, the ordinary and the usual into surprising and enthralling combinations. Impossible worlds are created which reflect, nevertheless, some of humanity's most profound experiences and attitudes. They charm and they threaten; sometimes they plunge into stunningly deep waters, only to surface with an elegant gesture. The suggestive capacity of Shakespeare's comedies is, at times, apparently without limitation; but the suggestions, rich and complex though they often are, irreverent and gay elsewhere, have no other status than that of theatrical sports. These plays are capable of haunting and delighting; they provide some of the most satisfying artistic experiences in literature, yet they frustrate those wishing to seek for a pattern of conduct or an organization of the common world into a philosophically or morally consistent point of view. The comedies tease and tantalize, they invite us to see all manner of possibilities contained in them, but they endorse none.

This comic mode, fundamental to Shakespeare's art, is present in almost every one of the comedies he wrote throughout his career. We must remember that comedy occupied him throughout his productive life—poetry, the history-plays and tragedies are, by contrast, restricted to more specific periods: the Shakespeare canon, in all probability, begins and ends with comedies. Moreover, these comedies display a remarkable variety of incidental detail, style, setting and characterization. Each comedy is a unique world—more so, perhaps, than in the case of Shakespeare's other works; as with so much truly great art, the work of art is self-contained, individual, incapable of being confused or conflated with others. The individuality of each of the comedies—created in terms of language, stagecraft and characters—reveals, nevertheless, the similarities and consistencies of attitude and artistic aim examined in this study. The variety of Shakespeare's comic world displays, notwithstanding the variety itself, preoccupations and priorities which persisted throughout his career, and these determined, as far as we are able to recover them, a consistent artistic stance.

By most canons of artistic propriety, the wealth of material to be encountered in the comedies should guarantee incoherence. Yet most of these plays retain a unity, despite their at times extravagant diversity. To identify how such unity is achieved may be beyond the skills of conventional literary discourse, for it is not to be found in any set of extractable meanings or concerns. No explanation of the comedies, whether in terms of moral preoccupation, symbolic structures or philosophical systems, will provide references enabling each of these worlds to be subsumed within a single coherent terminology. Almost every one of Shakespeare's strikingly varied comedies escapes such attempts to constrain it. Yet the coherence is there, growing out of an artistic and imaginative consistency which must be recognized. We may fall back upon certain shop-soiled terms like 'the genius of the poet' in order to discover a verbal or critical means of communicating this impression of coherence and consistency. But that term, like its kind, is too vague to be entirely satisfactory. We must conclude, perhaps reluctantly, that these fascinating and glittering works of art—so unlike other literary works, which often reach out beyond the world of their own confines towards the world of experience at large—cannot be discussed or evaluated in the common currency of critical discourse. For literary discussion operates best by means of analogies, and analogies in the comedies dissolve into smiling contradictions.

Shakespeare's comic world, a representative of an aristocratic and refined temperament (for all its liveliness and joyful tolerance of crudity) is a hall of mirrors where reflection meets beguiling reflection. It offers satisfaction and even, arguably, spiritual solace. The exhilaration (in the strict sense of the term) produced by these works is evident, especially in the theatre, where they rightfully belong. They appeal to sensations which are simultaneously child-like and sophisticated. But exegesis they resist. The nineteenth century saw this clearly enough when it stressed the charm, the whimsy and the enchantment it found in these plays. Yet, as with so many other things, the essential sentimentality of that age compromised its accurate discernment. The comedies are charming, whimsical and enchanting; but they deal with sterner matter as well—terror, alarm, panic and cruelty, and also with high idealism and sensuality. They are representatives of that aspect of European culture in which the artificial, the stylized and the playful become the repositories of significant, moving and enthralling emotional and aesthetic experiences. The amplitude of their concerns gives them that variety Johnson found so praiseworthy in *Hamlet* and Shakespeare in his own Cleopatra.

INDEX TO THE PLAYS